Dual Language Essentials
for Teachers and Administrators

Yvonne S. Freeman

David E. Freeman

Sandra P. Mercuri

HEINEMANN
PORTSMOUTH, NH

Heinemann
A division of Reed Elsevier Inc.
361 Hanover Street
Portsmouth, NH 03801–3912
www.heinemann.com

Offices and agents throughout the world

Library of Congress Cataloging-in-Publication Data
Freeman, Yvonne S.
    Dual language essentials for teachers and administrators / Yvonne S. Freeman, David E. Freeman, Sandra P. Mercuri.
        p. m.
    Includes bibliographical references and index.
    ISBN 0-325-00653-9 (alk. paper)
    1. Education, Bilingual.   2. Immersion method (Language teaching).
3. Curriculum planning.   I. Freeman, David E.   II. Mercuri, Sandra.   III. Title.

LC3719+
370.117—dc22   2004010667

Editor: *Lois Bridges*
Production: *Vicki Kasabian*
Cover design: *Catherine Hawkes/Cat & Mouse*
Interior design: *Jenny Jensen Greenleaf*
Typesetter: *Kim Arney Mulcahy*
Manufacturing: *Steve Bernier*

Printed in the United States of America on acid-free paper
08 07 06 05 04 EB 1 2 3 4 5

We dedicate this book to our daughter, Mary, and her husband, Francisco,
who are living bilingually; to our daughter, Ann, who is living trilingually
and sometimes quadrilingually. Our granddaughter, Maya Esmeralda, is
being raised bilingually, but our dream is that she and other future
generations become at least trilingual and, hopefully, quadrilingual
to live fully in our multilingual world.

—Yvonne and David Freeman

A mi esposo Freddy, que vive día a día el enriquecimiento de ser
multilingüe, y a mis hijos Aiko, Natascha, Jessy y Estefanía, que
ejercen y disfrutan sus habilidades bilingües y trilingües
en diferentes destinos del mundo.

—Sandra P. Mercuri

Contents

Acknowledgments

This book would not have been possible without the collaboration and cooperation of a great many people. We have attempted to list as many of them as possible here. However, there are undoubtedly others we have missed whose contributions have influenced our writing—presenters at conferences we have attended, teachers whose classrooms we have visited, and colleagues with whom we have had lively conversations about dual language.

First and foremost, Yvonne and David would like to begin the acknowledgments with Maura Sullivan from Heinemann. She is probably the main reason that this book has come out so soon after our last book, *Essential Linguistics: What You Need to Know to Teach Reading, ESL, Spelling, Phonics, and Grammar.* Maura has always supported our work but never before had she told us that we *must* write a book! She keeps herself informed on trends and issues in education and is passionate about the concept of dual language.

Others from Heinemann have also supported us over the years and on this book, in particular. Our editor, Lois Bridges, provides the kind of positive feedback that encourages us to keep writing, even when we feel overwhelmed with too many other responsibilities. She helps us see that our work might make a contribution, something that in the process of writing can easily be forgotten. Vicki Kasabian has been our production editor for four of our books. She is a dedicated and passionate professional who takes each book, no matter how complex, through the production process, giving it the careful attention to detail that is critical. We also wish to thank Beth Tripp, who, through her careful copy-editing, caught many mistakes and improved our style. Each summer we have the pleasure of visiting with all the staff at Heinemann at least once, and we are grateful, knowing just how much each contributes to the final published book.

The breadth and depth of this book would never have been possible without the help of colleagues from The University of Texas Pan American as well as that of administrators, resource specialists, and teachers in the Rio Grande valley of south Texas. Leo Gómez and José Ruíz-Escalante, two colleagues at the university where Yvonne and David teach, are dedicated to the concept of giving all students access to dual language education. Hilda Medrano, the dean of the College of Education, and Connie Guerra, bilingual director of Region One in south Texas, have supported their work and ours. These four people are largely responsible for the Freemans' move to south Texas where they have been able to see excellent dual language schools in action. One of those remarkable Texas schools is Runn Elementary School in Donna Independent School District (ISD), in Donna, Texas. Its principal, Ofelia Gaona, her vice principal, Noemi Green, and Domenica Sutti, the dual language resource specialist from the Region One office, provided support and authentic and detailed information needed to tell the story of their dual language school accurately. All of the wonderful teachers and staff at Runn Elementary welcomed Yvonne into their classrooms, but in particular, the Freemans would like to thank María Emilia Terrazas, María de Jesús Flores, María Maldonado, Araceli Garay, Melva Camacho, and Veronica Alemán.

Pharr Elementary School in the Pharr, San Juan, Alamo ISD is another excellent dual language school that provided Yvonne and David background and inspiration. Principal José Sepulveda has inspired his teachers for several years as they continually work to provide dual language education. Yolanda Vega, a teacher at Pharr, was especially helpful to Yvonne in providing an overview of her growth as a dual language teacher. District-level dual language and ESL specialists are led by Rosalva Silva and her assistant, Dela Alvarez, and are supported by Leonila Luera, the bilingual/ESL director. These staff along with specialists Lydia Villescas, Becky Sánchez, Oneida Cantú, Berta Medrano, and Elia Corona have made it possible for new dual language schools in the district to function effectively.

The Freemans want to acknowledge their students at The University of Texas Pan American. The preservice interns with whom Yvonne works in dual language schools help her evaluate through different eyes. The graduate students also helped Yvonne and David think through what is important in dual language. They thank them all, but in particular, Olivia Tovar Martínez from Mercedes ISD, José Rangel from Hidalgo ISD, and Emilian Martínez Barrera from Roma ISD.

Yvonne and David have also visited dual language schools in other parts of Texas. They are appreciative of the way district-level administrators as well as school site personnel have welcomed them and generously shared their insights. From Richardson ISD, they wish to thank Susan Foley, Nancy Kinzie, Nancy Stenberg, Maeli Dang, Mackie Kazdoy, Angela Ward, and Kay Reynolds. Their visits to schools there taught them much. They also wish to thank Evangelina Cortez for her invitation to visit Plano ISD schools. Without the patience and accommodation of Harcourt Achieve representatives Kristy Schulz and Tommy Mawk, the Freemans would never have been able to get to the schools.

People in other states also provided us with important information through interviews, on-site visits, and other types of assistance. Sandra was supported by Juan Sandoval, district bilingual services director of Parlier Unified School District. At Cesar Chávez, a dual language school in the district, she worked with vice principal Noemi Flores, resource specialist Rosie Barboa, as well as Ann Kauffman and Patricia Sánchez, two student teachers. Sandra also was supported by Hilda Trevino at Ann Leavenworth School, a school with a two-way strand in Fresno Unified School District. While working on this book, Sandra's dual language program assistant at Fresno Pacific University, Jennifer Huerta, often made contacts, found resources, and provided all three of us with needed clerical assistance.

In Nebraska, where Yvonne and David visited two dual language schools, an initial interview with Susan Mayberger, supervisor of English as a Second Language/director of Migrant Education of Omaha Public Schools, piqued Yvonne's interest in their dual language programs. Sharon Royers, Title VII director at Castelar Elementary, guided the Freemans through Castelar, a new two-way program. Under the leadership of Sharon and an innovative principal, Robert Acamo, teachers there like Juan Carlos Veloso, whom we feature in this book, can thrive. Pamela Cohen, the principal of Mars, the other two-way school in Omaha, will move on with students to be the principal of a new dual language middle school next year. Others educators in Omaha who supported their visit in a variety of ways include Collette Nero, Marsha Urban, and Adriana Vargas. The Freemans wish to especially acknowledge Arturo Vega, the district bilingual liaison, for helping get permissions from parents for photographs of their children.

In fall 2003, the Freemans were invited to the University of Northern Colorado to work with students and faculty by their longtime friend and colleague,

Elizabeth Franklin. A professor of bilingual education there, Madeline Milian invited them to visit Harris Bilingual Immersion Elementary School in Fort Collins, Colorado, a school she had worked with for some time. Principal Julie Schiola provided interview information for the book and served as a charming hostess for the visit with faculty and students.

Long telephone interviews and follow-up e-mails during the summer and fall of 2003 were critical to the formation of the essentials laid out in this book. Through a new colleague at the University of Texas Pan American, Alcione Ostorga, Yvonne learned of a growing dual language charter school in New York City. An interview with the parent codirector María Vega inspired Yvonne to write about the school, the Cypress Hills Community School.

Jeanna Hernández and Alma Rivas, two district dual language specialists in Wichita, Kansas, granted Yvonne an interesting interview. More details about that dual language program came from a former M.A. student, Marcela Pinzón, whom we feature among the dual language teachers.

A longtime colleague and respected expert in bilingual education, María Brisk, provided Yvonne with an overview of one of the oldest two-way programs in the country, the Amigos program, in Massachusetts. Since her grandchildren attend the school, María helped Yvonne also arrange an interview with her daughter, Angélica Brisk, a parent in a dual language school. We had another interview about dual language in Massachusetts with Ester de Jong, who has researched and written about a two-way program there. She provided important insights about different perspectives on how two-way programs should and should not be implemented.

Both public school educators and university faculty provided the Freemans with information about dual language education in parts of Florida. Yvonne interviewed Maritza Barbieri, dual language coordinator in the Palm Beach district, and Ann Jackman, a teacher educator and an ESOL coordinator there. Frank Ramos, at that time affiliated with Florida International University, provided some interesting insights into dual language in the Miami area.

At the 2003 La Cosecha Dual Language Conference in New Mexico, all three of us connected with several people around the country who are involved in dual language education. Among those were David Rodgers, a longtime advocate of dual language in the state and across the country, who provided critical information and inspiration, and Mary Jean Habermann López, who provided us with key information about the history of bilingual education and dual language in New Mexico. While at the conference, Yvonne and David were able to interview Annette Rickert Smith about the innovative international school she is piloting in the Las Vegas, Nevada, area, the J. Marlan Walker International School.

We especially want to thank the people whose stories we share, both students and teachers, who include Juan Carlos Veloso from Omaha, Nebraska; Marcela Pinzón from Witchita, Kansas; Jessica Mercuri, Victoria Rich, Vanessa Sue, and Sabrina Morilla from Fresno, California; Alexi Montemayor and Irma Villa from Sanger, California; Kari Bejar from Lemore, California; and Iris Welcome from Mariposa, California. All of these people shared important details of their lives that helped enrich this book.

A final, very personal, and loving acknowledgment goes to the Freemans' daughter, Ann, and their *ahijada* (goddaughter), Erika Jiménez García de López. Ann provided David and Yvonne with some critical references they needed during the writing. How nice it is when daughters begin to know as much as (or more than) their parents! The Freemans met Erika and her family when Yvonne was the *Directora de inglés* (English director) at a large dual language school in Mexico City. When Yvonne's memory for important details about the curriculum at that dual language school failed, she contacted Erika, who filled in those rich details that helped bring the description of that Mexican school alive.

Introduction

From a research journal:
As the United States becomes more diverse, and global economies increasingly affect the U.S. economy, language diversity should become increasingly appreciated and bilingualism-biliteracy more widely embraced. To accomplish the goal of creating a multilingual and multiliterate generation of students, two-way bilingual and biliterate education programs would have to be standard throughout the grades in elementary schools. (Fitzgerald 2000, 520)

From a research center:
Two way immersion education is a dynamic form of education that holds great promise for developing high levels of academic achievement, bilingualism and biliteracy, and cross-cultural awareness among participating students. (Howard and Christian 2002, 1)

From leading researchers:
This is not just a research report, this is a wakeup call to the field of bilingual education, written for both researchers and practitioners. We use the word *astounding* in the title because we have been truly amazed at the elevated student outcomes resulting from participation in dual language programs . . . Enrichment dual language schooling closes the academic achievement gap in second language and in first language students initially below grade level, and for all categories of students participating in this program. (Collier and Thomas 2004, 1)

From a teacher educator:
> We must steadfastly support dual language education in terms of its greater contribution to long-term education and preparation of students as life-long learners and successful citizens in an increasingly culturally, linguistically and ethnically diverse society. (Gómez 2003, 11)

From a teacher educator and public school resource specialist:
> Dual language is the greatest gift we can give our children . . . By providing instruction in two languages, children become bilingual, biliterate and multicultural. (Jackman 2003)

From a United States Secretary of Education:
> Proficiency in English and one other language is something that we need to encourage among all young people. That is why I am delighted to see and highlight the growth and promise of so many dual-language bilingual programs across the country. They are challenging young people with high standards, high expectations, and curriculum in two languages. (Riley 2000, 4)

These statements come from a variety of sources and are a reflection of the growing interest in and support for dual language. Researchers in literacy, bilingualism, and second language acquisition, teachers, teacher educators, and policy makers have taken an interest in these programs because they promote success for both language-majority and language-minority students. English language learners (ELLs) who have failed to realize high levels of academic achievement in English or their first language in various types of English as a second language (ESL) and transitional bilingual education (TBE) programs have made phenomenal gains in dual language programs (Collier and Thomas 2004; Thomas and Collier 2002; Lindholm-Leary 2001). In addition, native English speakers (NES) in these programs, despite learning through two languages, excel in their native English, scoring higher than peers studying only in English (Lindholm-Leary 2001). (A list of key terms and their acronyms can be found at the back of this book.)

Dual language programs are not new in this country, but the interest in dual language education has increased dramatically in the last fifteen years (Howard and Christian 2002). The Spanish/English programs in Florida and New Mexico and the French/English Ecole Bilingüe in Massachusetts were implemented in the 1960s. In the spring of 2004, the Center for Applied Linguistics (CAL) listed 294 dual language programs in twenty-four states (www.cal.org/twi/directory/). It is extremely difficult to keep track of the number of dual language programs, in part because of their rapid growth. The CAL listing is a low estimate because the programs self-report. If programs do not register with CAL, then they are not listed on the CAL website. We know, for example, that Texas has more than 194 programs (http://texastwoway.org/) and California has at least 100 programs (www.cal.org/twi/directory/tables.html#table1). Those two states have more programs than any others, but the total for those two states exceeds the CAL estimate for all states.

Common Characteristics

Although dual language programs vary widely in design and implementation, they all share certain characteristics. Students in the programs usually include some native English speakers and native speakers of another language. These two groups of students study together most of the day. In their classes, students learn language through academic content instruction in both languages. All students become proficient in using two languages for communication and learning. In addition, in this era of high-stakes testing, researchers have shown that both groups of students do as well as or better than students learning only in English on standardized tests given in English (Lindholm-Leary 2001; Thomas and Collier 2002).

Common Characteristics of Dual Language Education Programs
• Students include native English speakers and native speakers of another language.
• Students are integrated during most content instruction.
• Instruction is provided in two languages.
• Students become proficient in two languages.
• Student achievement in English for all students is equal to or exceeds that of students learning in English only.

Orientations Toward Language

In addition to the characteristics listed in the previous chart, those involved with dual language programs view language as enriching for everyone. Ruíz (1984) has described the historical development of three different orientations toward language: *language as a handicap, language as a right,* and *language as a resource.* He defines an orientation as a "complex of dispositions toward language and its role, and toward languages and their role in society" (16). Attitudes people hold about language come from their orientation.

During the fifties and sixties, *language as a handicap* was the prevalent orientation. Ruíz points out that at this time, educators saw English language learners as having a problem, so that "teaching English, even at the expense of the first language, became the objective of school programs" (19). In other words, educators with this orientation believed that to overcome the handicap they had, English language learners had to transition to English as quickly as possible.

Ruíz explains that in the seventies, the *language-as-a-right* orientation emerged. As a part of the civil rights movement, bilingual educators called for the rights of nonnative English speakers (NNES) to bilingual education. Students in bilingual programs could exercise their right to maintain their native language while learning a second language. Those who held this orientation demanded freedom from discrimination on the basis of language and the right to use one's first language in daily living. While this language-as-a-right orientation is positive, Ruíz notes that many people were resentful, especially when language rights were enforced.

More recently, a third orientation, *language as a resource,* has developed. Ruíz sees this orientation as a better approach to language planning for several reasons:

> it can have a direct impact on enhancing the language status of subordinate languages; it can help to ease tensions between majority and minority communities; it can serve as a more consistent way of viewing the role of non-English languages in U.S. society; and it highlights the importance of cooperative language planning. (25–26)

Dual language programs are all based on the *language-as-a-resource* orientation. These programs have raised the status and importance of languages other than English in many communities across the United States. In some communities they have eased tensions between groups who speak different languages. The programs have helped build cross-cultural school communities and cross-cultural friendships among students and parents, relationships that probably would not have developed without the programs. Dual language programs raise the status of non-English languages, because as native English-speaking children become bilingual, parents and students alike see the value of knowing more than one language. Finally, as community leaders, school board members, school administrators, and teachers work together to design and implement two-way bilingual programs, cooperation among groups enriches all parties.

Dual language education benefits both native speakers of English and native speakers of other languages. These programs serve English language learners in a unique way because the learners become proficient in English and, at the same time, develop and preserve their native language. Because their peers are also learning their language, they maintain pride in their first language and culture. Native English speakers add proficiency in a second language and increase their cross-cultural understanding. These benefits are the direct result of viewing all languages as valuable community resources.

Variations Among Programs

Although dual language programs share certain characteristics and are based on the same orientation, they vary in several ways. For one thing, they are called by different names. They involve different languages and different student populations. In addition, there are different program models and these models are implemented in a variety of ways.

Variation in Labels

While there is widespread agreement about the success of dual language programs, there is not the same agreement about what the programs should be called. As the opening quotes demonstrate, experts in the field use many different terms. Programs that share the characteristics listed on page xiv have been given a variety of names:

- dual language education (DLE)
- developmental bilingual education (DBE)
- two-way bilingual education (TWBE)
- two-way immersion (TWI)
- dual immersion (DI)
- enriched education (EE)

We have chosen to use the general term *dual language education* most often because that label captures the essential component, the use of two languages for instruction. The goal is for students to develop full conversational and academic proficiency in two languages. This term serves as an umbrella for several program models. We also use other terms when describing more specific programs.

Developmental bilingual education is a term that the U.S. Department of Education has used for the funding support for programs that take into account linguistic, psychological, social, and cognitive developmental issues (Torres-Guzmán 2002). DBE can refer to programs in which all or most students are English language learners, and though the students' first languages are supported, there is not the mixture of native and nonnative speakers of English learning one another's language that is characteristic of many dual language programs. For that reason, DBE programs may also be referred to as one-way dual language programs since the direction of language learning is the addition of English to the non-English language.

The term *two-way bilingual education* is a label that fits dual language programs with a mix of native English speakers and native speakers of another language. In these programs, some students are adding English and others are adding another language. The direction of language learning is two-way because about half of the students are adding English while the other half are adding a non-English language. A benefit of two-way programs is that classes include many native speakers of each language who can serve as models for the language. In addition, students can come to know others from a different cultural background. However, two-way programs can be implemented only if there are students from the two language backgrounds. In settings in which almost all the students are English language learners, dual language can still be implemented.

Immersion is a label used for some dual language programs. This label highlights an important feature—students are immersed in a new language. Immersion is a term strongly associated with the successful French immersion programs in Canada. In many of these programs, English speakers are immersed in French to become proficient in that language (Genesee 1987). These are one-way programs since all the students are native English speakers who are adding French as a second language.

The terms *two-way immersion* and *dual immersion* have been used to emphasize that, unlike the one-way French programs, these dual language programs have both native English speakers and native speakers of a second language, so the direction of language learning is two-way rather than one-way. However, some people in the United States object to the use of *immersion* because that label is also used to describe the Structured English Immersion (SEI) approach advocated by English Only (EO) proponents (Crawford 1997). In SEI programs, English language learners are immersed, or some would say submersed, in a new language with little or no support in their first language. Structured English

Immersion programs are not designed to develop students' native languages; thus, they are not dual language programs.

In addition to these labels, dual language programs have been referred to generally as *enriched education* programs. This label emphasizes that the approach to learning a new language is additive. Other models of bilingual education are subtractive because students often lose their native language in the process of learning English. They may also lose their primary culture and pride in their native language and culture. Dual language programs are not designed simply as a bridge to English. Instead, all students learn an additional language. Further, dual language programs share many of the characteristics of programs for gifted and talented students. There are high expectations and a challenging curriculum, not the watered-down curriculum found in some programs for English language learners. However, there are enrichment programs that do not include a second language component, so not all enriched education programs are dual language programs.

Variation in Languages and Student Populations

Dual language programs have been implemented in the United States for native English speakers and speakers of Spanish, Cantonese, Korean, French, Portuguese, Haitian-Creole, Tagalog, Arabic, and Japanese. Districts have also considered implementing programs in Hmong and Vietnamese. The Center for Applied Linguistics maintains a database of dual language programs (www.cal.org/twi /directory/tables.html). New programs are added frequently, and the list of non-English languages continues to expand. However, in the overwhelming majority of dual language programs, Spanish is the non-English language.

Dual language programs vary in both languages of instruction and student characteristics. In two-way dual language programs, about half the students are native English speakers and about half are native speakers of the non-English language featured in the program. In these two-way programs, though, there can be considerable variation in the ethnicity of the native English speakers. Native English speakers may include Anglos, Latinos, African Americans, and members of other ethnic groups. Often, the students come from different social and economic backgrounds.

In some dual language programs, most of the students come from the same linguistic and ethnic background. However, the parents may differ in their social and economic status, and the students may vary in their knowledge of English or the non-English language. In some areas, such as south Texas, where almost all the students are Latinos, some are English-dominant, some Spanish-dominant, and some are more balanced bilinguals.

Variation in Program Design and Implementation

As we began to conceptualize this book, we interviewed experienced teachers, preservice teachers, district and school administrators, resource teachers, teacher educators, and parents involved in dual language education across the United States. We spoke to experts in Massachusetts, Florida, Texas, Kansas, Nebraska, Colorado, Nevada, and California. We also read the research about dual language programs. All the programs we discussed and read about were considered dual language, but there was enormous variation in their design and implementation (Christian, Howard, and Loeb 2000). No two programs were being carried out in the same way, and, in fact, many programs varied widely from the basic models that are often described in the literature on dual language.

The two basic models, the 90/10 model and the 50/50 model, vary in how they divide the time each language is used for instruction. In the 90/10 model, the non-English language is used 90 percent of the time in early grades, and gradually more English is added until the sixth grade, when students have equal instructional time in both languages. Many schools have adopted this model with the early emphasis on the non-English language to help compensate for the dominant power of English outside the school context.

One variation within the 90/10 model involves literacy instruction. In most 90/10 programs, all students learn to read and write in the non-English language. However, in some programs, all students receive initial literacy instruction in their native language, and the rest of the day is divided, with 90 percent of the instructional time in the non-English language and 10 percent in English.

In the 50/50 model, students learn in English 50 percent of the time and in the other language 50 percent of the time throughout the program. Time for the two languages may be divided in various ways—half day and half day, alternate days, or even alternate weeks. This model is often used in areas with limited numbers of bilingual teachers. Teachers can team teach, and the bilingual teacher can provide the non-English language instruction to one group in the morning and the other group in the afternoon (or on alternate days or weeks). This maximizes faculty language resources.

Many programs labeled 50/50 simply divide up language use by time. However, in some 50/50 models, the division is by subject. For example, math may be taught in English and science and social studies in the non-English language.

Literacy instruction also varies in 50/50 programs. In some programs, all students receive initial language arts instruction in their native language, and then, by first or second grade, they have language arts together in both languages. In still others, all students receive language arts instruction in both languages from the beginning.

Not only are there variations within the basic models, there is also variation in how programs are implemented. Dual language programs may constitute a strand of one or two classes at each grade level within a school or the program may be implemented schoolwide or even districtwide. Many factors shape decisions regarding program design and implementation, including availability of bilingual faculty and materials, student population, and attitudes within the school and the community. Developing a successful program depends in part on choosing the model that best fits a particular context.

Our Involvement in Dual Language Education

Although we had experienced dual language education previously, we became actively involved again after Proposition 227, an English Only amendment, was passed in California. At that time, California needed a model that was legal, accepted by the general public, and effective for English language learners. Dual language fit that model. We were impressed by research results that showed that both native English speakers and English learners in dual language programs perform as well as or better academically than students in all-English programs. At the same time, all students in dual language programs become bilingual and biliterate (Lindholm 1992; Thomas and Collier 1997).

We began to visit local programs implementing dual language. We observed the classes and talked to teachers and administrators. While promoters of the programs at the schools were enthusiastic and teachers were working hard, it became clear to us that the presentation of the theory and research on dual language at conferences and during inservices had not provided all that was necessary for developing successful programs. Further, most schools lacked material resources in the non-English language.

Experts encourage schools to plan carefully for two to three years so that administrators, faculty, and parents can all understand the program, establish their goals, and support one another (Cloud, Genesee, and Hamayan 2000). With one or two exceptions, the new programs in our area were started very quickly. The need for effective programs for English language learners was so great that many schools launched a dual language program without adequate preparation.

We realized that those involved with the new dual language programs faced many challenges. Staff members were well meaning, but it was clear that they had not developed an in-depth understanding of program design or appropriate pedagogy. In most cases, former bilingual teachers or newly credentialed bilingual teachers were thrown into dual immersion classrooms without enough pre-planning or ongoing support. Some teachers did not really understand how dual language education differed from the transitional bilingual education they had taught for some time.

In addition, there were not enough materials to support content teaching in the non-English language, and teachers did not understand how to plan integrated units in two languages. To further complicate matters, most of these special programs were strands within schools, and teachers who were not involved in the dual language program resented the attention the new program was being given. Often, other teachers did not understand the purpose of the dual language program or share the enthusiasm for it.

As we reviewed the literature on dual language programs, we found that teachers in programs across the country were experiencing the same kinds of challenges that we observed locally. Howard and Loeb (1998) reported that in response to a survey and individual interviews, dual language teachers expressed the need to find more skilled teachers for their programs and to find support for in-depth training.

Yvonne and David wrote and implemented a grant to support both preservice and inservice teachers in dual language education. The grant provided coursework in theory and practice for dual language education. The coursework included a class that focused on the teaching of reading in Spanish and English. Sandra, the third author of this book, became the program coordinator of the grant. She worked with teachers in local dual language programs and ensured that students were placed in these schools for student teaching. Further, grant funds were used to establish a resource room with professional books, children's books in Spanish and English, and other resources for both student teachers and local teachers to use.

 Goals for This Book

Sandra continues to work with students wishing to become dual language teachers and with schools as part of the original grant initiated in California. David and Yvonne have moved to a university in south Texas where there are several dual language programs and colleagues who are experts in dual language education.

They have visited programs in their area and worked with preservice and inservice teachers teaching in those programs. In addition, they have interviewed educators and visited schools across the country involved in dual language.

We have come to realize that while teachers and administrators need to understand the big picture, the theoretical background and program models, they also need to understand how to implement effective practices in dual language classrooms. We have taught dual language teachers and worked with them to help them plan and develop curriculum. We have observed them in their classrooms and considered with them how best to teach the academic content areas and literacy in two languages. We have gathered books and other resource materials that support thematic teaching in Spanish and English and have shown teachers how to organize these materials for their teaching.

This book draws on our experiences, our reading of the research, and our understanding of teaching and learning. We hope to help readers as they plan instruction in dual language settings. Our goal is not to explain dual language in detail or to promote any particular model, although we will give an overview of the models and discuss dual language internationally. Instead, we would like to focus on the variety of implementation, characteristics of students and teachers involved in dual language, and essentials for success. We want to help educators envision the best curriculum for their students given their particular context.

With these goals in mind, we provide readers with what we consider to be dual language essentials. Through stories of dual language schools, of students and teachers, we hope to help readers consider what would be best for their program. In describing classroom practices, we show readers specific support strategies and outline how to plan for standards-based content instruction in two languages. Because Spanish is the second language in most programs in the United States and because our experiences are with Spanish/English programs, our classroom examples will be from Spanish/English classes. However, our hope is that the ideas we present can be applied in any dual language setting.

Organization of This Book

In Chapter 1 we describe dual language education models we have experienced in Latin America as well as a well-known European model of education that creates not only bilingual but also trilingual students. We offer these descriptions to help readers understand how common it is for schools to teach in more than one language. We then review typical programs that serve English language learners in the United States and report on the effectiveness of each. We also explain how dual language is part of what is called *enriched education* and conclude by giving a short history of dual language programs in the United States.

In Chapter 2 we open with scenarios of dual language schools across the country to give readers a taste of the possibilities for implementation. We then describe both teachers and students we know who are either studying in or teaching in dual language classrooms and discuss the variations in their characteristics and needs.

Beginning with Chapter 3, we present the essentials for effective dual language education. First we discuss essentials for whole schools when the entire school is a dual language school as well as when the dual language program is only a strand within the school. We see administrators as key, so our next section discusses the essentials for administrators. Since administrators who are effective work with their teachers, we then discuss administrator and teacher essentials. The final section in the chapter discusses essentials for teachers. We provide real examples of administrators and teachers who are implementing or working toward implementing the essentials.

In Chapter 4 we begin to present curriculum essentials for dual language. We organize the essentials in this chapter into three groups: curriculum essentials for overall organization, curriculum essentials for lesson delivery, and curriculum essentials for assessment. Our discussion of essentials for overall organization includes why it's important to organize around themes in dual language and how themes provide a natural preview, view, and review. In addition, we explain why language teaching in dual language must be done through meaningful content. Content-based thematic teaching is only effective if there is appropriate lesson delivery. We suggest that dual language teachers make the physical classroom environment predictable, and we include a discussion on how teachers might group students. We discuss several ways teachers can scaffold instruction. Routines are critical for students learning in two languages and provide a kind of scaffolded learning. Translation is not an effective way to scaffold, however. Teachers in dual language settings need to know why it is ineffective to use translation to help students as they are studying content in two languages. Throughout the chapter we give examples from classrooms we have seen and teachers we have known to help support an understanding of the curriculum essentials.

A meaning-centered literacy program is key to the success of dual language programs. Because we see this curriculum essential as so important, we have written an entire chapter on the teaching of reading and writing in two languages. In Chapter 5 we discuss the importance of understanding a meaning-centered reading theory in order to be certain that the methods for teaching reading match this theory. We specifically discuss why a meaning-centered, balanced approach is critical for dual language. In addition, we discuss key questions about developing literacy in two languages: What is the best language for initial literacy instruction? How does literacy transfer from one language to the other? Should the same methods be used in both languages to teach reading? What are the differences in learning to read in one's first and second languages? We conclude this chapter by listing specific essentials for a literacy program in a dual language setting.

In Chapter 6 we address the difficult question of planning. Planning is critical, yet not everyone knows how to go about it. We suggest beginning with the students and what we hope they will learn. This has sometimes been termed *backward planning*. We then explain the differences between long- and short-term planning as well as horizontal and vertical planning. To illustrate effective long- and short-term planning, we describe in detail a theme on community developed for a second-grade class. We conclude the book with a summary of the essentials and a list of the benefits of dual language education for our ever-changing global society.

Throughout the book we showcase wonderful schools and educators we have come to know as we have researched this book. We hope that these examples, along with the essentials, will assist teachers and administrators as they plan for or review dual language programs. We share a common goal: we all want to provide the best possible education for all students.

Bilingual Education Programs in Latin America, Europe, and the United States

Good morning, children.
Good morning, Ms. Freeman
How are you today?
Fine, thank you, and you?
I'm fine, thank you. What day is today?
Today is Monday, October 31.

This dialogue could well have been from any of the many English as a second or foreign language classrooms around the world. But it wasn't. Try to picture more than a thousand first- through fifth-grade children from different sections of the northern part of Mexico City lined up behind their teachers in thirty-two straight rows. All the students and the teachers are dressed in navy blue uniforms with white tops—boys in slacks and girls and teachers in jumpers. The children have overstuffed *mochilas* (bookbags) at their feet. They are standing within a huge outdoor fenced lot looking up to the second floor of their five-story school as administrators address them from an open overhang.

Dual Language Schools in Latin America

Mexico City ◆ This dialogue was part of the opening ceremony every week at the *Torres* campus of *El Instituto Ovalle Monday*. Following the greeting by Ms. Freeman (Yvonne), the *Directora de inglés* (coordinator of the English program), there was always a minilesson. On this occasion Yvonne told the students about Halloween in the United States, explaining in English how children dress up in costumes and pretend they are witches, ghosts, queens, or even Batman. She explained that the children go from house to house, ringing the doorbells and calling out "Trick or treat!" to get candy. Most of the children were very familiar with the tradition through television, movies, and even theme parties held in their own homes in Mexico. Next, the *Directora de español* (coordinator of the Spanish program) and the children exchanged greetings in Spanish, and she talked to them about *el día de los muertos* (the Day of the Dead) and the altar set up in the front of the school. Following these greetings and minilessons, students from one of the classrooms carried out the *escolta*, the flag-raising ceremony, which ended with the singing of the Mexican national anthem. Then, the *Directora* (principal) of the school excused teachers and students to their classrooms one grade level at a time.

El Insituto Ovalle Monday is a large English/Spanish bilingual school. It was started by a couple—the husband, Sr. Ovalle, was a Mexican national, and the wife, Ms. Monday, was a U.S. citizen. The first school housed four hundred children. The demand for a school providing instruction in English and Spanish in the area was so great that soon the school expanded to four campuses, including a preschool and kindergarten, two elementary schools, and a *secundaria* (sixth through eighth year) and a *preparatoria* (ninth through eleventh year). Most of the students are children of middle-class parents who pay the tuition and also pay for the books, the school supplies, and the uniforms required by the school. This school is similar to many throughout Latin American. The parents are prepared to make great sacrifices to give their children a chance to become bilingual. These parents believe that bilingualism in English and Spanish is critical for their children's future.

Yvonne worked at the *Torres* campus for almost two years. During that time she supported the English teachers with lesson planning, materials, and strategy training. All the teachers were native Spanish speakers who had various levels of English proficiency. The more proficient English-speaking teachers taught English through content all day long. The school was organized so that children in each class were taught one-half of the day in English and one-half of the day in Spanish. Their English curriculum included grammar, spelling, science, social studies, math, reading, reading comprehension, and listening. The children used books published in the United States, including basal readers, workbooks, and science, math, and social studies textbooks.

The Spanish curriculum was controlled and mandated by the education department of the Mexican government, SEP (*La Secretaría de la Educación Pública*). El Instituto Ovalle Monday offered all the required subjects, *español y ortografía* (Spanish and spelling), *ciencias sociales* (social studies), *ciencias naturales* (science), *matemáticas* (math), as well as enrichment courses in *dibujo* (drawing), *educación física* (physical education), and *educación musical* (music). Spanish textbooks were available either free from the government or for a nominal fee. However, for the most part, with the exception of early reading and language arts, these subjects were taught without textbook support. Literature was taught through the use of books from the rather limited school library selections.

The elementary school of El Instituto Ovalle Monday, like many English/Spanish dual language schools in Mexico City, was organized with two years of first grade. This allowed the children to be immersed in more English in the early grades. All children in the elementary school had what people from the United States would consider an extra year: *primero de inglés* (English first grade) and *primero* (first grade). The *primero de inglés* year was the only year that the time was not divided evenly for instruction. During this year children received 80 percent of their instruction in English and 20 percent in Spanish. During the Spanish time, they studied Spanish language arts. Because students took two years for the first-year curriculum, they had time to complete the curriculum required by the government and also begin to acquire both oral and written English.

Despite the fact that few of the English teachers had much preparation in second language acquisition theory and several did not have a teaching certificate, the results at El Instituto Ovalle Monday were really quite good. By second or third grade, most children could read, write, and converse in Spanish and English. By fifth grade, almost all of the children were proficient bilinguals. El Instituto Ovalle Monday has many of the characteristics of what we would call a one-way dual language school in the United States. Children learn language through content in their first language and in English, and they become proficient readers, writers, and speakers of both languages.

Cali, Colombia ◆ Across Central and Latin America, parents who can afford it send their children to schools like *El Instituto Ovalle Monday.* David and Yvonne had their first experience of living and teaching abroad as a young couple at a dual language school in Cali, Colombia. This American school, *El Colegio Bolívar,* included Colombian students as well as the children of Americans working in Colombia. Because the school was accredited by the Southern Association of Colleges and Schools and was the most prestigious (and most expensive) in the city, children of diplomats and businessmen from around the world also attended the school. David taught high school English and girls P.E. and Yvonne taught the English portion of the fourth-grade curriculum.

In elementary school, students studied content area subjects in English using textbooks from the United States and also followed the Spanish curriculum required by the government. Students were taught language arts and social studies, including Colombian history and government, in Spanish. The faculty included both native English and native Spanish speakers. Once students reached middle school, they could take an all-English track that would prepare them to attend a university in the United States or an even more rigorous Spanish/English program that would allow them to also earn the *Bachillerato,* the degree needed to attend a university in Colombia.

Guadalajara, Mexico ◆ Just recently, Yvonne and David's daughter, Mary, and their son-in-law, Francisco, took jobs at The American School Foundation of Guadalajara (ASFG) in Mexico, teaching high school English and drama and second grade, respectively. Francisco's second graders study content in Spanish from 8:00 to 10:30 using the government curriculum and textbooks. Then Francisco teaches language arts and reading in English until noon. After the lunch hour, he teaches the content areas of science, social studies, and math in English. He has access to extensive classroom and school libraries of children's literature and content books published in the United States, as well as up-to-date technology through a well-equipped computer lab. Mary teaches American literature to eleventh graders as well as drama, all in English also using textbooks published in the United States.

Like the American school in Colombia, this school is accredited by the Southern Association of Colleges and Schools and has a long waiting list of Mexican nationals trying to get their children into the school even with fees close to U.S.$8,000 per student per year. In 2002–2003 there were 1,404 students: 162 U.S. citizens, 1,190 Mexican nationals, and 52 children representing thirty-two other countries. The curriculum is similar to that of the Colombian school where David and Yvonne taught years ago, with instruction in English and Spanish in preschool through lower elementary and two tracks in middle and high school. The Mexican secondary program taught in Spanish and English includes three years of *secundaria* and three years of *preparatoria* or *bachillerato* and is considerably more demanding than the all-English upper-grade program. Students who graduate from this program have their choice of attending a university in Mexico or in the United States. In fact, 95 percent of the students who graduate do go to universities in the United States, often prestigious universities.

Mar de Plata, Argentina ◆ Sandra is from Argentina. She lived in a coastal town, Mar de Plata, until she came to the United States. Many of the people she knew as she grew up attended bilingual schools or are presently sending their children to bilingual schools. The schools that teach in both languages in her home city are called schools of *doble escolaridad* (double schooling) because students study all subjects in both English and Spanish. In the morning, they study subject areas required by the national curriculum in Spanish, and in the afternoon, they study those subjects and the same general, required content in English. The teachers of the English curriculum are generally native Spanish speakers who have different levels of preparation in English. In the elementary and middle schools, called *Educación General Básica (EGB)*, a person can teach in English if he or she has a certificate from an English Institute. However, for high school, the tenth, eleventh, and twelfth years of schooling, called *polimodal* in Argentina, teachers generally have to have a university-level degree in English.

The students in these bilingual schools are from upper-middle-class homes, and their parents are well educated. In Mar de Plata all the students are native Spanish speakers whose parents want them to be bilingual. Many of the students plan to attend universities in England or the United States.

In Buenos Aires, there are many English/Spanish bilingual schools. Some of the most prestigious are very expensive. Students study 50 percent of the time in Spanish and 50 percent in English from kindergarten through fifth grade. Teachers must be well prepared in English and are offered many of the same supports that U.S. teachers have, including access to materials and staff development, often provided by educators from abroad. In its promotional materials, the school considered the most elite claims to have an integrated bilingual curriculum that offers many advantages. It ensures a whole language approach, access to technology, and an enriched curriculum including art, music, information technology, physical education, and personal and social education.

In the *polimodal* portion of their education, students in the elite Argentine schools continue to study in both languages and are prepared to take the Cambridge IGCSE (International General Certificate of Secondary Education) exams in English, Spanish, and mathematics. While some schools prepare students to study in U.S. universities, the vast majority of the bilingual English/Spanish schools in Argentina prepare students to pass the Cambridge exams to study in England or even to pursue a career there. Not all students, however, want to go to the United States or England, so these schools prepare students to pass both the National Baccalaureate as well as the International Baccalaureate, a degree that is accepted in more than seven hundred universities worldwide, including forty Latin American universities. Students who pass all of the exams for these degrees are well-prepared bilinguals who have subject area expertise in Spanish and in English.

We began this chapter with a review of our personal experiences with dual language education in Latin America because the three of us have seen and experienced the power of dual language education in the settings described there. When dual language programs became more popular in the United States it was not necessary to convince us that this model could work because we had already seen it in action.

European Schools

The fact is that children are becoming bilingual, trilingual, and even quadrilingual around the world. One educational model that creates multilingual students is the European Schools, a network of nine schools in six different countries. European Schools has a reputation for promoting scholastic achievement, linguistic equity, multilingual proficiency, and multicultural awareness. The students' national, cultural, and linguistic identity is maintained through solid first language instruction, and a variety of courses are offered in different languages so that students become bilingual or, often, multilingual.

> On the one hand, they attempt to guarantee the development of the child's first language and identity, while on the other they strive to promote a European identity through instruction for all pupils in at least 2 languages, compulsory learning through a 3rd as a subject matter, and options regarding a 4th language. (Beardsmore 1995, 28)

The largest European School is in Brussels. This school offers instruction in all the official languages of the member states of the original European Economic Community except Portuguese. These include Danish, Dutch, English, French, German, Greek, Italian, and Spanish. Portuguese, a language spoken by many in the area, is offered in another European School in Brussels so that instruction is available for children whose native language is Portuguese.

The model of education in these European Schools is not like the models in the United States or Latin America because although the first language of every student is always the foundation and is always carefully maintained, "it gradually decreases in significance as pupils get older" (Beardsmore 1995, 29). Reading and writing are initially taught through the first language, and the second language is first taught as a subject and only later used to teach content. In other words, Italian children studying in a European School would receive most of their primary school content instruction in Italian, and a second language such as French would be taught as a subject, like a foreign language class.

In the third through fifth grades, students attend European Hours three times a week. Here students from all the language groups participate in hands-on activities taught by a teacher who speaks only one of the languages. During European Hours, students "work and play together, to make them aware of their common European heritage" (37). It isn't until middle school that students actually begin to study content through a second language, and even that begins with P.E., music, and art. Study of these subjects places lower linguistic demands on students than other content areas, such as social studies or science.

In sixth grade, students begin to study their third language as a subject. By eleventh grade, they begin to study a fourth language. It is important to note that throughout their schooling, students are constantly exposed to the languages of their peers, especially through the European Hours, and often several different languages are spoken commonly outside of school. While the European Schools are interesting to us, we agree with Beardsmore that "it is unlikely that a school as complex as the European School is either necessary or feasible in a different context" (33).

Dolson and Lindholm (1995) have looked at the European Schools model and compared it with dual language models in the United States. They found common principles that can provide useful guidelines for educators involved in dual language education:

1. Participants experience an additive form of bilingualism (or multilingualism). They are able to develop full proficiency in their mother tongue (L1) while gradually acquiring high levels of proficiency in a second language (L2);

2. Participants are offered subject matter and language lessons in both L1 and L2. Languages are kept separate for instruction with the sequence for most

participants being large amounts of L1 instruction initially with increasing amounts of L2 instruction over time;

3. Plentiful attention is given to maintaining a healthy identity with a heritage language group as well as the development of cross cultural knowledge, skills, and abilities needed to perform adequately in multicultural contexts;

4. Emphasis is placed on the authentic integration of students from different language and ethnic backgrounds. Substantial time allotments are dedicated to cooperative or communal hours aimed at fostering cross-cultural understandings, experiences and friendships;

5. Underlying the language and cross cultural aspects of the programs is a solid academic foundation made up of a high quality curriculum which allows students to meet both national and international scholastic standards expected of pupils at specified age/grade levels;

6. In route assessments are linked to the language used as a medium of instruction in the particular subject matter or course in question. Final examinations for the programs are conducted separately in both L1 and L2. Results are judged according to native speaker standards. (70)

All of these principles apply to two-way dual language programs in Europe and the United States. One-way dual language programs, such as those in Latin America do not have the "authentic integration of students from different language and ethnic backgrounds" because the student population usually consists primarily of students whose first language is Spanish and ethnic background is Latino. However, the other principles do apply to one-way dual language programs: additive bilingualism, subject matter teaching in two languages, keeping the languages separate, building a solid academic foundation, and assessment in both languages.

Overview of Programs for English Language Learners

Before we describe and analyze dual language programs in the United States, it is useful to compare dual language with other types of bilingual and second language education programs. As we will discuss later, dual language programs may or may not serve native English speakers, but all dual language programs serve English language learners. The population of ELLs in this country has grown by 95 percent since 1991, while the total K–12 enrollment has grown by only 12 percent. In 1991 there were 2.4 million English language learners out of the 43 million total students in K–12 schools. In the 2001–2002 school year the total enrollment had grown to 48.3 million while the ELL population had grown to 4.7 million, almost double what it was it 1991 (OELA 2002).

With this many students identified by official agencies as Limited English Proficient (LEP), it is important to look at which programs are being used to serve them and what the results of those programs are, especially when compared with dual language programs. It is important to also distinguish between programs that are subtractive, meaning a language is lost, and those that are additive, meaning a language is added (Cummins 2000; Soltero 2004).

Subtractive Programs

English Immersion and ESL ◆ English immersion programs are those in which students are immersed from the beginning in all-English instruction. If the programs are structured, their teachers may be given some specialized training that helps them support their English language learners as they teach in a language their students do not understand. For example, the teachers learn to use visuals, gestures, and graphic organizers to help make the English content they are teaching comprehensible. While these strategies do help students understand the content, there is much the students miss because they are learning the academic content through their second language. In California in 1998, Proposition 227 outlawed bilingual education and called for Structured English Immersion, promising that English learners would succeed academically in all-English programs. However, after five years of implementation, just 30 percent of the LEP students had conversational English and only 7 percent were able to follow academic instruction from school textbooks at grade level. Far from doing better, the English learners in California had fallen further behind (Crawford 2003). As native English speakers learn the content and progress, English learners are constantly struggling to catch up. Usually, the gap between native English speakers and English learners grows larger as students move up through the grades (Thomas and Collier 2002).

In many schools English language learners are given some type of ESL instruction. Often ESL is provided on a pullout basis. The variety of ways that ESL pullout is organized is probably as large as the number of schools. Some students may be pulled out for an hour a day, others for twenty minutes a day, and still others for twenty minutes twice a week. The ESL pullout class might consist of students at one grade level or students from kindergarten through sixth grade. The ESL teacher may also be pulled in to provide support in the mainstream classroom.

Sometimes ESL instruction is traditional. Teachers drill students on language structures and have them memorize vocabulary. In other cases, teachers who understand second language acquisition teach language through content organized around themes that connect to what the students are studying with their mainstream teachers. While students taught through content do somewhat better than students in traditional ESL, testing results show that most students in ESL classes do not catch up to their English-speaking peers (Collier and Thomas 1996). Perhaps the one exception is when the English learners are already literate in their first language. Research shows that students who are schooled in their first language do better in English than those who are not (Cummins 1981; Greene 1998). These students transfer the knowledge they gained in early schooling, including their ability to read and write, to English and catch up with native English-speaking peers fairly quickly.

Transitional or Early Exit Bilingual Education ◆ There are various types of transitional bilingual programs that serve to help English learners learn the content and literacy skills in their primary language as they are learning English. In Early Exit bilingual programs, students are taught literacy and content in their first language as well as in English for one to three years. Usually, students in these programs are exited as soon as they show enough ability in English to pass basic English proficiency measures for nonnative speakers of English. Often these exams do not test students' literacy in English but only their basic oral communication skills. Research shows that the greater the development of the first language, the better students do academically in English in the long run (Thomas and Collier 1997, 2002; Cummins 2000). For this reason, the Early Exit bilingual programs, which discontinue the use of native language instruction once students develop some English proficiency, do not show positive long-term results.

Additive Programs

Enriched Immersion ◆ This model is exemplified by the French immersion program in Canada, although this model has also been implemented in the United States in different languages. In the French program, middle-class

English-speaking children study from kindergarten through sixth grade in French and English. They are first immersed in French only and later, usually around second grade, begin to develop literacy in their first language, English. By the end of sixth grade, the children are quite bilingual and biliterate (Cloud, Genesee, and Hamayan 2000; Lambert and Tucker 1972). Because these children are from middle-class families and their parents advocate for the program, there are economic and sociopolitical influences on the positive outcomes of the program. We comment further on enrichment models of education and the French Immersion program later on.

Maintenance or Late Exit Bilingual Education ◆ In Late Exit programs, also called Maintenance or Developmental Bilingual programs, English language learners continue to receive first language support for an extended period, usually five or six years. Students also receive instruction in English and become bilingual and biliterate. Although the first language is maintained and developed, the emphasis is not on the full development of two languages. Rather, the first language is maintained as students learn English. While this model has been shown by research to give the most positive academic results of the traditional bilingual programs, it has also been the least often implemented (Ramírez 1991). In fact, states that allow bilingual education often mandate Early Exit rather than the more effective Late Exit programs.

Dual Language ◆ The most effective model for instruction of English learners is dual language education. In a dual language program, students develop high levels of proficiency in their first and their second languages, they achieve above grade level on academic performance measures, and they demonstrate positive cross-cultural attitudes and behaviors (Howard and Christian 2002; Thomas and Collier 2002). For English language learners, the positive view of their native language and culture demonstrated when other students are learning their language and valuing their culture is especially important. In addition, bilingualism is highly valued. This emphasis is critical in an atmosphere in which politicians and the general public call for English only.

Cummins (1996) has developed a useful framework for analyzing programs for English language learners. He contrasts schools that have an intercultural orientation and those with an assimilationist orientation. The program models we have identified as additive, especially dual language programs, have the characteristics of an intercultural orientation. The program models we identified as subtractive have many components of an assimilationist orientation.

Schools with an intercultural orientation develop programs in which all students add languages and cultures. In contrast, in schools with an assimilationist orientation, students often lose their first language and culture. In dual language programs, all students add a second language and an understanding of a second culture. In schools with ESL or transitional bilingual programs, language-minority students often lose their first language and culture.

Schools with an intercultural orientation develop collaborative relationships with parents and other community members. They include language-minority parents in decision making and adjust curriculum to meet the needs of all students. In additive dual language schools, parents are integral to the success of the program. School officials encourage parents to be part of both curricular and extracurricular activities. Parents of dual language children are involved because they understand and support the program. Schools with an assimilationist orientation often exclude, overtly or covertly, members of minority communities. Parents of second language students in assimilationist schools are seldom part of the PTA. They usually don't sit on the school board. Too often their concerns are not taken seriously. The message is "Fit in, and don't rock the boat."

Pedagogy in a school with an intercultural orientation is transformative. Students develop knowledge and skills they can use to improve their lives. Teachers often have a constructivist view and involve students in meaningful learning. Dual language teachers must use pedagogy that is meaning centered in order to be successful. In schools with an assimilationist orientation, pedagogy follows what Freire (1970) termed a banking approach. Teachers deposit knowledge in students and then withdraw it on tests. Students don't take ownership of their learning, and schools do not empower them to improve their life situation.

Assessment also differs in these two models. Schools with an intercultural orientation take an advocacy approach to assessment. Tests help teachers and students find strengths to build on. Teachers use test results to advocate for what their students need. In Chapter 4, we will share an example of one dual language school in which the entire staff supported struggling students and made sure they succeeded. In schools with an assimilationist orientation, assessment simply serves to legitimate the low grades language minority students receive. Eventually, the low grades also serve as reasons that the students cannot advance to higher education.

Cummins (1996) concludes that schools with an intercultural orientation produce students who are academically and personally empowered. In contrast, schools that take an assimilationist orientation produce students who are academically disabled or resistant. The framework Cummins has developed fits very well with the additive and subtractive program models for English language learners. The additive models—and especially dual language—has all the characteristics of the intercultural orientation. As a result, students in dual language programs develop both academic competence and personal confidence in their ability to use two languages.

Research on Dual Language Programs

Many schools have adopted dual language programs because of research reports that show that students in dual language programs score better on standardized tests in English than English language learners in other types of programs. The leading researchers Thomas and Collier (2002) have disseminated the results of their large, long-term studies widely. However, critics of bilingual education have questioned the research supporting dual language.

Much of the criticism has been unfounded, reflecting a general antibilingual bias. However, one academic, Christine Rossell (1990, 1998; Rossell and Baker 1996) has consistently critiqued studies showing the effectiveness of bilingual programs. She is concerned that some reports have not appeared in refereed journals and that in some cases, data supporting the reports' conclusions have not been made available.

Other researchers have responded to this criticism. For example, Greene conducted a meta-analysis of studies of bilingual programs (1998). His analysis showed that bilingual programs are effective in helping English language learners develop academic English. Collier and Thomas (2004) have also responded by publishing extensive data from their studies and by publishing in refereed journals.

Krashen (2004) has reviewed one aspect of the research on dual language programs, the progress of language minority students in acquiring academic English. To determine their progress, he looked at studies that reported students' scores on tests of reading comprehension in English. He excluded several studies because the scores of English language learners were combined with those of native speakers, because two-way students were not tested in English, or because the language minority students had already acquired a considerable amount of English before starting the dual language program.

The studies he reviewed fell into several categories: studies in which there were no comparison groups; studies in which students in dual language programs were compared with English language learners in mainstream classes; studies in which students in dual language programs were compared with students in transitional bilingual education; studies in which students in dual language programs were compared with students in developmental bilingual education; and studies in which students in dual language programs were compared with native English speakers in dual language programs.

Based on these studies, Krashen concluded, "Only a handful of studies exist, and they report generally positive but variable attainment in academic English among English learners . . . Thus a close look at the data shows that two-way programs show some promising results, but research has not yet demonstrated that they are the best possible program" (13).

Krashen's review did not consider studies such as the one conducted by Howard, Christian, and Genesee (2004). These researchers looked at reading and writing development of students in eleven two-way schools. The researchers found significant gains for third- and fifth-grade students in Spanish and English writing and in English reading. They conclude, "The fifth grade results are particularly encouraging, as they demonstrate that the majority of students received perfect or close to perfect scores on a grade-level assessment of English reading ability" (21). Although the researchers used rigorous methodology, they used their own test (a Cloze passage) rather than a standardized test that would allow comparisons with other students. Nevertheless, studies such as this one are compelling because they provide clear evidence of the gains students make in dual language classes.

To determine just how effective dual language programs are, it will be necessary to continue to collect data. It will be important to conduct studies that are both large-scale and long-term. However, the problem with large-scale studies is that the students come from different classrooms in different schools. For example, Thomas and Collier report results for large numbers of students in Houston schools. Even though the researchers visited schools and conducted interviews to ensure that programs were well-implemented, there would be variation across schools and within schools.

Like Krashen, we believe the results look positive. We are convinced that dual language programs can provide the best possible education for all students. Our observations have shown us, however, that programs vary widely in implementation. Dual language programs can only provide effective instruction if a number of elements are in place. Our goal in this book is to outline these essentials for developing and maintaining the best possible dual language programs.

Figure 1–1 summarizes the information on the types of programs for ELLs. In the last column a summary of the research shows which programs give the best academic results for the students involved (Thomas and Collier 2002, 1997; Collier and Thomas 1996; Cloud, Genesee, and Hamayan 2000; Crawford 2003).

Type of Program	Description	Language Result	Academic Result
English Immersion	English language learners are taught with mainstream students and given no special services.	Subtractive—Students learn to communicate in English but lose most or all of their native language proficiency.	Students show less progress in math and reading than students in ESL/bilingual programs. Highest number of dropouts is in this group.
Structured English Immersion	English language learners are taught only in English and teachers are trained to make the input comprehensible. This program has been widely implemented in California since the passage of Proposition 227 in 1998.	Subtractive—Students develop literacy and learn to communicate in English. All study is in English only. Students lose most or all of their ability to use their native language.	In California after five years of structured English, students had limited conversational English and had difficulty reading and understanding grade-level texts.
ESL Pullout Traditional Instruction	English language learners are given ESL support. They are taught basic vocabulary and language structure and are then integrated into all-English instruction.	Subtractive—Students develop literacy and learn to communicate in English. All study is in English only. Students lose most or all of their ability to use their native language.	These students show little academic progress and once mainstreamed, they rarely catch up. Many students drop out before graduation.
ESL Pullout Pull-in Content Instruction	English language learners are given two to three years ESL content support services and are then integrated into all-English instruction.	Subtractive—Students develop literacy and learn to communicate in English. All study is in English only. They lose most or all of their ability to use their native language.	By the end of high school many of these students drop out or are in the lowest fourth of their class.
Transitional Bilingual Education/ Early Exit Bilingual Education	English language learners receive a portion of their content instruction in their primary language for one to three years and then are integrated into all-English instruction.	Subtractive—Students learn to communicate and study in English only. They usually lose their first language.	At the end of high school these students are below the 50th percentile in tests of reading in English.

FIG. 1–1 Programs for English Language Learners

Type of Program	Description	Language Result	Academic Result
Enriched Immersion (example: French immersion in Canada)	Native English speakers are taught language through content instruction in a second language. English is introduced around second grade or later.	Additive—Students become bilingual and biliterate.	Students acquire a second language and achieve the same levels of competence in academic subjects as peers taught all in English.
Maintenance or Late Exit Programs	English language learners receive content instruction in both L1 and L2 for four to six years.	Additive—students become bilingual and biliterate.	ELLs outperform students in English-only programs. Students achieve above the 50th percentile on standardized tests of English reading by sixth or seventh grade.
Dual Language Education	English language learners and native speakers of English learn language through content in both English and the first language of the English learners.	Additive—Native English speakers and English learners become bilingual and biliterate.	Students from both language groups outperform students in transitional and developmental bilingual education and score above the 50th percentile on standardized tests of English reading by seventh grade.

FIG. 1–1 Programs for English Language Learners (*continued*)

Enrichment Programs: Some Distinctions

Dual language programs are a type of enrichment education:

> Enriched Educational programs are programs that emphasize challenging standards in the core curriculum domains while enriching students' development in both their first and second language. These programs aim for full proficiency in two languages, an understanding and appreciation of the cultures associated with those languages, and high levels of achievement in all core academic domains. (Cloud, Genesee, and Hamayan 2000, 205)

The French immersion programs in Canada that we described earlier are enrichment programs because they do all of the above: they aim at full proficiency in two languages, an understanding and appreciation of two cultures, and high levels of academic achievement. All the students are English speakers learning in French and English. Their parents are usually middle class and have not only chosen the French immersion program but have also advocated for it. The students do very well academically in both languages. However, because they do not interact in school with native French speakers other than their teachers, research has shown their French is not entirely nativelike. Swain (1985) found that the grammatical competence of grade 6 French immersion students was not equivalent to that of native speakers, "in spite of 7 years of comprehensible input in the target language . . ." (251).

In the United States there has been a recent growth in enrichment programs similar to the French immersion programs in Canada. Often these programs arise because of the growing interest in dual language. School district administrators, often with parental encouragement, but not always, start what is often called an international school. Students in these schools are all native English speakers who learn in two languages throughout elementary school. The programs differ from the French immersion programs in that literacy is usually developed in two languages from the beginning, and often students study 50 percent of the time in English and 50 percent of the time in the second language. Students become bilingual and biliterate and develop positive attitudes toward the target language and speakers of the target language. Research on these programs in the United States is not as extensive as that of programs in Canada, but students do become bilingual and biliterate.

Maintenance bilingual programs in the United States are also considered enrichment models. In most of these programs, Spanish speakers identified as LEP are taught in both Spanish and English from kindergarten through the upper grades. In this process, they develop English and maintain their Spanish. However, there is seldom a model for language use, and in some programs, most instruction is in Spanish. Since there are no native speakers of English in these programs, the programs are considered one-way, rather than two-way, programs. The parents of these LEP children are often low income. They do not usually have a voice in school decision making, and the general public may not look at these programs as enrichment. In addition, there may be resentment about these special programs being provided for Latino children but not for others.

In contrast, students in dual language enrichment programs, even when all the children are Latino, do not all start with the same first language. Some are native English speakers and some are not. Usually, students come from both low-income and middle- or upper-middle-class families. The students learn together in two languages and become competent in both. When students come from two or more cultural groups, they also build important friendships

Type of Enrichment	Students	Curriculum	Results
French Immersion	English speakers	Immersed first in French and then learn in French and English.	Become proficient readers and writers of French and English, although French is not entirely nativelike.
One-Way Enriched Education for Native English Speakers/International Schools	Native English speakers	Usually taught literacy and content in two languages from the beginning.	Become proficient readers and writers of a second language and English.
Maintenance Bilingual Education/One-Way or Enriched Immersion for Nonnative Speakers of English	Speakers of one non-English language (usually Spanish)	Taught literacy and content in both English and Spanish from the beginning.	Become fluent readers, writers, and speakers of two languages. May not enjoy positive image.
Dual Language Education	Native speakers of English and native speakers of another language	Taught literacy and content in two languages.	Become fluent readers, writers, and speakers of two languages. Positive cross-cultural attitudes develop.

FIG. 1–2 Enriched Education Programs

and come to appreciate one another's strengths, languages, and cultures. Figure 1–2 shows the similarities and differences among the types of enrichment programs: French immersion, international schools, maintenance bilingual, and dual immersion.

 ## Historical Context for Dual Language

Bilingualism and encouragement of linguistic diversity have been common since ancient times. The early Greeks, for example, conquered large areas of the Mediterranean and schooled those whom they conquered in the Greek language and culture. However, they did not try to replace local languages. When education was available, it was common to provide formal schooling in more than one language. In fact, since there was so little written material available, a literate person had to be able to read in more than one language. When the Romans conquered Europe, formal schooling included Latin for all students. Like the Greeks, the Romans did not attempt to replace the native language. The precedent for learning in more than one language in Europe was well established by the early occupations (Lessow-Hurley 1996).

In the United States, multilingualism was common when this country was founded. Crawford (1999) reports that "in 1664, when the settlement of New Netherlands was ceded to the British crown, at least eighteen tongues were spoken on Manhattan Island, not counting the Indian languages" (21).

Teaching in languages other than English is not new to the United States. In the 1800s, with the influx of large numbers of immigrants, schools in more than a dozen states provided instruction in a variety of languages, including German, Swedish, Norwegian, Danish, Dutch, Polish, Italian, Czech, French, and Spanish (Lessow-Hurley 1996; Ovando and Collier 1998). There were German/English schools in Baltimore, Cincinnati, Cleveland, Indianapolis, Milwaukee, and St. Louis. Louisiana authorized instruction in English, French, or both languages, and the Territory of New Mexico passed a law authorizing bilingual instruction in Spanish and English. Native Americans also provided instruction in their indigenous languages and English. In fact, Crawford (2004) reports that by 1850, the Cherokees had achieved a 90 percent literacy rate and used bilingual materials "to such an extent that Oklahoma Cherokees had a higher English literacy level than the white populations of either Texas or Arkansas" (92).

Even though the early history of America reflects an acceptance of instruction in languages other than English, attitudes toward bilingualism became increasingly negative. For example, the accomplishments of the Cherokees were resented, and by 1879 the government began to force Native American children to attend boarding schools in an attempt to eradicate native languages and replace them with English. About the same time, Italian, Jewish, and Slavic immigrants began to outnumber the already established Irish, German, and Scandinavian immigrant populations. Public sentiment toward these newcomers was negative, and those who did not speak English were criticized.

In 1906, Congress passed the first federal language law requiring knowledge of English for naturalization. Proficiency in English began to be equated with political loyalty. Around the time that the United States entered World War I, it was clearly un-American to speak a language other than English in public. By the 1930s, bilingual instruction "was virtually eradicated throughout the United States" (Crawford 2004, 91), and there was little interest in learning in two languages in public schools for the next thirty years.

The New Mexico Bilingual Education Story

New Mexico, a state whose people have been multilingual since before it became a territory, stands out as an exception in its openness to bilingual education. From the 1200s, around sixty Pueblo tribes spoke different indigenous languages including Tewa, Tiwa, Towa, Keres, and Zuni. Navajo and Apache Native Americans arrived around 1500. Between the early 1500s and the mid-1800s, Spain and then Mexico ruled the area and the governance was known for encouraging bilingualism and cultural pluralism. Under Mexican rule, native New Mexicans were even appointed to government posts, giving New Mexicans both the responsibility for and voice in self-governance. When New Mexico became a U.S. territory around 1850, New Mexicans could run for the legislature. During this period, the territory officially authorized bilingual education in Spanish and English. In the early 1900s when some in the United States were mandating English-only instruction, New Mexico still acknowledged the importance of Spanish and bilingualism, even passing constitutional provisions to maintain a bilingual citizenry. In 1935 a state house bill called for rural teachers to teach Spanish reading to Spanish-speaking pupils and to English speakers who wanted to learn Spanish (López 2003).

Between 1935 and the mid-1960s, New Mexico was the site of much interest in language learning and teaching. In 1961 state language educators were instrumental in the formation of the Teachers of English to Speakers of Other Languages (TESOL) organization, which now is a well-established international organization supporting the teaching of English around the world. In 1963, the state department of education funded one of the earliest bilingual projects in the country. The Pecos Bilingual Education Project taught social studies and language arts to Spanish speakers in Spanish to show they could develop literacy skills in standard Spanish.

One of the earliest dual language programs in the United States was initiated through National Defense Education Act (NDEA) funding in 1967. Las Cruces Public Schools began an innovative 50/50 K–3 sustained bilingual program with mainly Spanish speakers but including around 10 to 15 percent English-speaking participants. Children became very bilingual and a study of the students through twelfth grade showed there were no dropouts from this program (López 2003). Between 1967 and the present, New Mexico is one state that has continued to support bilingualism by passing a bilingual education act, providing state guidelines for bilingual certification, forming an educational partnership with Spain, increasing state funding for bilingual programs, and calling for proficiency in English and another language. In 1996 the state department of education piloted a four-year program to support two-way dual language immersion in five schools in the state. Later funding through Title VII allowed for a longitudinal study of five dual language pilot programs across the state (López 2003). In view of the state's history, it is not surprising, then, that

New Mexico hosts the annual La Cosecha Conference, one of the country's most important dual language conferences.

Two-Way Programs: The Florida Story

The 1959 revolution in Cuba brought back bilingual education to the south when privileged, professional Cuban refugees arrived on the Florida coast with education, job skills, and pride in their language and culture. Feinberg (1999) describes how dual language education programs developed in Miami. By the early 1960s the huge influx of Cuban refugees into the area brought more than eighteen thousand Cuban students into the Miami Dade County public schools. The school district, overwhelmed by the enrollment of more than three thousand non-English-speaking students per year, began recruiting experienced Cuban teachers and, through the Miami Cuban Teacher Retraining project, gave them special certification. With the help of these educators and grants, Coral Way Elementary School, a bi-ethnic, bilingual school, was opened in 1965. By 1975, eight bi-ethnic, bilingual schools were established and bilingual curriculum was available in eighteen secondary schools.

However, as the Latino community expanded, antagonism toward Latinos and the Spanish language grew; so, for the next ten years, between 1978 and 1988, there was a yearly battle to maintain any of the bilingual support that had been provided. Most of the bilingual programs disappeared. These battles did serve a creative purpose. They empowered bilingual advocates who became active in community-based organizations such as the Spanish American League Against Discrimination (SALAD) and the American Hispanic Educators Association of Dade (AHEAD). Professional organizations such as the Florida Bilingual Association, the Florida Foreign Language Association, and Florida Teachers of English to Speakers of Other Languages became proactive. In 1982, when the school board considered the total elimination of programs in Spanish for Spanish speakers, AHEAD leaders were responsible for working to change the membership of the school board and to gain influence with district superintendents.

Other events supported the rise of dual language education in Miami. In 1985 the Southern Governors' Association featured a discussion of the business-related educational needs of an emerging global economy and multicultural society. One of the results of this meeting was a call for drawing on the linguistic resources of language-minority students. At about this time, a local study of language-related workforce needs called for more job applicants who were bilingual and biliterate. In the English Only atmosphere they had grown up in, very few native-born Latinos had more than a rudimentary command of oral Spanish and did not read or write the language well. In 1996 the new school board responded to this need for bilingualism and biliteracy and voted financial support for a bilingual expansion plan. By June 1999, five dual language schools were established, and seventeen other schools offered support for the development of bilingualism and biliteracy. Feinberg (1999) explains what happened in Miami despite anti-immigrant sentiment and political attacks on bilingual education throughout the rest of the country:

> The combination of increased Hispanic representation on the board, the influence of prestigious community and chamber organizations, academic support in the form of well publicized research studies, and the active involvement of politically savvy members of the bilingual education community was successful in repelling if not eliminating resistance to bilingual schools and programs. (60)

Growth of Dual Language Programs Across the Country

The reasons for the resurgence of dual language in Florida are similar to the reasons for the growth of these programs across the country. Howard and Christian (2002) explain that between 1963, when Coral Way opened, and the mid-1980s, the growth of dual language programs was relatively slow. However, since then the growth has been rapid because of the need to compete in a global economy, the needs of an increased number of second language learners, and the obvious success of the programs.

Policy makers and educators have recognized how critical it is for Americans to become multilingual in the growing global economy. In 2000, when then Secretary of Education Riley highlighted the dual language approach as the most effective way to teach English and encourage biliteracy, he pointed out that the United States needed to invest in programs such as these because "in an international economy, knowledge—and knowledge of language—is power" (2000, 4). Brecht and Ingold (1998) explain clearly the importance of multilingualism in this country:

> Because the United States interacts with virtually every nation in the world, and because U.S. society includes individuals and communities from many of those nations, the need for proficiency in their languages and for use in social, economic, and geopolitical areas has never been higher. (1)

Considerable research has pointed to dual language education as the best way for English learners, as well as native English speakers, to achieve biliteracy and experience high academic achievement. Research reports from districts across the country repeatedly credit dual language education for higher test scores (Lindholm-Leary 2001; Thomas and Collier 2002; Christian, Howard, and Loeb 2000). Some particularly well-known programs have been the basis of much research and study. These include the Oyster School in Washington, D.C., begun in 1971; the Amigos Two Way program in Cambridge, Massachusetts, begun in 1985; Francis Scott Key Elementary School in Arlington, Virginia, begun in 1986; and River Glen Elementary in San José, California, begun in 1987. Even English Only advocates cannot deny the success of these programs. In California, despite the English Only initiative, Proposition 227, districts are looking at dual language as a way to help English learners succeed because Structured English Immersion programs mandated by the proposition have not resulted in academic gains. English Only immersion programs are not teaching children English (Crawford 2003). In contrast, English language learners in dual language programs do well on standardized measures in English and also maintain and develop their native language.

Success stories from dual language programs have been widely disseminated throughout the education community. Specialists from successful programs have spoken about the benefits of dual language to teachers and administrators at conferences and district meetings across the country. Videos have been made with experts, teachers, administrators, and parents explaining why two-way bilingual education works. State and national education conferences have held institutes to promote dual language programs and have formed special interest groups on dual language to help educators network and support one another.

Educators support dual language education not only because it helps students succeed academically but also because they know that dual language schools promote increased cross-cultural understanding (Torres-Guzmán 2002; Lindholm-Leary 2001). Cabezón, Nicoladis, and Lambert (2003) report in their study of the Amigos program in Massachusetts what has been the experience of schools implementing dual language across the country.

> We notice . . . that both English- and Spanish-Amigos enjoy learning about a new and different cultural group through long-term daily contact with members of a second ethnolinguistic group, who become like brothers and sisters to them. (11)

Studies of the Amigos program, as well as studies of other early dual language programs such as the Oyster program (Freeman 1995), reflect how important it is that children from different languages and cultures learn together in two languages. Genesee and Gándara (1999) point out that dual language programs provide data that support the contact hypothesis. This hypothesis holds that improved relationships result when students work and study together—when there is increased contact between cultures:

> Dual-language programs present a particularly interesting case for examining the contact hypothesis because they provide sustained opportunities for direct intergroup contact and, in principle, they incorporate at least some of the situational characteristics that are considered critical for positive intergroup outcomes, namely, the potential for close and cooperative contact in a context that is anxiety reduced and equitable for all participating groups. (667)

Contact promotes cross-cultural understanding among the children participating in dual language programs. However, the discrepancies between the socioeconomic status of English speakers and Spanish speakers can work to hinder positive intergroup relationships. For that reason, it is especially important that administrators, teachers, and parents maintain high expectations for students from both groups. Students are more likely to develop positive attitudes toward their classmates in a school where all students are expected to succeed. A school in south Texas provides this kind of positive atmosphere. At a recent orientation, Yvonne and her student teachers were visibly moved as the principal passionately explained that:

> All our students are special. All of them have potential. It doesn't matter if they live in a *colonia* with no electricity or running water. It doesn't matter if their parents work in the fields. Everyone here is becoming bilingual and biliterate. Everyone can and will learn.

 Conclusion

As we interviewed administrators, teachers, parents, and teacher educators across the country about Spanish/English dual language programs, we asked them what they saw as the benefits of these programs. The answers they gave mirrored the answers others have reported. They told us that schools needed to prepare children for a global economy and that children needed to be prepared for the twenty-first century. They also said that all the dual language schools in their area were *A*-rated, that the children, both native English and native Spanish speakers, had the highest test scores in their districts, that the children in their schools were becoming bilingual and biliterate, that their students appreciated each other's cultures, that their students were open to and accepting of diversity, and that lifelong intercultural friendships had been formed. In fact, the only negatives that interviewees expressed about dual language education had to do with implementation questions.

In the rest of this book, then, we hope to address some of the struggles that educators face as they develop and implement dual language programs. As has been typical in our previous books, we begin with scenarios from schools, and we tell stories of students and teachers. In the next chapter, we first describe twelve dual language programs across the country that represent some of the variety in program models. We then profile types of students and teachers who are part of different dual language programs. We also suggest what kinds of support each type of teacher and student needs. As you read about these schools and the students and the teachers, try to identify characteristics of the programs, students, and teachers in your area and consider what might be learned from those comparisons.

 Learning Extensions

1. In Figure 1–1, we summarize several types of programs for English language learners. We list the language result and the academic result for each type of program. Describe a program in your local school: which type of program is it, and what are the language and academic results? Be prepared to discuss this with others.

2. This chapter discusses subtractive programs for ELLs. Have you or has anyone you know experienced subtractive schooling? Which type of subtractive program was it? What were the effects?

3. In California, Proposition 227 calls for English immersion. Other states in the United States have similar propositions or English Only requirements. Have you seen the effect of these propositions on students and/or communities? Discuss this.

4. Interview someone who is working in a school with one of the types of subtractive programs described in this chapter. Be prepared to give a description of the students involved, the program itself, and the language and academic results. Do the results match the results listed here?

Dual Language Programs, Students, and Teachers

Across the country dual language classrooms are giving parents, teachers, school administrators, school boards, and communities a new vision of the potential of an enriched model of bilingual education. As we interviewed people about their programs and, in many cases, visited the schools where programs had been implemented, we were continually struck by the diversity within the programs. There were different reasons that schools or programs within schools were begun. There were many different adaptations of the basic dual language models. Student populations varied widely, as did the communities where the programs existed. Teachers working in the dual language programs also varied in their backgrounds, their bilingual proficiency, and their reasons for teaching in dual language programs.

Programs grow out of a vision from within the school or the community. In order to create new programs and maintain the quality of existing ones, those involved in dual language education must seriously consider who their students and teachers are. While no program can maintain long-term success without knowledgeable leadership, programs must also develop in ways that are responsive to the needs and skills of both students and teachers.

In this chapter we provide an overview of programs, students, and teachers. First, to show how varied dual language programs are, we present snapshots of twelve dual language schools and one international program. Next, using examples from real students, we describe the types of students found in dual language programs and identify the differing needs students have. Finally, we provide case studies of teachers either teaching in dual language programs or preparing to teach in them. Because of their different backgrounds and language proficiencies, these teachers need different kinds of support. It is our hope that these examples might help readers reflect on their own programs, students, and teachers and consider how best to meet their varied needs.

Dual Language Programs Across the United States

Northeast

A dual language strand was created in 1990 in a school in Framingham, Massachusetts, because the district was concerned both about the social segregation of Spanish-speaking students in regular bilingual programs and the "white flight" of middle-class parents. The program had two purposes. On one hand, it was meant to attract middle-class Anglo parents with the idea that their children could become bilingual and biliterate. On the other hand, the program was created to meet the academic, language, and social needs of the mainly lower socioeconomic Latino children who made up one-third of the school population. Most of the Spanish speakers were U.S.-born Puerto Ricans or Central or South American children and most of the English speakers were Anglos.

The program model evolved as neither a pure 90/10 nor a 50/50 model. Those working with the program saw development of literacy in the primary language as key. In kindergarten, Spanish speakers have all their instruction in Spanish with the exception of specials, including music, art, and physical education. Native English speakers are given language arts, math, and specials in English, so they are taught in Spanish with the native Spanish speakers about 40 percent of the time through science and social studies units. In first grade, students are taught math and language arts in their primary language and are integrated for instruction in other subject areas. This means that students are taught in their nonnative language only about 30 percent of the time. However, by third grade, students are integrated for language arts instruction in both languages, so instruction is 50 percent of the time in English and 50 percent of the time in Spanish. An emphasis in the program is to keep academic work at grade level in both languages at all times despite the fact that there are always some students learning in their second language. Talented bilingual teachers, both native and nonnative speakers, were recruited to teach in the program and are largely responsible for the continuity and success of the program (de Jong 2002b).

New York City

Parents and community members in a working-class neighborhood in inner-city New York were concerned that students in their schools were not achieving. Their district had been identified as one of the poorest in the country. Proactive parents visited schools throughout the city to see what programs were successful and found that students in dual language schools in more affluent neighborhoods were showing high academic success. Since almost 70 percent of the neighborhood school population consisted of Latino immigrants from all over the Spanish-speaking world, supporters for change decided that it would be good to consider a two-way bilingual program in which Spanish speakers could build on the strength of their primary language and, at the same time, develop the needed academic skills in English. Representatives from the large African American and growing Asian groups in the area also supported a dual language program because they knew their children would benefit from becoming bilingual.

Working together with some educators, neighborhood advocates applied for and got a New Vision grant, one of many granted in New York City, to create a Spanish/English dual language school. The school opened with 54 students in 1997 and by 2003 had 256 students. In the short period since the school began, test scores have risen dramatically. In 2002 the students scored first in their district in math and fourth in English reading.

The school is unusual in that the codirectors are a teacher from the program and a parent advocate. They have worked with dual language consultants to provide inservice for the staff and to develop a program appropriate for their needs. After analysis of a more traditional alternate-day 50/50 model, the teachers and administration decided that kindergarten and first-grade children needed longer periods of immersion in their second language, so they chose a model with alternate weeks in Spanish and English for those two grades. For second through fifth grades, the program uses an alternate-day model.

Teachers in the program represent the diversity of the community, though some of the Spanish-speaking teachers are Anglo, a group not representative of the neighborhood. The benefits of the program go beyond academic achievement. Program developers and faculty notice that students show respect for diversity and that the different ethnic groups, both students and parents, work together and have formed important friendships that should have a positive effect on the whole community. In addition, many of the parents who advocated for their children's education have become even more empowered and active. More than $11 million have been raised to establish a new dual language school site and presently that site is being refurbished for occupancy in the near future.

Florida

In a district on the east coast of Florida, several dual language programs have been established to meet both the academic needs of the students and the language needs of the large bilingual community. The population of area schools ranges from 60 to 70 percent Latino. Students in the two-way programs include English-speaking Anglos, Latinos, and African Americans as well as native Spanish speakers from Mexico, Cuba, Puerto Rico, Venezuela, Peru, Argentina, and Uruguay. Most programs also include Haitian Creole speakers who have recently immigrated into this region.

Teachers work in bilingual pairs. At first, the dual language schools tried an alternate-day model. However, teachers and administrators felt that the English learners needed some curriculum in English every day, so they changed the model. Presently, in kindergarten through second grade, the English teacher teaches one group of students language arts, social studies, and math in the morning. While that group receives their instruction in English, another group receives language arts, social studies, and science in Spanish. Teachers switch groups after lunch and teach students the same content in the same language to the other group. Thus, each teacher sees about fifty students daily. Note that in these three grades, math is taught only in English and science is taught only in Spanish.

From third grade on, the models vary widely within the district. In some cases, the students' exposure to Spanish is drastically reduced to a short Spanish language arts time. This causes concern for those who understand the importance of the continual development of both languages.

Teachers in the program are both native English speakers, who teach the English portion of the program, and Spanish speakers with various levels of proficiency in Spanish. Some are native speakers and others are second- or third-generation Latinos who struggle with academic Spanish. A special program recruits exchange teachers from Spain to teach in several of the schools. However, the teachers from Spain have to make adjustments to teach in a completely different environment with different kinds of curricular expectations.

Despite the variations and struggles, there is overall success with the programs. Schools that were previously *D*-rated have become *A*-rated after implementing dual language programs. Latino parents feel comfortable in these schools, and staff members have noticed a much-improved attitude toward cultural and linguistic diversity.

Urban California

A large, inner-city elementary school in Fresno, California, with a community population made up primarily of immigrants from Mexico, Central America, and Southeast Asia began a Spanish/English dual language strand in 1997. Some of the English-speaking students in the program come from other neighborhoods and are transported by parents who value bilingualism. Other English speakers are Anglos, African Americans, or Asians living near the school.

The school has maintained a fairly pure 90/10 model for its program. Students in kindergarten and first grade learn in Spanish for most of the day. By second grade more English is added, and in third grade literacy is taught to all students in both languages. By fifth grade, students have approximately one-half of the day in English and one-half of the day in Spanish.

Teachers in the school are native Spanish speakers from Mexico or Central America as well as second-generation Spanish speakers who have maintained or relearned Spanish. Administrative support for the dual language strand in the school has been high and different grants have supported both research of the program and the acquisition of needed resources. The entire school, and especially the dual language strand, is consistently recognized for high student success.

Rural California

A rural school district in central California with a transitional bilingual program had experienced problems with students' low academic achievement and gang involvement. The school board brought in a new bilingual director who believed in meeting student needs through dual language programs. However, the student body was more than 95 percent Latino with a large percentage of English language learners. Most programs the new director knew about had a more equal number of native English speakers and English language learners. The philosophy and curriculum of dual language programs, however, intrigued him. He applied for and received a grant that allowed him to provide financial support so many of his teachers could complete an M.A. degree in bilingual education. At the same time, he implemented two-way bilingual education in two different schools.

The programs began as 50/50 models with one-half of the day in English and one-half of the day in Spanish. With time, the new director changed these programs to 90/10 models because of the research in California that showed greater success for the 90/10 model (Lindholm-Leary 2001). He felt that this model offered more potential for the students in his district.

The teachers in his two-way programs, mainly local second-generation Mexican Americans who had experienced negative attitudes in their own schooling, were excited about this new program. However, the necessary curricular changes, especially in the upper grades, presented a challenge. It was not easy to implement appropriate curriculum and find credentialed teachers with the academic Spanish proficiency needed to support teaching academic content. A local university faculty member works with the teachers to support the strong content- and theme-based curriculum that students need for academic success.

Nebraska

Omaha's second language population was largely Polish until a recent influx of immigrants from Mexico found work in the meatpacking plants and the service industries in the city. As is typical for most new immigrant populations, the newcomers settled together in inner-city neighborhoods and impacted two elementary schools in particular. A new second language specialist with experience in two-way bilingual education arrived from New York City and encouraged the development of dual language strands in the two schools. Presently several middle-class Anglo parents have enrolled their children in these programs, but the majority of the children are Mexican-origin English language learners.

The first school to implement the program has used bilingual teams to provide instruction in each language. Teachers work closely together to plan opening activities for the students in each language and then teach literacy and content around the same themes in each language. Students switch teachers and languages halfway through the day. Some teachers plan so well together that they actually physically mirror each other's rooms in the two languages. For example, in first grade when students study family, the related sections of both the Spanish teacher's and the English teacher's rooms are arranged to show similar brainstorming and graphing activities, art projects, and key-word charts.

Perhaps the biggest challenge for program coordinators in this Midwest community has been finding teachers whose Spanish is adequate or native Spanish speakers with the teaching credentials required by the state. These challenges have required adaptations in program structure. In the second school, which is just implementing the dual language model, the preschool uses a native English-speaking teacher learning Spanish and a bilingual para-educator rather than a pair of credentialed teachers because the school cannot find enough Spanish-speaking teachers. Still, despite these challenges, after three years, the first school to implement two-way education is already showing impressive scores on standardized tests.

Kansas

In Wichita, Kansas, the dual language strand in one school was so successful that administrators, teachers, and community members promoted the building of a dual language school in the city. In fall 2003, the new dual language K–3 school opened to much celebration in the entire community. This school will eventually house a K–8 dual language program.

In the old school, there were two dual language classrooms at each grade level and teachers taught in Spanish/English teams. Students were given ninety minutes of language arts daily in their native language and then teachers taught science, social studies, and math through alternate-week themes. For example, after the daily language arts period, a group of integrated Spanish- and English-dominant children studied science, social studies, and math around a rural communities theme with the Spanish teacher for a week while the other integrated group of children studied urban communities in English through science, social studies, and math. Then the groups switched and the teachers taught their units again to the other group. Specials such as music, art, and physical education were all taught in English.

This year at the new school, there are three classes at the first-, second-, and third-grade levels, so teachers are organizing the curriculum differently than before. Two of the three teachers for each grade level teach in Spanish. Each teacher has a different content specialization. One teacher teaches language arts and social studies in English, another teaches language arts and social studies in Spanish, and the third teaches science and math in Spanish. Mainly because of staffing limitations, specials are also taught in English at the new school.

When the program first began at the old school, the school was only able to recruit 25 percent English-speaking students. The interest of the English-speaking community in the program has grown so that in the new school, 40 percent of the students are native English-speaking Anglos, African Americans, and Latinos. Many people now believe that this program has the potential of impacting the entire community by promoting not only bilingualism but also unity and cross-cultural understanding.

Colorado

When one Colorado school district called for proposals for the establishment of innovative programs in an old building no longer being used, a proactive transitional bilingual teacher organized parent and community support to start a dual language school. After ten years, the program has grown from 88 students to 325 students. Recently, a several-million-dollar expansion was added to the building to accommodate the student growth. Fifty-four percent of the school is Latino, and many Latino parents choose this school for their children. Most of the families come from Mexico, and the school works to be sure they feel welcomed and supported. Many of the native English speakers at the school are Anglos whose parents bring them to the school each day from other areas in the district. The program has evolved and attracts more students each year. There is a long list of both English-speaking and Spanish-speaking parents who hope to have their children in the program.

When the program began, Spanish/English teachers teamed to teach combination grade levels in their respective languages, but as the program developed, the school decided that any teacher working in the program should be a model of bilingualism. Most teachers are able to teach in both Spanish and English and all have at least receptive knowledge of Spanish.

At this school, students in first through fourth grade are integrated for instruction during a morning homeroom opening time and in the afternoon for math, science, and social studies. The afternoon content areas are taught to all students in Spanish one week and in English the next. In the morning, English-speaking students have language arts in English and Spanish as a Second Language (SSL) while Spanish speakers have Spanish language arts and ESL. Students are integrated for language arts time by fifth or sixth grade.

Urban Texas

A large district in North Dallas includes neighborhoods that vary a great deal. Two interesting neighborhood schools in the district meet the needs of their student populations with different kinds of dual language programs. One school in a middle-class neighborhood has a two-way bilingual strand. Another in a section of the community with many new immigrants from Central America has a strong one-way dual language program. Students in both programs have succeeded academically in both languages, and parent involvement, though different in nature, has been high.

Two-Way Strand School ◆ One school of around five hundred students is located in a middle-class neighborhood. Many Spanish speakers living in the area have moved to this country from South America. Other students come from Mexico and Central America. The school, which began its two-way program six years ago, has a strand that now goes from kindergarten through fifth grade. Advocates for the two-way program received funding from a grant and then carefully laid the groundwork necessary for implementation. Before the program was implemented, parents of both native English and native Spanish speakers were shown the positive research results of two-way programs. Videos of successful programs helped participants understand the goals and the value of two-way bilingual education. As the program has developed and staff and parents have interacted, parents have become more informed and involved.

Approximately 60 percent of the students in the program are native Spanish speakers and 40 percent native English speakers, though this division varies a bit from class to class. Teachers and administrators have worked together to develop a 50/50 model that works for them. Although classes began with an alternate-day model, teachers found that they could not finish projects they had begun or teach the content they wished thoroughly enough, so the teachers have moved to a two-day/two-day model—two days are taught in Spanish and two days in English.

Literacy is developed for both native Spanish speakers and native English speakers in their primary language first. For example, fluency, comprehension, and knowledge of vocabulary in Spanish are evaluated before native Spanish speakers are given literacy instruction in English. Because of their lack of Spanish knowledge, native English speakers are not admitted to the program after second grade, though Spanish speakers are able to enter the program at any time. Those Spanish speakers are usually literate in Spanish. Their teachers are not only bilingual but also ESL-certified and can provide the strategies students need to make the content taught in English comprehensible. As an additional resource to the model, the grant resource specialist provides small-group tutoring for ESL students during guided reading.

Careful planning has gone into the program. All teachers are given time to plan together every six weeks, and as a result, the teachers collaborate to develop lessons and strategies that give students access to content taught in both languages. Teachers do not share students but do help each other organize around themes as much as possible.

Both Spanish-speaking and English-speaking parents are very supportive. There are good reasons for this support, as students do well academically, form strong friendships, and become empowered learners. Standardized test scores show that the English speakers outscore most English speakers in the school despite the fact that they are learning in two languages. Their Spanish scores are adequate but not quite at grade level. By third grade, tests show that Spanish speakers are at grade level when tested in English and above grade level when tested in Spanish.

One-Way School ◆ Beautifully mounted native costumes and artifacts, a world map, and a huge, colorful sign saying "We Are the World" welcome all to a PreK–1 school serving a neighborhood with a high immigrant population. The commitment to high parent involvement, beginning when children are still infants, is evident throughout the school. Several classrooms are dedicated to parent education during the day and in the evenings. The school has been a gathering place for parents in the community for more than ten years. Classes include ESL, GED, parenting, and nutrition. The daytime classes for parents attract more than a hundred families. The evening classes have more than five hundred adults and children in attendance. In addition, every Wednesday for the past twelve years, parents have come and worked in the halls, in the cafeteria, and in classrooms, helping teachers with many different tasks.

Six years ago the school district decided to offer the largely Spanish-speaking student body a 50/50 Spanish/English program. Spanish speakers make up much of the student body of approximately seven hundred students. Only two classes at each grade level provide English instruction for native English speakers. The bilingual teachers in the 50/50 program organize instruction around themes connected to the TEKS (Texas Essential Knowledge and Skills). Initially in prekindergarten, most of the instruction is in Spanish, but within a few weeks, teachers begin to use an alternating schedule between Spanish and

English. The exact language delivery model may differ from teacher to teacher and depend on the time of year. Teachers have the flexibility to adjust the delivery based on classroom needs as long as they stay true to the 50/50 model for all subjects.

Literacy is developed in both languages from the beginning. While instruction alternates for other subjects, literacy may be taught in more extended blocks so that students can complete some literacy activities in one language before moving on to new activities in the other language. For example, language arts might be in Spanish for a week and then in English for a week while other subjects alternate on a daily basis. Emphasis is placed on the similarities between the two languages. For example, one kindergarten teacher has developed an alphabet chart with pictures of words that have the same initial sound in both English and Spanish for each letter. For example, *B* shows a baby (*bebé*) and *C* has a castle (*castillo*). All the other teachers now use this chart, and it is posted in the halls and the cafeteria.

Students are succeeding academically in this school and transfer from this school to another neighborhood school that continues the 50/50 program through the sixth grade. Students in the program become truly bilingual and biliterate.

South Texas

An elementary school of 360 students is located one mile from the Mexican border amid fields of sugar cane. Many of the students the school serves live in unincorporated *colonias,* neighborhoods often without sewer service and sometimes even without water lines. Ninety-nine percent of the students are from low-income Latino families. Some of the students come to school speaking only Spanish, some come speaking only English, and many come with varied proficiency in both languages. The test scores at the school were dismal eight years ago until a passionate, committed, and innovative woman became principal. Her dedication and persistence have resulted in a beautiful new school building that replaces the substandard buildings that housed students in the past and in the establishment of a dual language program.

The principal worked with a local university professor who had developed a model of dual language education that fit the uniquely Latino population of the valley of south Texas. It is a 50/50 model in which language use is divided by subject area and by time. Students are taught to read and write in their primary languages in preschool and kindergarten. Starting in second grade, students have language arts in both languages. Math is always taught in English and science and social studies in Spanish. Specials, including music, art, physical education, and computers, and daily openings are done one day in Spanish and the next in English. Also, on alternate days all the business of the school is carried out in Spanish or English, so secretaries greet guests and answer the phone in Spanish on Spanish days and in English on English days. This gives both languages equal value at the school.

In only a few years, the school's atmosphere and physical appearance and the students' academic achievement have had a complete turnaround. The school was recently recognized by the State of Texas for outstanding academic achievement. It has been featured in magazines and on national television. The students are proud of themselves and their learning, and this is reflected in their work and the school environment. With innovative planning, grant writing, and persistence, the principal provides inservice for teachers by nationally and internationally renowned experts. Even with support, however, the challenges are many. Administrators and teachers constantly work together to provide effective instruction. This includes giving native Spanish-speaking students the academic Spanish they need to be able to also acquire academic English. The teachers are almost all second- or third-generation Mexican Americans who have lived in the valley all their lives. Some need to work on improving their academic Spanish. Everyone realizes that in order to help students, it is necessary to constantly reevaluate, continue to learn, and be prepared to change.

A Nevada One-Way Enrichment Model

An international school was started in Henderson, Nevada, south of Las Vegas, when an area superintendent became intrigued by the idea that native English speakers could receive an enriched program and become bilingual and biliterate. He recruited a dual language specialist who had been working in the district in a two-way school to begin a program in another school. The specialist and the administration of the new school worked together to plan and implement a truly international curriculum. The program not only creates bilinguals but also reflects a commitment to international education. The school is located in a middle- to upper-class suburban neighborhood in which nearly all the students are native English speakers. This is a one-way program. English-speaking children are adding Spanish as a second language. The school is not a magnet school. Only children who live in the school area attend this school.

The curriculum is organized around integrated themes based on social studies content including governments, architecture, exploration, immigration, the environment, and the imagination of children as seen through literature. During the first year, the PTA supported the hiring of a local artist, who created an impressive mural with flags from around the world and sections reflecting the themes in intricate detail. The children watched the mural being created and now use the mural for several projects as they study the themes.

The program has been implemented at the kindergarten and first-grade levels at this point. New grade levels will be added each year. Teachers work in bilingual teams. One week, students learn in English in the morning and Spanish in the afternoon, and the next week, they learn in Spanish in the morning and English in the afternoon.

Parents are extremely supportive of the program. In fact, the success of the program has encouraged the opening of two other international schools in the area. Student progress at this early stage is perhaps best reflected in a story told by the program coordinator and assistant principal. One parent who was concerned about the program began asking lots of questions of one of the Spanish teachers. The Spanish teacher, who was committed to speaking only Spanish in front of the children, answered the frustrated mother in Spanish. However, the mother's young son came up and helped out by translating everything the teacher said. The mother was so amazed that she immediately went to the coordinator's office to admit her concerns were unfounded. She has since visited classes and come to understand how well her son is learning academic content through Spanish.

 ## Variations and Similarities

During our interviews and visits to these schools, we noted both variations and similarities. As school representatives told us their stories and showed us their schools, we were continually impressed by how the different schools had adapted their dual language programs to fit the needs of both their students and their teachers. While experts have laid out some basic dual language education models and requirements for successful programs, the context of each school determines how the program will be implemented.

Program leaders, working with teachers, have improvised to adapt proven models to fit the students, teachers, and available resources. Dual language education has had such spectacular results, especially for English language learners, that educators are willing to make the necessary modifications to implement a program that will help their students. Results from the programs we have investigated show improved academic achievement, the development of bilingual and biliterate students, and positive cross-cultural relationships.

Advocates of two-way bilingual education are concerned with the many variations in implementation (Christian, Howard, and Loeb 2000). There is a danger that if some programs are poorly implemented and produce poor results, critics will use those schools as examples and condemn all dual language programs. Historically, bilingual programs have been targets for individuals and groups who favor English-only instruction. On one hand, there is a need to provide English language learners with the best possible education; on the other hand, there is the very real possibility that poorly implemented programs will fail, attract public attention, and lead to the rejection of dual language education in general.

While we cannot solve the problems that individual school districts face as they try to implement dual language education in a variety of settings with varied resources, we can help educators think carefully about how to develop programs that fit their students and their teachers. In the next section we provide profiles of students from some of the programs described earlier.

 ## Students in Dual Language Programs

One of the first things we noticed as we studied dual language schools across the country is that the student population often drives the curriculum. This is as it should be, as education should be responsive to the needs of the learners. Our discussion of students in dual language programs begins with those students for whom English is the native language and then moves to those for whom Spanish is the stronger language. A third group includes those students who are somewhat bilingual when they begin school. Finally, there are a few students in dual language Spanish/English programs who speak neither English nor Spanish when they enter. We describe these different types of students and discuss the differing needs of each group. Readers can compare these students with their students and consider how to configure their programs to best meet the needs of their students.

Native English Speakers

There are three common types of native English speakers in dual language programs: native English speakers whose parents are middle-class or upper-middle-class Anglos, second- or third-generation Latino children who enter school speaking English, and native English speakers whose ethnic background is African American, Asian American, Haitian Creole, Portuguese, or any of the many groups represented in this country. The parents of the children in these three groups usually choose the dual language program for their children because they believe in the program's benefits. There is, however, also a fourth kind of native English speaker. They are found in programs in which there are neighborhood dual language schools. These children come from various socio-economic and ethnic backgrounds and attend a dual language program because it is the only option in their neighborhood school. Their parents may or may not understand, approve of, or support two-way bilingual education.

Native English speakers with adequate preparation and support ◆ Victoria, or Tori, as she is affectionately called by all, is a native English speaker whose parents are well-educated professionals. Victoria's family lives in an affluent area in the northern part of their small California city. They have to drive thirty minutes each day to take Victoria to an inner-city school where there is a Spanish/English dual language program. Victoria's mother is a teacher who understands the importance of bilingualism. When asked why they chose the program, her parents explained, "We chose to place Tori in the dual immersion program because multilingualism is a bridge to a wider worldview and provides a broader learning base." Tori's parents wanted her to have the opportunity to learn a second language at an early age and become bilingual and bicultural.

Victoria's parents explain the benefits they have seen for their daughter.

> Tori is in her seventh year of dual immersion. We have seen her world perspective grow; she appreciates different people, different cultures, and different learning opportunities. She is comfortable speaking Spanish often with people she doesn't know well. Her second language ability routinely puts others at ease, and we're certain it will help her as she progresses toward a career. She reads and writes on grade level in both languages and scores above average on standardized tests in both languages. She is a healthy, well-adjusted person.

Both Tori's parents and her teachers comment that she is a great problem solver and is a big-picture thinker inside and outside the classroom. They attribute this to her bilingual, bicultural education. Tori is proud of being bilingual and brags about being the only kid in her neighborhood who can speak Spanish.

Students like Victoria are usually excellent students to have in any two-way program. They have the advantages of their home environment, which almost always includes rich literacy experiences in English and their parents' positive encouragement to become bilingual. Children like Victoria have all the incentives they need to succeed.

Many students are like Tori. However, interviews with parents of English-speaking children surfaced some concerns that were unique to this group. Middle-class parents know the importance of helping their children with their homework and reading to and with them at home. However, when their children are studying in a language parents do not understand, speak, read, or write, at least not fluently, the parents become anxious and concerned. One could point out that this is the situation for the many immigrant parents who send their children to all-English programs, but this insight does not help middle-class English-speaking parents who want to be sure their children have academic success. Parent anxiety seems to be especially high with younger children—kindergartners and first graders.

Schools and teachers have developed different strategies to relieve the concerns of these parents. They have sent home weekly packets with familiar activities. For example, schools might send a list of spelling words to practice. Even though the words are in Spanish, parents understand how to help their children study for a spelling test. Parents get used to the routine and work to help their children with their homework. Another possible support is sending home Spanish children's books that are accompanied by tapes. These materials provide opportunities for parents to read with their children and also learn with them.

Second- or third-generation English speakers ◆ Alexandra is also called by her nickname, Alexi. She represents a large group of children found in many dual language programs. Alexi's grandparents on one side and great-grandparents on the other came from Mexico to seek a better life in this country. Her maternal grandparents were born in Arizona and Texas, and her mother grew up speaking English. Her father, though born in Mexico, grew up in California, speaking English. Both parents graduated from high school. Her father finished junior college and now works as a communication specialist for AT&T. Her mother went to secretarial school, worked for a school district, and now works at a local university. She has been the administrative assistant for a grant program and presently works for the dean of professional development.

Though Alexi's parents speak and understand Spanish, they never learned to read or write Spanish since their schooling was all in English. Their two older boys were raised as monolingual English speakers. Alexi and her two older brothers could not speak to or always understand their grandparents on their father's side. When Alexi reached school age, her parents investigated a local dual language program and decided they wanted to enroll their daughter. This turned out to be a difficult decision. While some relatives were supportive, others believed that, since English was spoken at home, Alexi would get confused being taught in Spanish at school. They also seemed convinced that learning in Spanish would impede her academic development. Criticism was not just from family members. A local teacher told them that dual immersion was just for non-English speakers and implied that the program was remedial.

Alexi's mother was not to be discouraged. She consulted with Yvonne and other educators involved in bilingual education at the university where she was working. With their encouragement, Alexi's parents decided to send their daughter to the dual language program. This decision meant sacrifice on their part, as they both work nine to five. Their sons attend school in the town where they live, but they have to transport Alexi to a neighboring town so she can attend the dual language school there.

Alexi is now in the second grade and doing well. Her mother wrote the following testimony.

> Since we started the program with Alexi in kindergarten, we have really seen her growth in speaking Spanish, her writing and reading. Our two older boys have seen her progress in Spanish so they are now trying to learn it. My oldest son, Andrew, just started high school and is taking Spanish. When he has trouble reading words in Spanish he asks his little sister for help in understanding the meaning of the word in English. From a total of 17 grandchildren between my husband's family and mine, the ages ranging from 3 years old to 22 years old, Alexi, who is 7 years old now, is the only grandchild that can speak, read, and write fluently in Spanish.

Latino parents, like Alexi's, need support. First of all, the parents need encouragement from those who understand dual language education and its purposes, so that they can trust that their children will become bilingual and biliterate in both Spanish and English. Alexi's parents are extremely proud of her Spanish-speaking abilities, and they are now encouraging other Latino parents to try dual immersion. Her mother told us, "I have had positive responses from other parents who have been impressed with Alexi's bilingualism. Some are considering putting their young children in a dual immersion program." Second- or third-generation families may be culturally ambivalent. They may need to develop pride in their cultural heritage and develop an appreciation for different cultural groups. In addition, some English-speaking Latino parents may not be as well-educated as Alexi's parents and may be less able to support their children in a dual language program.

Native English speakers with a third culture background ◆ Sabrina and Vanessa are both in the Fresno Spanish/English dual language program described earlier. They are also both native English speakers whose parents speak English and another language. Sabrina's father grew up in Venezuela speaking Spanish and her mother, born and raised in Singapore, speaks English and two dialects of Chinese. Vanessa's father is Chinese and her mother is Mexican. Both sets of parents wanted their monolingual English-speaking children to be able to communicate with Spanish-speaking grandparents who live in the United States. Sabrina's and Vanessa's parents are well aware of the advantages of bilingualism for their daughters and realize that in this global society, everyone should know at least two languages.

Sabrina's father told us, "In most countries in the world, particularly in Asia and Europe, people speak a minimum of two languages. The more languages you know, the more you will exercise your brain, the smarter you'll become." Vanessa's father was also supportive of the program:

> We figured the program could provide our daughter with more job and schooling possibilities as well as allow her to communicate with her grandfather who speaks only Spanish. The dual immersion program has surpassed our initial expectations.

Children like Sabrina and Vanessa should be encouraged to appreciate their own cultural backgrounds. They bring special richness to dual language programs that should be drawn on and shared. In addition, of course, they may need support in understanding the cultures represented in the dual language program. In Sabrina's and Vanessa's cases, they should learn about their Latino and Chinese heritages as well as come to understand the culture of the mainstream English-speaking population.

Neighborhood children ◆ Some children are in two-way bilingual education not because their parents chose the program, but because they happen to live in a neighborhood where the local school provides dual language education for all students. Usually, school districts will try to accommodate parents who do not wish to have their children in these special programs, but sometimes transporting children elsewhere is difficult. As dual language becomes more popular, there are also some districts that have chosen this model for all their schools. This leaves parents without a choice.

The children in these situations need special attention. Their parents may be Anglo or Latino or represent other ethnic groups. However, these parents often do not understand the dual language program and have fears about whether their children will learn English well. In addition, sometimes Anglo or African American parents are mistrustful of their Latino neighbors and vice versa. Schools need to help both parents and children appreciate the value of two-way bilingual education and work to help everyone appreciate diversity and learning in two languages.

Native Spanish Speakers

Within dual language programs there are always children whose first language is not English. A major goal of these programs is to help English language learners succeed at a higher rate than in other types of programs. A key to assuring the success of the students is identifying the types of non-English speakers in the program and responding to their different needs. In this section, we describe young Spanish-speaking newcomers, young second- and third-generation students who speak Spanish and/or English at home, older newcomers with formal schooling who enter school speaking only Spanish, and older newcomers with limited schooling who enter school speaking only Spanish.

Younger students with limited preparation and support ◆ Pepe started school in kindergarten in a dual language border school in south Texas. He missed the preschool that the neighborhood dual language program offered because his family was working in another state that had no preschool program. Pepe is the middle child of seven. His family originally came from Mexico and his father now has found work doing local agricultural jobs. In an effort to make ends meet, his mother sells tamales and tacos to people at the school, in some of their local small-town businesses, and in their *colonia*.

Neither of Pepe's parents went to school in Mexico. They don't have the academic background to help him with schoolwork, and they are too exhausted or too busy even if they could. Although his parents speak no English, Pepe's older siblings have attended school and speak some English at home. Sometimes these older brothers and sisters can help Pepe with his homework.

Because children like Pepe are or have been migrants who live in poor neighborhoods, they often suffer from lack of self-esteem. Dual language programs need to help these students build pride in their culture and language and support them academically in ways their families cannot. This may include assistance during school from resource personnel or volunteers. Oftentimes, well-planned after-school programs can also help a student like Pepe begin to catch up to his peers. However, it is important that Pepe and others like him are made to feel that they can succeed and that they have potential. A key to the success of dual language programs is the underlying belief that all children, despite their circumstances, can and will learn with appropriate support.

Native Spanish speakers with some English proficiency ◆ In a dual language school in a small agricultural city in south Texas, students in a kindergarten class are mostly second- or third-generation immigrants from Mexico. A few children are newcomers recently arrived from rural Mexico who speak no English. Those born in the United States make up two basic groups: students who are English-dominant with at least some receptive knowledge of Spanish and those who are Spanish-dominant with varied competency in English.

The parents of the English-dominant children usually have had some education in the United States and at least one parent often has a job in which he or she uses English. Usually, older siblings also speak English, and both English and Spanish are spoken at home. Occasionally, only English is spoken at home except when grandparents or other relatives who are more recent immigrants visit. Depending on their competency in English, students in this kindergarten class have been identified as LEP (Limited English Proficient) or FEP (Fluent English Proficient).

The second group of U.S.-born students come from homes where Spanish is spoken most of the time. These students are Spanish-dominant. Because of the English they hear on television, in stores, and from older siblings and neighbors, they also have receptive knowledge of English and can express themselves in English in basic conversation.

Certainly, students like these need support to develop academic English as well as academic Spanish. In addition, many times these students are aware that English is the language of power outside of school, and they need to come to value their Spanish language and culture and appreciate the opportunity they have to develop not only English but also their native Spanish.

Older native Spanish speakers with adequate academic preparation ◆ Alma came to the United States from a city in northern Mexico when she was in the fourth grade. When she entered her two-way bilingual school, she was at grade level in writing, reading, and math in Spanish. She had also had studied social studies and science.

At first Alma was overwhelmed at the differences in the way school was conducted in the United States. Group work, hands-on activities, and the movement of students for computers, library, and other specials confused her. In addition, she had no English beyond the little English she had been taught in Mexico. In those classes students studied grammar and vocabulary but seldom actually used the language.

During Spanish instruction, however, Alma's teacher took advantage of her high levels of academic Spanish and often had her work with her peers. Alma was eager to participate and one of her most common responses when asked to help another student was "*No hay problema, maestra*" ("No problem, teacher").

Alma is one of four children. Her parents have been involved in her education in the United States from the beginning. Her mother did have some schooling, so she can help Alma with her homework in Spanish. Though both parents work in the fields, they have found time to volunteer for field trips and to help bring food and assist the teachers during parties.

By the time Alma got to the sixth grade, she was able to read and write in English as well as in Spanish. A good part of the reason for her success was the enriched dual language curriculum she experienced in both her native language and in English. Alma entered school in the United States with academic Spanish and subject matter knowledge that transferred to English as she became more proficient in English. She went on to junior high school and continued to compete well with her peers in coursework, though standardized tests were a challenge.

Students like Alma usually thrive in the enriched curriculum that dual language provides. They come academically prepared, and in dual language programs they continue to be supported in their primary language as they acquire English. Although students like Alma need extra support in catching up in English, they serve as rich resources during Spanish time. In appropriately implemented dual language programs, English-speaking peers help newcomers with English and native Spanish speakers enrich the Spanish development of their English-speaking classmates.

Older native Spanish speakers with limited academic preparation ◆ José began school in the United States in kindergarten. However, at the end of that first year, his family returned to Mexico, where he lived on a remote *rancho*. Although he attended school there, his rural school did not adequately prepare him to enter third grade when his family moved back to the United States. He entered his dual language third-grade classroom speaking and reading Spanish, but his literacy in Spanish was not at grade level. In addition, he had forgotten most of the English he had learned in kindergarten.

José was frustrated. His mother confided in the teacher that he cried every day when he got home from school because he knew he was so far behind his classmates. Fortunately, the school provided extra support in English from resource teachers and volunteers and also helped José with reading and writing in Spanish.

Soon José began responding to shared reading experiences in class. His teacher found that he was good working in groups though he needed to have individual, differentiated assignments, especially at first. Once he caught on to the classroom routines, he participated more. He had fairly good math skills, so he could often help his peers with math. At the end of fourth grade, he had learned to write in both Spanish and English, but he was below grade level in both languages. His teacher recommended that he continue to receive extra support in fifth grade.

Some two-way bilingual program administrators would not be willing to accept students like José. They would argue that he could not catch up academically in Spanish or in English. However, as dual language becomes more common and as whole schools and even districts decide to implement two-way programs, educators need to consider how they will serve the needs of older students who enter their schools with limited formal schooling.

Obviously, there need to be extra supports available for students like José. Peers can provide some support, and teachers can work to differentiate instruction, but, in addition, students will probably need tutoring to accelerate their literacy development and to help them catch up in the academic content they have missed. In addition, it is critical that these students do not receive the message that they cannot learn. A key to dual language programs is that all students are valued members of the learning community and that their language and culture are valued. When students come with limited preparation, the whole school needs to embrace them, help build their self-esteem by finding their strengths, and then provide the academic support they need.

Native Speakers of a Third Language

Kou entered kindergarten in an inner-city school as a dominant Hmong speaker. The school's overall population consists of many students who are immigrants from a variety of countries and speak several different languages. However, the majority of the students identified as English language learners speak Spanish or Hmong. Kou's older brothers and sisters convinced their parents that it would be good for Kou to be part of the school's Spanish/English two-way bilingual education strand. They believed that it would be to Kou's advantage to learn Spanish as he grew up.

Kou's parents work in agriculture outside their city. Neither of them is literate in Hmong. They do not speak much English. Kou is the youngest of ten children. The older children in the family take care of most of the family business translating for the family and providing the information the school needs about the younger children. They are often in charge of younger siblings. Kou's older brothers and sisters help him with his homework in English. One brother is studying Spanish in high school, so he also can help some with Spanish.

Kou needs support beyond what his older siblings can provide. He entered school speaking some English because his older siblings spoke some English at home. However, he started in the dual language program as a limited speaker of both English and Spanish. If the two-way program provides the usual extra-linguistic supports as well as the context-rich content curriculum that it should, Kou will probably acquire both Spanish and English. However, his teachers should be careful to ensure that he progresses at the same rate as his peers. It is easy to be impressed by the small gains that students like Kou, who are acquiring a second and third language, make and not hold them to the same standards as other students.

Another key concern for third language speakers is the possible loss of their first language. As these children study Spanish and English, there is little incentive to continue with their first language, especially in situations like Kou's. His parents may not understand the importance of maintaining the Hmong language, and older brothers and sisters value the acquisition of both Spanish and English more than Hmong because they see those as languages of more power. Students like Kou may also have difficulty developing a clear cultural identity.

Additional Concerns

Because dual language programs are fairly new in the United States and because empowered Anglo parents are often anxious about their children's progress, there is a tendency for teachers and administrators to give more positive reinforcement and support to native English speakers learning Spanish than to native Spanish speakers learning English. In other words, it is expected that Spanish speakers will learn English, so there is little excitement when they do. However, when native English-speaking children, especially those from middle-class Anglo homes, begin to learn Spanish, they are often applauded and given special attention. Publicity for the programs in newspapers and on television often features those English speakers learning Spanish or another second language. While this is important especially in recruiting for and promoting two-way bilingual education, educators must be sure to be equally positive about their Spanish speakers acquiring English (Valdés 1997). Delgado-Larroco (1998) found that English-speaking children had higher status in dual language classrooms and were given more praise and support for learning a second language than their Spanish-speaking peers. This finding supports the concern that even dual language programs are not free from the tendency to hold different expectations for the two groups of students.

A related concern involves the academic challenge of the curriculum. Because both English speakers and Spanish speakers are always learning in their second language, teachers must always scaffold instruction. However, at the same time, students must be given academically challenging curriculum that is at grade level in both languages. At times that may mean that students will need to work in monolingual pairs or groups to be challenged in their first language. In addition, teachers may need to plan special units of instruction or different grouping configurations when they notice that students are not developing the advanced literacy they need or are not keeping up in content in either language (de Jong 2002a). We will return to these points later in the book.

Teachers in Dual Language Programs

Everywhere we have traveled across the country, administrators and specialists working in dual language programs have talked to us about the importance of finding quality teachers. Because all three authors are involved in teacher preparation programs that specialize in preparing teachers for two-way bilingual education, we are often approached by administrators eager to recruit our students. In many areas, the English language learner population has grown rapidly and there is community support for the establishment of dual language programs, but it is difficult to find qualified bilingual teachers.

In the following sections we describe several teachers who are currently teaching in or preparing to teach in dual language programs. Some of these teachers are native Spanish speakers who have come to this country for various reasons. They speak Spanish but may struggle with English. Some are immigrants who have lived and studied in this country long enough to become quite bilingual. In fact, they may have taught as credentialed bilingual teachers and now find themselves teaching in a dual language setting. Two other types of teachers in two-way bilingual classrooms are Spanish speakers who were born here and have various levels of proficiency in their native language and native English speakers who have acquired at least some proficiency in Spanish.

We give examples of these different types of teachers and also identify the supports they need to succeed. Since the teacher and the teacher's language proficiency are crucial to the success of any two-way bilingual program, those involved in establishing or maintaining programs need to carefully consider the characteristics of their teachers and the supports they need.

Native Spanish Speakers with Academic Preparation in Spanish

Recent immigrants who are native speakers of Spanish and have been educated in their own country can provide excellent Spanish language models. These immigrants come to the United States for a variety of reasons. Some come in search of fulfilling the American Dream. Others arrive because they have married a U.S. citizen, or they come for other reasons and then marry here. Still others come with family or to join family living here. Some are actually educators by profession, but many are not. Juan Carlos, Marcela, and Jessica serve as examples of recent immigrants who are teaching in dual language classrooms.

Juan Carlos ◆ Juan Carlos arrived in the United States in 1993 from Chile with only very basic English. He explains that he knew "the verb 'to be,' a couple of words here and a couple of words there, and that was it!" He had always dreamed of becoming a teacher in the United States and had the long-term goal of earning a Ph.D. in education here. He studied both music and elementary education pedagogy in Chile and taught there for fifteen years. When a pastor friend in California offered to sponsor his coming to this country if Juan would lead the music ministry at his Spanish-speaking church, Juan Carlos jumped at the chance.

After four years in this country, Juan Carlos was hired by the Los Angeles Unified School District to teach in a first-grade dual language classroom in inner-city Watts. Juan Carlos had good success with his students: one-half African American and one-half Latino. However, with his limited time to acquire English and understand the U.S. school system, he could not pass the CBEST, the exam for teacher credentialing in California. He went to the district office to plead his case, but the answer at the many offices he entered was always "I'm sorry. I can see you are a good teacher, but there is nothing I can do." Juan Carlos explains that that rejection was "the biggest frustration of my entire career!"

Juan Carlos did not give up. He knew bilingual teachers were needed in this country. He found another ministry job in Omaha, Nebraska, this time in Christian education. In 1999 he moved to Nebraska. He explored the idea of teaching there and found an advocate in the city's district office. The ESL coordinator had implemented dual language in one school and needed fluent speakers of Spanish for another program that was starting. Juan Carlos worked with small groups of children at first as an independent consultant. Then, he got a provisional certificate, and the following year, he was given a contract in a dual language classroom. However, again the state teacher certification requirements were overwhelming. The district officials did not want to lose Juan Carlos, so they hired a substitute to be in his classroom while he taught for several months. In the meantime, he took the required coursework and passed the state certification test. Juan Carlos summarized his experiences:

Challenges? Frustrations? Many!!! The school district did their part and I really value and appreciate that, and I believe I did my part too. Teaching in the USA is an honor for me as a Latin American teacher. It is amazing the amount of resources available for teachers. My last memory as a teacher in Chile is forty-five students in my classroom, no paraprofessional, and a piece of chalk in my hand as the only supply.

Presently, Juan Carlos is teaching kindergarten in a dual language school and working on an M.A. in educational administration at the University of Nebraska.

Marcela ◆ Marcela was born in Colombia and educated at a university there. She received a degree in modern languages. After graduation, she moved from her home city of Bucaramanga to Bogotá to teach first and second grade at the American school. She taught there for four years, but she wanted to go to the

United States to live and to study more, so she applied to several universities in the United States and eventually went to study elementary education in Missouri.

During her studies in Missouri, Marcela continued her interest in second language acquisition. When she heard there was going to be an ESL conference locally, she decided to attend. David and Yvonne had just published their first book on working with English language learners and were presenting at the conference. Marcela bought their book to use for a research project and asked them to autograph it. In conversation, Marcela learned they had lived and taught in Colombia and that they directed an M.A. in TESOL program in California. David encouraged her to come study in that program.

Marcela finished her M.A. in elementary education in Missouri but suffered a car accident before returning home. After a long recovery, she went back to Colombia and taught again at the American school for two years. Because she still wanted to study English language teaching, she contacted the Freemans, applied to their program, and went to California. She planned to return to Colombia to teach English as a foreign language. However, during this period she fell in love and got engaged. Her husband-to-be lived in Wichita, Kansas, so she prepared to move there after finishing her second M.A. degree.

As chance would have it, the Freemans gave a presentation in Wichita about that time and learned the school district was beginning a dual language program. School district officials were delighted to hear that a native Spanish speaker with such strong educational preparation would be coming to their city. Marcela began talking with them and actually changed her M.A. thesis topic. She chose to write about cooperative learning in two-way bilingual classrooms. For the past five years Marcela has taught first grade in a dual language classroom in Wichita, and in the fall of 2003, she helped open a new dual language school.

Marcela was certainly well prepared for her teaching through her university coursework. In addition, she is a native Spanish speaker. However, the paperwork required to get her teaching credential was extremely complex. Like others who come to this country and want to get a license or credential, she had to get all her transcripts from Colombia translated and evaluated for equivalency. This was a tedious and expensive process. In addition, she had to study for the state teachers exam, which covered math, English, and the history of U.S. education. She studied for more than three months, spending long hours poring over study manuals and reviewing math with her husband. When it came time to apply for the teaching job, Marcella also needed letters from the professors she had studied with in Colombia years earlier. Getting these letters was another tedious and time-consuming process. Her memory of all this paperwork still leaves her frustrated. Marcela and her husband are moving to New

Mexico next year. She has already been offered a job working in a dual language school in Las Cruces. Marcela wonders how complex the credentialing in New Mexico will be.

Jessica ◆ Jessica came to the United States from Argentina with her parents and younger sister just before her eighteenth birthday. Her parents had decided to emigrate from Argentina because of the growing economic problems and political instability there. Jessica's father was involved in Rotary and the family was able to find sponsors from that organization to help them move to the largest city in central California.

Jessica had finished the equivalent of high school in Argentina, so when she first arrived, she studied English for a few months and then enrolled in the local junior college. Her major was microbiology. However, several factors led her to change her major to liberal studies, the degree needed for elementary teaching in California. In the first place, her mother had been able to get working papers through a school district because she took classes to become a credentialed bilingual teacher. Jessica knew that she would also need to get legal status. She hoped to find a school to sponsor her. In addition, Jessica went to her mother's school several times and worked with her mother and found she really loved teaching.

After completing two years at the junior college, Jessica transferred to a small local university and began studying on a student visa. She finished her B.A. degree and became part of a special program designed to prepare bilingual teachers to work in dual language classrooms. Jessica's greatest hurdle was to pass the state teacher credentialing exams. Although she did well in her coursework at the university, she found the context-reduced exams given in English quite difficult. In addition, many of the questions assumed background knowledge Jessica lacked. She finally passed all sections of the required exams, one on the third try.

Jessica did her student teaching in a dual language third-grade classroom. Her program was based on a constructivist approach. She learned how to organize around themes connected to standards and to engage students in collaborative, inquiry-based activities. This approach was certainly different from her own learning experiences in Argentina. Jessica's master teacher was extremely pleased with her work with the children and her Spanish proficiency. Recently she was hired by another school district to teach in their dual language program. The district will sponsor her so that she can get the necessary working papers.

Juan Carlos, Marcela, and Jessica have had to overcome extra hurdles in order to teach in the United States. Their experiences in their countries were often with traditional teaching approaches, but here they were expected to teach using a student-centered approach. All three also faced difficulties in getting credentialed. They had to pass exams for which they lacked background knowledge. Juan Carlos had studied almost no English before coming to this country, so the decontextualized standardized tests in English were a special challenge. He also had to take additional coursework despite having earned two degrees in Chile. In both his case and Marcela's, because they had studied education in their country as well as in this country, they had to do extra paperwork to validate their Latin American education.

Teachers like Juan Carlos, Marcela, and Jessica need support to pass the required exams and fill out the extra papers. Often they also need to find school districts that will provide various kinds of aid including at times support documents so that they can work in this country legally. The teaching approach in dual language must be learner-centered and should be theme-based. These approaches are quite different from the past schooling experiences of many immigrant teachers. In addition, the entire school system is different. Newcomers need mentors to help them understand and adjust to a new way of teaching and learning.

There is one last concern that may arise when schools hire newcomer native Spanish speakers. Sometimes newcomers who come from middle- to upper-class families in their native countries are not accustomed to working with children of lower socioeconomic status or with parents with little or no educational background. Those teachers need some sensitivity training to help them empathize with the children, their families, and their needs. This includes a sensitivity to the dialect of Spanish the children bring to school. It is important that the children learn academic Spanish but at the same time not be made to feel that the language spoken at home is inferior.

Juan Carlos, Marcela, and Jessica were fortunate to attend universities in the U.S. where these issues were discussed. All of these fine teachers understood linguistic and cultural diversity and were respectful of it. However, not all native Spanish-speaking teachers are, especially if they are hired on emergency credentials and have not had the training in language acquisition and cross-cultural communication that is so critical to being a teacher of bilingual children. We will return to a discussion of this concern later.

Francisca ◆ Francisca moved across the border from Mexico when she was thirteen. She had attended school in Mexico but had never studied any English. When her parents got jobs working in the fields in a border town in south Texas, she and her seven siblings were suddenly thrown into school taught all in English. During that time, children from Mexico were sometimes treated poorly. Francisca remembers being segregated in the classroom and admonished not to speak any Spanish. She also remembers being insulted by teachers and other students who could speak English well.

Francisca is a very strong person. Though she struggled academically in English, she never gave up. Her parents encouraged her to continue in school even though they could not help her with schoolwork. Their belief in her kept her going. After high school, she worked and went to junior college and then transferred to the local university. It took her eight years to get her B.A. degree because she had to work full-time and also help take care of family members, including a terminally ill father.

In college she majored in education and specialized in bilingual education. When she graduated, she got a job in a transitional bilingual education program in which students transitioned to all-English instruction in fourth grade. As a third-grade bilingual teacher, she provided some first language support in reading and content areas. However, since she was the third-grade teacher, she was expected to try to get her students into English as quickly as possible. She was concerned about how her students struggled and believed that the program was harming some children.

Francisca wanted to understand bilingual education more fully. She sensed that the program at her school was not the best, but she could not articulate why. When a grant designed to support future administrators in dual language schools became available, she decided to go back to school to get an M.A. degree. As she studied second language acquisition, she realized why she and the students in her transitional program struggled in school. She also came to understand how the academic Spanish she had developed in Mexico had helped her make it through college.

When Francisca had an opportunity to transfer to a school beginning a dual language program, she took it. Now she is learning how to provide a better educational experience for Spanish-speaking children than she had. She is empathetic toward recent immigrants and knows the importance of helping them develop academic Spanish to the highest possible level. She sees that the dual language program is doing that.

Francisca struggled through school in English with limited support. Now, as she works on her M.A. degree, she continues to need help with academic reading and writing in English. However, her strengths are obvious. This teacher has the needed academic Spanish, and she is developing an understanding of teaching and learning that will support her own students now and students in other dual language schools later when she becomes an administrator.

Native Spanish Speakers with Limited or No Academic Preparation in Spanish

Irma ◆ Irma came to the United States from Mexico before she was old enough to attend school. She spoke only Spanish at home with her family, so she entered kindergarten as a monolingual Spanish speaker. She attended school in a period when Mexican children were punished for speaking Spanish at school. Although Irma maintained some conversational Spanish at home, she lost most of her ability to communicate effectively in Spanish because she was schooled entirely in English.

At her school there was no real support for English learners. Since her parents were not educated, they could not help Irma with her homework. She struggled academically throughout her schooling. As she approach high school graduation, no one at her school encouraged her to further her education, so she went to work in the fields and later in a fruit-packing plant.

During those years working at the packing plant, Irma asked a coworker to reteach her Spanish. She took this endeavor as another job and over the next five years, she forced herself to use the language as much as she could with her coworkers in order to regain some of her Spanish.

Eventually, Irma applied to the local school district and became a bilingual aide. When she heard about a grant supporting paraprofessionals in getting their teaching credential, she decided to go back to school. After a difficult period of finishing basic requirements at the junior college, she went on to the university and earned her B.A. degree. She entered a teacher education program that prepares dual language teachers. She studied Spanish at the university and is now able to read and write Spanish. She is not fluent, but she continues to refine and further develop her Spanish abilities by working with the bilingual students in her classroom.

Irma represents a large group of Spanish speakers in this country who have lost or nearly lost their first language. Often these students have struggled through school taught all in English. In order to teach in a dual language classroom, these teachers need to improve their conversational and academic Spanish and often their academic English as well. Even with the effort she has already put forth, Irma knows that she will have to continue to work to make herself truly bilingual and biliterate.

Kari ◆ Kari, although of Latino background, grew up as a monolingual English speaker in a middle-class neighborhood. In high school and college she decided to study Spanish. Her Spanish classes, however, did not give her either the conversational or the academic Spanish she really wanted. Kari had family in Barcelona, Spain, so she decided to go there to study and reconnect with her relatives. She went to Spain twice.

When she returned from her second trip, Kari decided that she wanted to teach second language learners and use the Spanish language she was regaining. Preparing herself to teach in a two-way bilingual education program seemed to be the best way to do this. During her student teaching experience Kari was placed in a dual language classroom where she was able to use and further refine her Spanish.

Kari, unlike Irma, developed strong academic competence in English in school. When she got to high school and wanted to develop her heritage language, she had the underlying competence in English to help support the acquisition of a second language. At the same time, she had to seek out opportunities to improve her Spanish. She was fortunate that she had Spanish-speaking friends in Spain. Her study in Spain helped her develop both conversational and academic proficiency in Spanish. Both of these kinds of proficiency are necessary for teaching in a dual language setting.

Native English Speakers with Receptive Knowledge of Spanish

The teachers we have discussed to this point are all either bilingual in Spanish and English or native Spanish speakers who also can function in English. Many dual language programs, however, also use teachers who are native English speakers with receptive knowledge of Spanish. Iris provides an example of this kind of teacher.

Iris ◆ Iris took a few Spanish classes in high school and college. It was her church work with Latino youth, however, that convinced her that she wanted to teach English learners. Iris saw how even her minimal knowledge of Spanish helped her reach the Spanish-speaking young people more personally. That experience motivated her to become a teacher. She knew that she lacked the ability to teach in Spanish, but she entered the dual language teacher education program to learn theories and strategies to work more effectively with second language learners and to support the English instruction in two-way bilingual schools.

Throughout her teacher education program, Iris has demonstrated her commitment to Latino students. She took an intensive summer seminar to improve her Spanish skills, and she forced herself to use Spanish to do presentations in her education classes. Her coursework and her efforts have helped prepare her to better meet the needs of her English language learners.

 ## Conclusion

There is a great deal of variety in dual language programs and in the students and teachers in these programs. A key to either developing or improving two-way programs is a thorough understanding of the context of the program. This includes understanding who the students and teachers are. The different types of students and teachers we have described have varying strengths and needs. Those wishing to develop or improve a dual language program should select a program model that capitalizes on the strengths and meets the needs of both students and teachers.

In this chapter we have pointed out some of the variations in dual language programs, students, and teachers. In the following chapters, we outline the essentials for all dual language programs. In these chapters we provide specific examples and scenarios to bring these essentials to life.

Learning Extensions

1. Look over the descriptions of the various dual language programs described in the first part of the chapter. Choose two that interest you. Using a Venn diagram or some other compare-and-contrast graphic organizer, make a comparison of the two you chose.

2. Consider a dual language program you are familiar with or visit a local dual language school. Then, compare that program with one described in the chapter. Which features are the same? Which are different?

3. Review the case studies of students in dual language schools who are native English speakers, native Spanish speakers, and speakers of other languages. Think of students in a dual language school who represent two of these groups. If you do not know students studying in a dual language school,

interview some. Which of the case study students in this chapter is most similar to the students you know? Explain.

4. Teachers in dual language settings come with different strengths and backgrounds. Which of the teachers described in this chapter is most like you?

5. Do dual language schools you know have difficulty finding qualified teachers for their programs? What types of teachers are they looking for? How do they recruit and support teachers in their programs?

School, Administrator, and Teacher Essentials

As we have visited schools, interviewed educators, and worked with student teachers planning for and teaching in dual language settings, we have seen a great deal of variation in the programs, teachers, and students. However, even with that variation, it is clear that programs must have certain essential elements to fully meet the academic needs of the students they are intended to serve. In this and the following chapters, we offer what we consider to be the essential elements of effective dual language programs. In this chapter we address essentials for whole schools, for administrators, for administrators and teachers working together, and for teachers.

We have developed these essentials based on the information that we have read, our own background of working in schools, and the ideas we have gained from interviews and visits to dual language schools. For those thinking of implementing a dual language program or for those wishing to reflect on an existing program, a number of publications can serve as useful resources. In Figure 3–1 we list books and articles we drew on as we developed and refined our dual language essentials. The following references can serve as a starter list.

Christian, D. 1994. *Two-Way Bilingual Education: Students Learning Through Two Languages*. Washington, DC: Office of Educational Research and Improvement.

Christian, D., C. L. Montone, K. J. Lindholm, and I. Carranza. 1997. *Profiles in Two-Way Immersion Education*. Washington, DC: Center for Applied Linguistics.

Cloud, N., F. Genesee, and E. Hamayan. 2000. *Dual Language Instruction: A Handbook for Enriched Education*. Boston: Heinle & Heinle.

Freeman, R. 2004. *Building on Community Bilingualism: Promoting Multilingualism Through Schooling*. Philadelphia: Caslon.

Howard, E. R., and D. Christian. 2002. *Two-Way Immersion 101: Designing and Implementing a Two-Way Immersion Education Program at the Elementary Level*. Santa Cruz: Center for Research on Education, Diversity and Excellence, University of California, Santa Cruz.

Howard, E. R., and M. I. Loeb. 1998. *In Their Own Words: Two-Way Immersion Teachers Talk About Their Professional Experiences*. (ERIC Document No. EDO-FL-98-14). Washington, DC: ERIC.

Howard, E. R., N. Olague, and D. Rogers. 2003. *The Dual Language Program Planner: A Guide for Designing and Implementing Dual Language Programs*. Santa Cruz: Center for Research on Education, Diversity, and Excellence.

Howard, E. R., J. Sugarman, and D. Christian. 2003. *Trends in Two-Way Immersion Education: A Review of the Research*. Baltimore, MD: Center for Research on the Education of Students Placed at Risk.

Lindholm-Leary, K. J. 2001. *Dual Language Education*. Clevedon, England: Multilingual Matters.

Montone, C. L., and M. I. Loeb. 2000. *Implementing Two-Way Immersion Programs in Secondary Schools*. Education Practice Report No. 5. Santa Cruz: CREDE.

Pérez, B. 2004. *Becoming Biliterate: A Study of Two-Way Bilingual Immersion Education*. Mahwah, NJ: Lawrence Erlbaum Associates.

Soltero, S. W. 2004. *Dual Language: Teaching and Learning in Two Languages*. Boston: Pearson.

Torres-Guzmán, M. E. 2002. *Dual Language Programs: Key Features and Results*. No. 14. Washington, DC: National Clearinghouse for English Language Acquisition and Language Instruction Educational Programs.

FIG. 3–1 Dual Language Resources

Many journal articles also provide valuable information on dual language programs, and new articles are constantly being published (de Jong 2002a, 2002b, 2004; Alanís 2000; Christian, Howard, and Loeb 2000; Montone and Loeb 2000; Fern 1995; Freeman 1995; Collier and Thomas 2004). It is important to stay current in this field as more and more programs are being implemented, and different schools are discovering innovative ways to make programs work well in a variety of settings.

Whole-School Essentials

Whether a dual language program is a strand within a school or encompasses the entire school, there are three essentials that all school personnel must follow for the program to succeed.

Whole School Essentials
• Understand and support the goals and benefits of the program.
• Be flexible and open to change.
• Be committed to academic and social equity and the promotion of equal status for both languages.

While these three essentials may seem obvious, if any one of them is missing, the program will not be as effective as it could be. In the following sections we discuss each of these essentials and offer specific examples from our experiences to help readers understand both what to avoid and also how to provide for the essentials.

Understanding and Supporting the Goals and Benefits of the Program

In a recent publication by CRESPAR (Center for Research on the Education of Students Placed at Risk), Howard, Sugarman, and Christian (2003) review the research on two-way immersion education. In this report they summarize the common features of successful programs. The first item on their list supports our first whole-school essential:

> 1. It is important to have all stakeholders involved in program planning from the earliest stages in order to ensure that everyone understands the model, has a shared vision for implementation, and is clear about others' motivations for starting the program. (19)

We have seen that if there are even a few at a school site who do not understand and/or support the dual language program, the program can be sabotaged from within. The following example shows what can happen.

A California example ◆ After the passage of Proposition 227 in California, administrators in a large urban school district began to consider how they could continue to serve the large numbers of Spanish speakers who had been in bilingual programs up to that time. The new proposition banned bilingual education, but ESL/bilingual specialists in the district believed that there was a better alternative to Structured English Immersion mandated by the initiative. At a principals' meeting, one principal who had implemented a two-way English/Spanish strand at her school several years earlier reported on the success of her program and, in particular, the success of her Latino students. She invited the other principals to attend an all-day district training designed to inform both administrators and teachers about two-way education, including the rationale, research results, and the many positive outcomes.

The incoming principal of Edwards School decided to attend this workshop. She knew that she had a challenge ahead of her in leading this large inner-city school, and she was looking for something that could improve the school's dismal record in academics and the general school climate. Her school of around one thousand students had had a bilingual strand for Spanish speakers, but that program was now in danger of being dismantled because of the new antibilingual law. She hoped the workshop would provide the answer that she needed.

The workshop presenters described the success of the two-way school in the district. They also shared the results of the large-scale study reported by Thomas and Collier (2002). Although the presenters stressed the necessity of careful planning and involving all parties, including parents and teachers, the Edwards principal could not wait to get this program going. Her school needed change right away. To get started, she enlisted the help of the district bilingual office by calling on one of its resource specialists. She also involved her vice principal, who had no background in bilingual or two-way education. The three planned to start a two-way strand in the school and wrote a grant for funding for the following year.

The principal announced at a spring faculty meeting that there would be a two-way strand at the school in the fall. There was initial interest from teachers who were presently teaching in the school's transitional bilingual program, but after those teachers were sent out for an initial training and visitations to dual language schools, some of them decided they did not want to be involved in a program that seemed to require so much extra work and planning. This did not deter the principal. She hired the needed new teachers for the strand. Since she could not find teachers with experience in dual language, she hired newly credentialed bilingual teachers. To recruit students into the program, she advertised to English-speaking parents that an innovative program would be started in the fall to help their kindergarten and first-grade children become bilingual.

Over the summer the principal and teachers who were to teach in the program attended the state dual language conference, and the teachers were given a week to work on planning. They decided to use a 90/10 model because the other school in the district had chosen that model and the California research they had heard at the conference supported that model (Lindholm-Leary 2001). However, the grant that the administrators had written was not funded, so there was no additional money in the school budget for further inservicing or support from outside consultants. In addition, there was no extra money to buy needed resource materials in Spanish.

When school started in the fall, the determined principal implemented the program in two kindergartens and two first-grades. There were many problems. At an early informational meeting, parents raised questions that neither the principal nor the district resource person could answer. Parents of Spanish-speaking children were concerned that their children were receiving so little instruction in English, and parents of English-speaking children complained that their children didn't understand any of the instruction.

Parents were not the only ones who did not fully support the program. It soon became obvious that teachers who were not part of the dual language strand felt marginalized and resentful. They didn't understand the program and were suspicious of it. They believed that too much attention was being given to the two-way program. Bilingual paraprofessionals didn't understand why they needed to speak only Spanish in the two-way classes when they believed the Latino children needed to be practicing more English. Even school secretaries showed resentment toward the program because it involved extra work for them. The fact that most of the school's meager resource money was being spent on the new program did not help either. Soon the principal had a divided faculty and staff.

At about this time, a local university received a grant to train both preservice and inservice dual language teachers. The principal asked university faculty members for help. The university team visited classes and interviewed teachers. The team then met with the principal and vice principal and made specific suggestions. The principal obviously felt overwhelmed and was not sure she could carry out the suggestions. In the end, one of the university's bilingual faculty members agreed to teach a series of seminars on dual language for all the teachers on campus, offering them university credit. In addition, she attended a parent meeting and answered parents' concerns.

These efforts were too little too late, however. The negative climate at the school kept all but the teachers teaching in or planning to teach in the two-way language strand from attending the seminars. In fact, more teachers from other schools contemplating dual language attended the class than teachers at Edwards School. Teachers from Edwards who took the course benefited from what they learned, but they also realized that the essential groundwork for a successful program had not been laid. Other teachers at Edwards still did not understand or support the program; the school still lacked Spanish language resources; and the teachers were still not confident that they could implement the new teaching methods and techniques they were studying. To make matters worse, at the end of the year, the principal retired, leaving a serious leadership vacuum.

Flexibilty and Openness

Even when schools do take the necessary time to plan and prepare for dual language programs, there still are challenges. The faculty and administration need to be flexible and open to new ideas. They need ongoing professional development. Fern (1995) described one of the oldest two-way schools, the Oyster Bilingual School in Washington, D.C., which was started in 1971. The school has received national and local honors for excellence. Yet, as Fern points out, to maintain this excellent reputation, the whole school community needs to work together:

> It is important that everyone in a school community be aware of the vision and mission of the school . . . All members of the learning community should be targeted for professional development, from cafeteria/maintenance personnel to teachers to parents and other community members/organizations to administrators and politicians. To paraphrase the observation of a New York State Education Department staff person, professional development plans which neglect any part of the learning community are analogous to constructing a really sound house but stopping before the roof is completed. (509–10)

Other researchers have analyzed Oyster Bilingual School as well (Freeman 1995, 1998). The administration, faculty, and staff have taken the results of this research into account as they have continually worked to improve their program. They have not been content with past accomplishments. Instead, they are open to new ideas and willing to make changes.

Not all schools have had the benefit of reports from outside researchers. However, as programs develop, administrators and teachers need to remain open and willing to make needed changes. A description of two dual language schools in one large, Midwest city helps exemplify the need for the first two whole-school essentials but makes especially clear the necessity for flexibility and openness to change.

A Midwest example ◆ A city in the Midwest, like many others in the country's heartland, had experienced a huge growth in its Spanish-speaking population over the past five to seven years. Jobs in the meatpacking industry as well as a growing service industry attracted new immigrants from states like California, Texas, and Florida. As in many cities, the immigrants settled in concentrated areas and created their own Spanish-speaking neighborhoods.

Schooling for the children of these newcomers became a serious concern about five years ago, especially for administrators and faculty in schools in the rapidly changing neighborhoods where immigrants were settling. An unprepared district administration was faced with supplying ESL and bilingual support, a need that had been almost nonexistent in the past. Two district people who were interested in the new immigrants were recruited to help. In addition, new hires included people who could lead the district in the right direction. A key addition to the district office was an educator with experience in two-way bilingual education from the East Coast. In turn, she recruited both teachers and staff who would support two-way bilingual education. For example, she hired an elementary teacher with an M.A. in early childhood education to lead the implementation of a new dual language program under a Title VII grant because this teacher understood good curricular practices and was willing and eager to get an ESL endorsement. This teacher was also interested in being trained in dual language. She attended conferences as well as the summer institute, Dual U, sponsored annually by the Illinois Resource Center.

Unlike the principal at Edwards, the new specialist found an openness to looking for new solutions to serve English learners. The principals in the two schools most impacted by new immigrants were eager to learn about innovative programs. The East Coast expert encouraged administrators and some faculty who would be involved in the two-way program to attend the National Association of Bilingual Education (NABE) conference. They planned carefully to get as much information as possible during the conference. They chose sessions on dual language and spent mealtimes as a group discussing what they had learned and considering ways they could use this information to develop a plan to implement a two-way strand in their schools. The administration and faculty were open to new ideas and worked together, guided by the expert. As a result, the programs they developed have had very positive early results.

The first year was spent with planning, visits to dual language schools around the country, and meetings with parents. It soon became apparent that one of their biggest challenges would be to find enough credentialed bilingual teachers who could teach content in Spanish. However, they were able to identify several potential candidates who would need district support to complete college coursework and pass state teaching exams, and they began to provide that support.

Even with careful planning and a solid base of support, two-way programs face challenges, and faculty and staff must remain flexible and open to change. This school implemented a two-way strand following all the recommended steps. The program now extends through third grade. There is a constant effort to be sure that all the teachers in the school understand the program and support it. This is not always an easy task, and teachers in the two-way program admit they sometimes feel alienated.

Teachers work in bilingual teams consisting of an English teacher and a Spanish teacher. Students spend half the day with each teacher. This arrangement allows the school to make the best possible use of the limited number of Spanish-speaking teachers, since they use Spanish to teach one group in the morning and another group in the afternoon. However, team members need to plan together and cooperate. Some teams work together better than others, and team members need to be open to ideas from their partners and remain flexible in their planning.

In addition, it soon became apparent that the office and custodial staff needed to be informed about the program. When they began complaining and making negative comments, they were included in some early orientation meetings. Now, they are often consulted about how the new program impacts them. Without the support of the whole school community, a program cannot succeed.

As this program moves beyond third grade, the challenge is to find teachers with the academic Spanish needed to teach subjects in the upper grades. In addition, since students from this school move to a middle school for fifth and sixth grades, the district has already designated the principal of the elementary school to be the principal of the middle school to maintain the needed leadership continuity. That principal is currently researching and visiting other middle schools around the country that have dual language programs.

The second school in this Midwest city has just begun to implement two-way education. This school has also struggled to find bilingual teachers and to help those teachers involved in the program learn to work and plan together effectively in bilingual pairs. Since the pairs must work well together and agree on the content to be taught and the strategies they will use, some have said that being part of a bilingual two-way team is like being in a marriage. If the partnership doesn't work, there needs to be an amicable divorce!

It has become clear to both the teachers and administrators at this school that two-way education is much more than teaching in two languages. For example, the bilingual resource person at the school was concerned about how to diplomatically help a very traditional kindergarten teacher with no ESL training teach the English curriculum comprehensibly to her native Spanish speakers. The principal helped solve this problem by hiring a new kindergarten teacher who was studying for her ESL endorsement and who had a strong background in early childhood education and then moving the traditional teacher to second grade, where the Spanish-speaking children know much more English. This move also probably avoided a "divorce," since the traditional teacher did not plan well with her Spanish-side partner. In addition the bilingual resource specialist was able to move some native Spanish-speaking teachers into the upper grades, where their Spanish expertise was needed to teach the academic content area subjects. Administrators at the school have been open to change, and teachers have been flexible and willing to take on the challenge of working with a partner, often at a new grade level.

Equality or Inequality in Dual Language Programs?

It is critical, then, that all stakeholders understand the dual language program at their school site and that they be flexible and open to change. In addition, all school personnel must be committed to academic and social equity and the promotion of equal status for both languages. Developing a program that provides equality in academics, social status, and language status is extremely difficult. Yet equity issues cannot be ignored if the goals of dual language, including high academic achievement for all, development of bilingualism and biliteracy, and demonstration of positive cross-cultural attitudes and behaviors, are to be achieved.

In their discussion of equity issues, Bourdieu and Passeron (1977) use the terms *social capital*, *linguistic capital*, and *cultural capital* to explain how social status, linguistic knowledge, and cultural background function in a society. Certain groups in a society have capital that is highly valued, and others possess less-valued capital. For example, in any society, belonging to a certain social group, knowing a certain language, and coming from a certain cultural background confer status. In schools the capital that some students bring is more highly valued than the capital other students bring.

All students come from some social, linguistic, and cultural background, but different backgrounds carry different values. *Capital* is an appropriate metaphor to explain differences in value. When we traveled to Mexico recently, our dollar was worth about eleven pesos. The dollar was more highly valued than the peso. However, if we had gone to Europe, our dollar would not have been worth as much as the Euro. These differences in the value of the U.S. dollar are arbitrary and have nothing to do with the intrinsic value of the coins or bills we use to buy and sell goods and services.

Students who enter U.S. schools speaking English have more linguistic capital than those who come speaking Spanish even though their proficiency levels in their native languages may be the same. In most schools, instruction is provided in English, books are in English, and tests are in English. Textbooks and tests are written with the assumption that students reading the books or taking the tests speak English and come with mainstream cultural knowledge and at least middle-class status. The ways in which schooling is organized mean that students with certain social, linguistic, and cultural capital are more likely to succeed than others.

Dual language programs attempt to counter the norms of the wider society by promoting academic and social equity and equal status of the two languages. Studies have shown that both minority- and majority-language students in dual language programs reach high levels of academic achievement (Lindholm-Leary 2001; Thomas and Collier 2002). Both groups do as well as or better than their peers studying in English-only classrooms. In addition, studies have shown that students in two-way programs have more positive attitudes toward bilingualism and multiculturalism (Cabezón, Nicoladis, and Lambert 1998).

However, several researchers have found that, even in dual language programs, achieving equity is a challenge. Valdés (1997) posits, for example, that Spanish speakers may not develop high levels of academic Spanish in dual language classrooms because teachers are teaching native English speakers as well as native Spanish speakers and, therefore, may be watering down the Spanish they use for instruction. Valdés asks whether "hispanophone children acquire native-like academic Spanish?" (416). In addition, some dual language teachers themselves lack high levels of academic Spanish and so have difficulty modeling the academic register for students.

Valdés also questions whether there is true equality in the value placed on developing bilingualism for both groups. She points to the fact that reporters emphasize how well English speakers in two-way programs develop Spanish but ignore the English development of Spanish speakers. "For minority children, the acquisition of English is expected. For Mainstream children, the acquisition of a non-English language is enthusiastically applauded" (417). Genesee and Gándara (1999) share similar concerns, fearing that despite the friendships that form in two-way classrooms and the positive views that students develop about each other's culture and language, "language minority students may still harbor feelings of inferiority and low self-esteem" (678).

Valdés also raises the concern that two-way programs are giving future advantages to previously privileged monolingual English-speaking children by making them bilingual. In the past "skills in two languages have opened doors for members of minority groups" (1997, 419). However, in successful dual language programs, all students become bilingual. Valdés' point is that the one advantage language-minority children might have may be usurped by English speakers who become bilingual.

Native English speakers may enjoy other subtle advantages over their native Spanish-speaking peers. Delgado-Larroco (1998) carried out a yearlong study of a two-way immersion kindergarten classroom. She examined student discourse, patterns of interaction, and instructional strategies used by the teachers. She concluded that English Native Speakers (ENS) were given more attention than Spanish native speakers (SNS) because of the parents' status and concern about their children's progress.

> Mainstream parents' influence placed ENSs as the focus of instruction. Instructional strategies ensured ENSs' Spanish acquisition and ENSs' and SNSs' access to the curriculum. SNSs served as linguistic models, and facilitated ENSs' conceptual understanding and participation. A macroanalysis of the findings suggests a subordinate/superordinate relationship between SNSs and ENSs in this classroom. This relationship mirrors their parents' status in the society. (vii)

Thus, even in a two-way setting, Spanish speakers were not getting equal treatment.

Freeman (1996) found that despite the efforts of the Oyster Bilingual School personnel to create an environment of equity, constant efforts needed to be made to fight societal values and the movement toward the status quo. Race and social class had strong influences on social grouping even at the school. For example, dark-skinned Latinas sat apart from light-skinned Latinas in the lunchrooms. In addition, subconscious responses from teachers in two-way schools often showed that teachers held low expectations for language-minority students. Despite the teachers' best intentions, these expectations were evident in their teaching (Freeman 1995). Fern (1995) had also asked questions on the same theme about Oyster:

> Is Oyster a truly "multicultural" school in the sense that all cultures are not only appreciated, studied and respected, but also integrated into the curriculum and the decision-making process? While it is certain that substantive and successful efforts are in place to proceed toward this ideal, there is still room for improvement. (507–508)

Even in dual language programs, students understand that English is the language of power. Griego-Jones (1994) studied the emergent literacy development of Spanish-dominant children in a two-way program. She found that the children showed a strong preference for using English even when their Spanish skills were much better than their English skills. Even though school personnel and parents had committed themselves to the bilingual development of the children in the two-way school, "children regarded Spanish as acceptable to use but seemed to view it as a vehicle they leaned on as they worked to become proficient in English" (82). Griego-Jones and others have found that students receive indirect messages about the importance of English over Spanish. For example, when teachers or students code-switch, it is usually from Spanish into English. Seldom have researchers found frequent code-switching into Spanish during English instructional time (Howard, Sugarman, and Christian 2003).

Teachers and administrators should work to promote the equal status of both languages in dual language schools. McCollum (1999), in studying middle school Mexican-background students in a two-way program, found that devaluing the Spanish dialect of the students led them to abandon Spanish and choose English. She observed one teacher who insisted that students use what she viewed as correct Spanish. This teacher corrected students' Spanish and made statements about the Spanish dialect of the students that made them feel their Spanish was inadequate. Students preferred to use English rather than be criticized for their Spanish.

The students were left in a double bind. Their Spanish was not deemed acceptable in school, and they struggled with English in their English classes. This led students to look for approval from their peers. McCollum documents how Spanish speakers "saw English as more prestigious due to the rewards that accrued from speaking it" (126). Students believed that those Mexican-background students who spoke English were more popular because they could talk back to teachers in English and generally disrupt classes. They perceived this ability as important for joining the status peer groups at the school. Thus, the Spanish-speaking students at this school not only rejected their language but moved toward becoming trouble makers.

Social pressures do have a large influence, especially as students move beyond their elementary years. Freeman (1998) found that students who had positive attitudes toward bilingualism and biculturalism in their two-way elementary school chose English over Spanish in junior high and even rejected their own cultural background to remain popular among Anglo peers. Their linguistic and cultural capital, their Spanish language and culture, was not valued in their new school. Instead, the Anglos held both the linguistic and the cultural capital and the only way Latinos could be equal was to reject their own language and background.

Alanís (2000) found that even in a dual language program in Texas close to the border, students favored English over Spanish. While in early grades students in the program used both languages, in the upper grades almost all students moved toward using English. This preference for and stronger ability in English were due to factors within and outside the classroom. In the first place, the school's goal was only oral proficiency in Spanish rather than equal levels of bilingualism and biliteracy in both languages. The emphasis on the TASS (Texas Assessment of Academic Skills) and the tendency to encourage students to take the test in English also led students to believe that English was what really mattered. Teachers at the upper grades used mostly English and lacked the needed resources to really teach content in Spanish. In fact, teachers bragged that most of their students took the TASS in English because those scores were the ones that really counted.

Asymmetry in dual language programs ◆ As a summary of this section on inequalities in dual language programs, we review three kinds of asymmetry that programs should avoid. In a study of a dual language program in Phoenix, Arizona, Amrein and Peña (2000) noted instructional asymmetry, resource asymmetry, and student asymmetry, which kept the program from accomplishing all of its goals. While, as the authors point out, every program is unique and is affected by the context in which it is developed, consideration of these three types of asymmetry could help those developing programs elsewhere to meet the goal of academic, social, and linguistic equity.

Instructional asymmetry refers to how the two groups of students receive instruction in the classroom. Amrein and Peña, like other researchers, found that English was more valued than Spanish and was often the measure of student success. In addition, Spanish instructors were all bilingual, but English teachers were monolingual. Therefore, during Spanish instruction, English-speaking children could be understood by their teachers when they used English, but Spanish-speaking children could not be understood by their teachers when they used Spanish during English instruction. This asymmetry was negative for both English speakers and Spanish speakers. Spanish speakers had more difficulty understanding the English curriculum, and English speakers had less need to use and understand Spanish during Spanish instruction.

Resource asymmetry was also a concern at the Phoenix school. In the Spanish instruction classrooms, books were available in Spanish and in English, and posters around the room were in both languages. However, in the English instruction classrooms, all books and environmental print were in English. In the school library, books in Spanish constituted only 20 percent of the entire collection. In addition, the Spanish books were located in a separate and isolated part of the library, making students who chose Spanish books feel different and uncomfortable. Overall, there were more materials of all kinds available in English. This asymmetry sends a clear message about the importance of English. In many schools, the resources in Spanish are not of the same quality and quantity as those available in English.

Amrein and Peña also found student asymmetry at the school. Despite the program director's claims that students in the school interacted all the time and thus were developing cross-cultural abilities, the researchers noted that there was a great deal of self-segregation among the students. Whenever students had a choice inside or outside the classroom, they broke off into homogeneous groups that "reflected imbalances existing in the larger society" (10). Further, the Latino students who were more bilingual and served as language brokers for other native Spanish speakers were seen as a kind of elite group. They either associated with other language brokers or joined the monolingual English groups rather than interacting with the students they were most intended to help.

In summary, many obstacles may keep dual language programs from reaching the goal of academic, social, and linguistic equity. Certainly, dual language programs provide non-English-speaking students more opportunities for access to academic achievement and cross-cultural friendships than other program models. In addition, native English speakers have opportunities to become bilingual and broaden their understanding of cross-cultural issues. However, those implementing dual language programs must understand the subtle influences that can keep their programs from achieving equality, and teachers and administrators should take specific steps to ensure equal status of both languages and both language groups. The dual language model developed by Gómez (2003) includes one way to help schools achieve equal status of the two languages.

Gómez' Language of the Day

In his 50/50 model for dual language schools, Gómez has included one extremely important element. In this model, the 50/50 division extends beyond the instructional time. Outside the front office door and on each classroom door, there is always a sign that says either "Este es un salón de estudiantes bilingües. Hoy es día de ESPAÑOL. This is a classroom of bilingual learners. Today is SPANISH day" (see Figure 3–2) or "This is a classroom of bilingual learners. Today is ENGLISH day. Este es un salón de estudiantes bilingües. Hoy es día de INGLES." This does not mean that the subjects are all taught in either English or Spanish that day. The division of languages in his model is by subject matter. Math is always in English, science and social studies are in Spanish, and reading/language arts is in both languages. The signs mean that *all* business outside the classroom, including office business, announcements, specials like P.E., music, and computers, and hall passing times, is to be conducted in the language of the day. In addition, teachers use the language of the day for the daily news time when they review the calendar, complete some basic math facts, and engage students in a language experience activity.

FIG. 3–2 Today Is Spanish Day

A visitor entering a school using this model on Spanish day is greeted in Spanish. Phones are answered first in Spanish too. If the person visiting or calling doesn't speak Spanish, a translator is provided, just as Spanish-speaking parents are given assistance on English days. As students move around the school, they are reminded of the language of the day if they forget. Music and P.E. teachers conduct their lessons in the language of the day. All these practices give everyone the message that both languages matter. This model does require that administrators, office staff, and teachers of specials be bilingual. This also means that the administration must ensure that the language-of-the-day procedure is followed by everyone. In so many ways, it is the administrator who is key to the success of a dual language program. In the following sections, we lay out administrative essentials for dual language programs.

Administrative Essentials

Whether the dual language program is implemented schoolwide or is a strand in the school, strong administrative leadership is critical for the program's success. The school site principal must be knowledgeable about dual language education and committed to the program. This means that there must be an investment of time and energy on the part of the principal. In many schools, a resource specialist has direct responsibility for the day-to-day operation of the program. The principal and the specialist form a team, and each person takes on some of the duties involved in establishing and maintaining a successful program. There are five essentials for administrators.

Administrative Essentials
• Monitor to ensure consistent planning, curriculum implementation, and classroom organization.
• Provide and participate in ongoing professional development for teachers through consultants, school visits, and conferences.
• Provide necessary funding for rich and varied materials in both languages in all content areas.
• Provide time for teachers to plan and problem-solve together.
• Provide positive feedback to encourage students, teachers, and other staff and make them feel appreciated.

Monitor to Ensure Consistent Curriculum

Educators often talk about how the pendulum swings. One year a certain philosophy, an approach to teaching, or a set of materials is promoted as the way to succeed. The next year something quite different is in style, something that might be considered at the opposite end of the pendulum swing from the previous practices. These shifts often leave teachers and students confused and frustrated. Dual language programs cannot constantly shift philosophies, approaches, or materials. Administrators are key to providing the stability a dual language program needs to achieve consistent planning, curriculum implementation, and classroom organization. In a research summary of their work with dual language programs, Collier and Thomas (2004) explain the key role good dual language administrators play, their commitment to the challenges, and the importance of consistency.

> Administrators of dual language schools talk about the enormous amount of planning time needed and the complications of what they are doing. But they add they absolutely love their jobs and are fully committed to making dual language work for the whole community . . . A principal's commitment to and vision of this reform requires great sensitivity to culturally and linguistically diverse communities and the willingness to stick with the decision to implement a full enrichment model that enhances the achievement of all student groups. (12)

Dual language programs must follow a curriculum that is consistent with bilingual education theory and best practices and that all teachers understand and can implement in their classrooms. Since dual language programs require teachers to implement specific strategies and to teach language through content in a setting in which about half the students are learning in a second language, there is a need for ongoing professional development. Sometimes consultants can be brought into the school, sometimes teachers and administrators can visit other dual language schools to get ideas for their own program, and often local, state, and national conferences can provide dual language educators with important information. It is essential that administrators make school visits and attend inservices and conferences along with their teachers so that they can fully understand and support effective practices.

Provide Necessary Resources

A good administrative team also makes sure that teachers are provided with the necessary resources. Too often the resources in English are adequate, but there are not enough appropriate resources in the second language. As we discussed earlier, this not only limits learning in the minority language but also sends students the message that English is the valued language. For example, schools should have equal numbers of books in Spanish and in English, and the books should be equally attractive. If English books are glossy hardbacks and Spanish materials are black-and-white photocopies, students get the message that the school does not value Spanish.

Providing adequate resources in both languages is critical for the literacy development of students in dual language programs. Many programs have adequate resources in English, but lack comparable resources in Spanish, especially at the upper grades. McQuillan (1998) shows high correlations between National Assessment of Educational Progress (NAEP) scores for different states and measures of access to books for students in those states. To determine access to print, he assembled data from studies of the number of books in students' homes, classroom libraries, school libraries, and public libraries. He also reviewed data from studies of how many books students read during free or sustained silent reading (SSR). McQuillan presents a convincing argument that access to books is the crucial variable that separates groups of students into good and struggling readers. The studies he reviews show that good readers have access to more books and read more.

Krashen (2003) also presents extensive data from research studies, including studies of English language learners, showing the importance of access to books and time spent in free voluntary reading. Some of the most compelling studies on the value of access to books are reported by Elley (1991, 1998; W. Elley and Mangubhai 1983) who provided extensive resources for children learning English in third world countries. Elley reports remarkable gains in English proficiency and English reading comprehension for students with access to many interesting books.

In dual language programs, it is necessary to find books in two languages. Students in programs with more resources do better than those with limited access to books. Krashen (2004) reports on a study by Ajuira (1994), which found that Hispanic children in a two-way grade one class did better than a comparison group in a mainstream class on a modified version of the Iowa Test of Basic Skills. However, as Krashen points out, students in the mainstream class had very limited access to books. There was only one big book in the room, and the classroom library fit on less than one quarter of one bookshelf. In contrast, students in the two-way class had access to many more books, including more than twenty big books in Spanish and English. The higher scores for students in the two-way class can certainly be attributed to both the kind of program and the much greater access to books. If the number of books in the two classes Ajuira studied had been reversed, it is not likely that students in the two-way program would have scored so much better than students in the mainstream program. Access to books is critical for high student achievement in dual language classes.

Provide Time to Plan and Positive Feedback

Administrative support to provide for appropriate dual language curriculum, ongoing professional development, and adequate materials, is important, but not enough. Administrators in dual language schools need to provide teachers and resource specialists with the time they need to work together to plan and solve problems that inevitably arise. We have seen that implementing a successful dual language curriculum can be overwhelming, but when people work together, they create a positive atmosphere that energizes all those involved in the program. Often teachers take their lunch or preparation periods to work together, but this is asking a lot of teachers who already feel stretched to the limit.

Administrators can help teachers find the time they need for collaboration by providing release time during scheduled inservice days when students are not there or by providing substitutes so groups of teachers can work together. Some very creative administrators occasionally arrange the school schedule so that different groups of teachers can meet while groups of students go to their specials (P.E., music, art, and the computer lab).

Providing planning and problem-solving time is important and is one way that administrators can show teachers they are valued. In addition, everyone needs positive reinforcement, especially when they are working hard. Excellent administrators find several different ways to positively reinforce the good work that their teachers and other staff members are doing. They compliment them publicly in many settings, including at faculty meetings, school board meetings, parent meetings, or meetings with community and university members. Some administrators write notes to teachers who have made an extra effort. When reporters from local newspapers come to gather information about the dual language program, good administrators make sure that the teachers are also interviewed and featured. However, perhaps the most meaningful support comes from daily encouragement that includes details about specific things that the administrator has noticed teachers and specialists doing.

Of course, it is not only teachers and resource specialists who need support. When administrators compliment clerical and custodial staff and occasionally take them to lunch, these staff members feel appreciated too. They come to see their work as critical and take a personal pride in the dual language program. The atmosphere that they help create is evident when anyone enters the school.

Finally, and perhaps most important, good administrators encourage the students in the school. They take an interest in the students, both native English and native Spanish speakers, equally. Rather than simply disciplining students they catch doing something wrong, good administrators take the time to talk to and joke with students informally in the halls or at school events such as fairs and sports events. This is especially important in dual language programs because students need to feel their program is special and that they are the key to making it that way.

One particularly poignant example comes from Ms. Gaona, the principal at Runn Elementary School, a rural Texas school on the Mexican border in which many students live below the poverty level. In Texas, students must pass the standardized third-grade test in order to go on to fourth grade. Third-grade teachers and their students had worked quite hard to prepare for this test by teaching reading, writing, and content in a meaningful context. They also worked on test-taking strategies. On the day of the test, Ms. Gaona brought the students gifts that she had bought using her own money. Every third-grade child received a stuffed animal to hug as he or she took the test. Ms. Gaona explained to each child that she knew they had worked hard, and she wanted to show them that she knew they were all going to do the best they could. She appreciated their hard work and she had confidence that they would do well. In fact, the students did very well, and on the day the results came in, to show her appreciation for all their hard work, the principal treated all the teachers to lunch!

Good administrators, then, make sure that planning time, materials, and ongoing training opportunities are available to their staff. Everyone in effective dual language schools works hard and is dedicated to what he or she is doing. But because there is so much to do, to understand, and to keep track of, people can get discouraged. Administrators must also be the cheerleaders, the people who show that every person's hard work is appreciated. When staff members know their work is valued, they work harder and do so willingly.

 ## Administrator and Teacher Essentials

I believe it is important to mention that the teachers are here because of the administrative support. Nowhere else in the district will you find a principal that will make it a point to make home visits to discuss problems with students and/or offer to bring in parents for meetings. The staff is loyal to her for her unwavering support of the dual language program and as a strong administrator; but *every* teacher here believes in the academic success and lifelong achievement for our students through the Dual Language Program, or we wouldn't be here. (quote from María Maldonado, a teacher at Runn Elementary Dual Language School)

As the section on the essentials for administrators makes clear, administrators must support teachers in every possible way. This, however, cannot happen in a situation where the administrator is only considered the boss and does not include teachers in important decisions that affect teaching or program planning. Administrators and teachers must form a team, one in which the administrator provides leadership and support without dictating. In dual language, this requires a leader who can help all the players—including teachers, secretarial and custodial staff, parents, and students—work together effectively toward the common goal of educating the students in two languages.

While it is possible in some schools for administrators to administrate and teachers to teach without really understanding theory and research, this is not true in dual language schools. It is critical that teachers and administrators understand bilingual education theory and research. They must also understand the importance of teaching language through content, how to apply second language teaching strategies, and the differences among dual language models. In addition, both administrators and teachers must understand the importance of having students develop literacy and academic competence in their first languages and understand how knowledge transfers to a second language. When the administrators and teachers develop a thorough understanding of dual language, they can explain and defend the program to parents, school board members, and the community. There are seven essentials for administrators and teachers.

Administrator and Teacher Essentials

- Collaborate on the development and implementation of all aspects of the program.

- Understand that academic competence in two languages takes time to develop.

- Work for consistency in program planning, classroom organization, and literacy instruction across and within grade levels.

- Respond to parental concerns and needs.

- Include parents from both language groups in program planning and implementation.

- Promote and explain the dual language program to parents, the school board, and the community.

- Display a passion for the program, the students, and the families.

Both administrators and teachers play important roles in the implementation and development of a dual language program. In the section that follows, we provide an example of one school in which an outstanding administrator, Ofelia Gaona, whom we introduced earlier, and her hardworking teachers exemplify all the essentials listed here. We hope that this example will help readers visualize both administrative and administrator and teacher essentials. While she is the first to tell everyone, "We make mistakes. We have a lot to learn," Runn Elementary School and Ofelia Gaona's leadership have much to teach us all.

A Texas Border Dual Language School

Ms. Gaona provides both tangible and intangible supports to her teachers and the students at her school. She is principal of a rural preK–5 dual language school in south Texas. The school lies one mile from the Rio Grande River, in the middle of sugar cane fields. Ofelia and her staff provide all the essentials listed previously, including the important characteristics of passion and caring. Upon entering the school, visitors feel the warmth, see evidence of the learning, and experience being welcomed with open arms, often literally. Added to the feeling of warmth is one of pride in the new school additions and new landscaping. No longer do students learn in converted army barracks and run-down portables or have to play in muddy fields.

Of the total of 364 students in the school, 99.7 percent are listed by the state department of education as Hispanic, 328 as limited English proficient, and 348 as economically disadvantaged. All students receive free lunch. Many of the students live in extreme poverty, but the children, according to Ms. Gaona, "are not deprived. They are all special. They all can succeed." And they do. In 2002 the state TASS (Texas Assessment of Academic Achievement) rated the school as acceptable and listed it as "well above average" when compared with similar schools.

The school has not always been considered acceptable. In 1993–1994, when Ms. Gaona joined the school administration as the curriculum specialist, the school's achievement level was one of the lowest in the state. Only two students passed all sections of the state's achievement test (Rips 1999). However, by 1997 the Texas Education Agency recognized Runn children for high performance. And the students' continued success over the next years led to recognition of the school in a state magazine, a spot on the national television show, *CBS World News: An American Dream Series,* and an official resolution by the state's legislators commending "all those associated with Runn Elementary School for its designation as one of the state's top schools" (Texas House of Representatives 1999).

Ms. Gaona credits her teachers, the administrative staff, and the dual language program that started seven years ago. However, Ms. Gaona's leadership has been the key. Ofelia Gaona knows her school community, her students, her parents, her teachers, and all her staff. Most mornings, she greets students, teachers, and parents as they enter the school. She knows them by name. When parents come to school unannounced with questions or concerns, she answers them patiently in Spanish or English. She knows how to make everyone from university professors to migrant workers feel they are not just welcome in her school but they can, and should, help. She knows the needs at her school and finds the support that parents, students, and teachers require.

The amazing 97.9 percent attendance rate at the school reflects the fact that Ms. Gaona knows her students. When students struggle academically, are absent, or cause discipline problems, she goes to the home so she can discuss with the parents how the child can be helped. She tells stories of children living in impossible conditions. Some students are locked out of their homes by parents who have problems of their own. When one student came to school riding an old bicycle along the highway rain or shine, concerned faculty and staff formed a team to pick the boy up. Ms. Gaona, with sympathetic tears, tells anyone who will listen, "You look at their living conditions and wonder how they do it." It is hard for her to see the conditions in which some of the children live, but her understanding of the children and their families helps her be the determined educator she is. She insists on good attendance, insists that parents help, and insists that students do their best. She helps students succeed by her example of hard work and by inspiring others to help her do it.

Ms. Gaona reminds rowdy children that there is no running in the halls and explains to them how important it is to respect their new school buildings. She calls visitors over to proudly show off the singing talents of a young bilingual boy whose migrant parents trust the school to do what is best for their children.

At Christmas for the past several years, every child in the school has received a present from church members in a nearby town or from members of different churches in Stanton, North Dakota. Ms. Gaona visited churches near the school to ask for ideas for ways to brighten Christmas for students at her school. Some North Dakotans, escaping the winter cold, heard Ms. Gaona at the Lutheran church and wrote friends in their hometown, asking for help. Members of several churches in North Dakota have responded generously every year since. Reflecting on this experience, Ms. Gaona commented, "Even for me, as principal, it's a support system, someone that cares, somebody you go to and say, 'This is what we're facing.' It's not always financial, sometimes just support and ideas" (Associated Press 2004, 1).

The administrative staff is as committed as the principal. The staff includes Ms. Sutti, a bilingual specialist from the regional support center, whose work at Runn is funded by a Title VII grant. Ms. Sutti has several years of experience supporting teachers in dual language settings. She knows bilingual education and has taught university courses in bilingualism and biliteracy. She coaches teachers and advises them on important issues related to teaching strategies and student assessment. She works closely with Ms. Gaona and the vice principal, Ms. Green, at the school. Ms. Green recently completed an M.A. in administrative leadership and bilingual education. All three know the school, the students, the teachers, dual language, and bilingual education. They make a powerful administrative team.

Ms. Gaona supports her teachers and works with them. Whenever there are concerns, teachers and administrators work together, meeting over lunch or during teacher work days. When teachers, resource specialists, or librarians ask for something that will improve instruction for the students, Ms. Gaona's answer is always, "We'll find money. Get what you need." The Title VII grant and an Accelerated Schools Grant help her provide materials and professional development. She rejected one consultant the district had hired to provide the schools with professional development. She explained to Yvonne, "That presenter won't help my teachers help my kids." Instead, she used grant money to bring in the country's expert on cooperative learning, Spencer Kagan (1986), to work with her staff. In fact, she insisted that Kagan himself come for the workshop. She also hired a literacy specialist to help teachers with guided reading and a hands-on math expert who works in classrooms giving demonstration lessons. The teachers have all enthusiastically implemented his strategies because they have seen him work with their students!

Planning days are provided at the school so that teachers can do horizontal planning across each grade level or vertical planning across several grade levels. This type of planning ensures that curriculum is coordinated across and within grade levels. Faculty and administration also get together to problem-solve. Recently, when a teacher noticed that ten third-grade students were not doing well on standardized tests in English, Ms. Gaona and Ms. Sutti called a meeting of the kindergarten and first-grade teachers to study the cumulative folders of those children to see where early instruction and support went wrong. They asked Yvonne as well as the region's bilingual director and the student teachers to be part of that meeting. They invited everyone to give input. A review of student records showed that the struggling students had not received adequate literacy development in Spanish before starting their English literacy program.

Throughout the meeting, Ms. Gaona made it clear that the problem had to be solved. She admitted, "We haven't always done things correctly, but that is going to change." The group decided to increase the number of sections of Spanish literacy instruction at the school. The administrative team also sat down with third-grade teachers and discussed with them concerns about the academic Spanish of the third graders. They all talked together about how to support students to give them access to Spanish content at grade level.

It is understood at Runn Elementary School that everyone works together. Everyone works hard and takes their responsibilities seriously. Several teachers at different grade levels were asked to take their personal time after school or on Saturdays to work individually with one of the struggling third graders. No one refused. These tutoring sessions supported these students in reading in their primary language, Spanish, as well as in English. Just recently, Yvonne received the latest report on the students' progress from Ms. Gaona, who had just gotten home from a Saturday session at her school. She excitedly told Yvonne that the students, identified just three months earlier as failing, were making remarkable progress. Some had jumped two to three years in growth in their Spanish reading. All were progressing well in Spanish and in English reading, too.

A final example of how the Runn principal and teachers together promote success comes from experiences Yvonne had with her university student teachers last semester. In the initial meeting with the twenty-five student teachers, Ms. Gaona paired the aspiring teachers with their school site mentor teachers. Then she made sure everyone knew that "the teachers at Runn Elementary School work hard." She continued, "They are wonderful teachers. Our students are wonderful too. We are lucky to have you young people here, but you are lucky to be here too!" The student teachers from the university were welcomed to the school and regarded as valuable resources. After only six weeks, Ms. Gaona was able to tell Yvonne the strengths of the different student teachers working in her school and made it a point to compliment two in particular for a wonderful lesson she took the time to observe. In fact, she made it a point to observe all the student teachers!

Ms. Gaona values not only the students, teachers, and other staff but also the parents who come to the school. She somehow always has time for everyone who needs her. This includes taking time with Latino parents concerned that the dual language program isn't teaching their children enough English. Yvonne has observed how Ms. Gaona has calmed their fears, knowing that these parents see English as the road to success. They do not understand how full development of a student's first language leads to academic success.

Because she visits many of the children's homes, Ms. Gaona knows that many parents struggle to provide for their children. They often lack the benefits of schooling themselves so they need different kinds of support. Yvonne attended a workshop at the school for parents on redirecting children's behavior. This workshop was part of a program developed by the International Network for Children and Families (INCAF). The facilitator, who was bilingual, had parents role-play different everyday interactions and discuss how those situation s should be handled. For example, in pairs, one parent role-played a child trying to tell her parent something exciting that had happened that day at school. The other parent played the role of a parent who was too busy to listen to the child. As parents debriefed the role-play experience, one parent showed that she had really understood how important it is to listen to children. She had played a child and said, "*¡Casi me dio ganas de llorar! ¡No me estaba escuchando!*" ("I almost wanted to cry! She wasn't listening to me!").

Ms. Gaona makes sure that what's important gets attention. Her dedication inspires everyone who works at the school. When the leadership is so strong, teachers appreciate the children and their parents. They feel comfortable supporting the dual language program and explaining the philosophy of the program. It is, though, more than advocacy that makes Runn the school it is. It is a combination of hardworking, knowledgeable, caring teachers and administrators committed to helping children become bilingual and biliterate. Ms. Garay, a teacher with seven years' experience, explained this well: "Ms. Gaona trusts us enough to say, 'You know what you're doing.' That, in a sense, is a big responsibility for me. I better know what I'm doing if she trusts me with these kids."

 ## Teacher Essentials

The essentials we discussed in the previous section apply to both teachers and administrators. Teachers and administrators should collaborate on building a thorough understanding of theory, developing the curriculum, and explaining the program to parents. Some additional essentials relate specifically to teachers. Teachers need to be competent bilinguals themselves or, if teaching in only one of the two languages, be proficient in that language and have receptive knowledge of the other. While it is important to be competent in the language of instruction and provide a model of conventional language use, teachers must also be tolerant of their students' native dialects. Teachers should build upon students' backgrounds and expand their knowledge. In addition to having language competence and developing their students' language proficiency, teachers in dual language settings must be able to work collaboratively with others. In successful programs, teachers plan together, both horizontally and vertically. They understand short- and long-term planning that starts with student needs. Finally, teachers must work together to find and share resources. When teachers plan and share together, they expand the potential for student learning.

Teacher Essentials
• Develop high levels of proficiency in two languages or proficiency in one language and a receptive knowledge of the second language.
• Recognize and appreciate language variation but model conventional oral and written language when providing instruction in either language.
• Collaborate to articulate curriculum within and across grade levels.
• Collaborate for both short- and long-term planning.
• Collaborate to locate resources in both languages.

Teachers Are Competent Bilinguals

A key essential is that the teacher be competent in the language of instruction. We realize that this is one of the most difficult essentials to achieve in dual language programs. Research tells us that people do not become competent bilinguals in a short period of time. It takes four to nine years, depending on different factors, for someone to be able to compete academically with native speakers of a language (Collier 1989; Cummins 1981). Often, aspects of a second language, such as pronunciation or command of idioms, may never be completely mastered. Because developing high levels of academic language proficiency is so difficult, nonnative speakers of Spanish face a challenge in teaching academic content in Spanish to children, especially at the upper grades. Yvonne provides a personal example. She has been studying Spanish since high school. She majored in Spanish at the university she attended and has lived in Colombia, Mexico, and Venezuela. Still, she knows she has an accent when she speaks Spanish. When she teaches her biliteracy course at the university in Spanish, it takes more energy than when she teaches in English, and she does not always feel confident. She realizes some of her syntax is not always nativelike, and she sometimes lacks certain technical vocabulary because her academic studies of this subject were primarily done in English.

Native Spanish speakers in this country may also struggle with Spanish. The Freemans are living in the Rio Grande Valley in south Texas, ten miles from the border with Mexico. The community is very bilingual. In stores Spanish is spoken as often as English. The university where they teach is 87 percent Latino, and Spanish and English are heard in the halls and classrooms. Still, English is the language of power, and students who have spoken Spanish with families and friends often have had little formal schooling in Spanish. Dual language programs did not exist when they were younger. When local students decide to study bilingual education and get a bilingual credential to teach in dual language settings, one of their biggest hurdles is gaining the academic Spanish they need. They are proficient users of Tex-Mex, but to teach academic content, they must be able to read and write conventional Spanish.

In some dual language programs, schools have chosen a model in which teachers are hired to teach in only one language. Teachers work in teams. One teacher teaches in English and the other in the non-English language. In these cases, it is important that both teachers have receptive knowledge of the other language of instruction. This is critical for teachers in the earlier grades, when students may be able to express themselves only in one language. Teachers need to understand their students' needs and respond to them. An English-speaking teacher can maintain the language of instruction by responding in English to a child who asks a question in Spanish, but to do that, the teacher must understand the question.

Teachers who know only one language do not always understand the struggles of second language learners. Receptive knowledge of Spanish and/or a willingness to develop higher levels of Spanish proficiency is an entrance requirement for the dual language preparation program that Sandra directs. Students planning to teach English and working on their Spanish talk about how important their own struggles with learning Spanish have been. They are much more understanding of the native Spanish-speaking children's challenges as those children try to learn in their second language, English.

Native Speakers Appreciate Language Variation

There is a kind of reverse side to concerns about teachers having language competence. Native Spanish speakers teaching in a dual language program are sometimes not tolerant of the Spanish dialects their students speak. McCollum (1999) documents how Spanish-side teachers in a two-way program criticized students' local Spanish dialect. This caused students to reject their native language and turn to English. Teachers should model and teach conventional forms and vocabulary, but standard Spanish can be considered an addition to the dialects students bring to school. Native speakers of a language should always validate the languages students bring to school and help those students develop conventional language forms as well. Yvonne watched one teacher work with Spanish-speaking children to help them understand that "*Stá bueno,*" meaning "OK" or "Fine," is all right to use in informal conversation and is used widely by local Spanish speakers, but another way to say "OK" that is more formal and more appropriate to use with elders including teachers is "*Está bien.*"

Another example of acceptance of students' language comes from Pérez' (2004) description of the San Antonio schools. Although teachers discourage code-switching in their classes, bilinguals in San Antonio are accustomed to switching back and forth from one language to the other within a sentence or a conversation. Since code-switching is common in the community, some teachers questioned the practice of eliminating code-switching in school. In some classes, teachers chose to read books that included instances of code-switching, and they encouraged students to make purposeful use of code-switching as they wrote. Teachers in the San Antonio programs viewed their students' language as a resource and attempted to develop that resource by showing students effective ways to use two languages in their writing. In the process, they validated the local language variety that both students and teachers often used.

Code-switching shows a command of both English and Spanish. Those who code-switch have control over the underlying structure of two languages and understand social communication. An example showing how competent bilinguals code-switch comes from one of Yvonne's graduate students, who works as a dual language strategist. She was talking to bilingual colleagues at her school about her language proficiency. She said, "*Yo soy bien* fluent *en español* (I am really fluent in Spanish)." The interesting thing about her code-switch to English in the middle of the sentence is that she probably used *fluent* subconsciously because she understands the underlying structure of both languages. Many times Spanish speakers would say, "*Yo hablo con fluidez en español*" (literally meaning, "I have quite a bit of fluency in Spanish"). Since she had started her sentence with the structure "I am quite . . .," she had to use an English adjective, *fluent*, because *fluidez* is a noun and could not fit the syntactic pattern she had begun. Bilinguals never insert a noun where there should be an adjective.

Code-switching can become a topic for linguistic investigation in a dual language class. In the San Antonio schools, teachers helped students understand how writers could use code-switching effectively in their writing. Teachers could also engage students in a comparative study of the two languages in the classroom, since some students are experts in each language. For example, students could look at how idioms differ across languages. In English, a person gets married *to* someone. In Spanish, a person gets married *with* someone. A shady deal in English might be conducted *under the table*, but in some dialects of Spanish, it is carried out *under the water*. In addition, students could look at differences in syntax. In English, adjectives usually precede nouns and in Spanish, they follow nouns. They could also look at similarities and differences in spelling patterns. For example, the /k/ sound is spelled with *c* in both languages when the following letter is a consonant or *a, o,* or *u*. On the other hand, when the following vowel is *i* or *e*, English words use *k* to represent the /k/ sound and Spanish words use *qu*. By engaging students in linguistic study of the two languages, teachers can increase students' metalinguistic awareness, their knowledge about language. Further, as they study differences and similarities between their two languages, bilingual students become more aware of conventional patterns of use in each language and increase their language competence.

Code-switching can serve various purposes when the speaker and listener are both competent bilinguals. The two primary reasons that bilinguals code-switch are for more effective expression and for social group solidarity. A monolingual who has read extensively and has developed advanced vocabulary has more linguistic resources to draw on than someone whose vocabulary is less developed. In the same way, a bilingual has greater language resources than a monolingual. A competent bilingual person may choose to insert a word or phrase from one language into a conversation in a second language just because that vocabulary communicates more effectively.

An example of code-switching to access vocabulary resources comes from another graduate student of Yvonne's. The student had just begun to share rides to class. When she got into her friend's car she said, "Wow, your car is so *amplio* (spacious)!" She probably knew the word *spacious*, but it just did not convey the same feeling that she knew *amplio* would for the listener. Somehow *amplio* has a connotation of more positive space to the bilingual speaker and served as more of a compliment.

In addition, bilinguals use code-switching to signal that they are part of a social group. All people use the forms of language in ways that are appropriate for the social context. Teachers use different registers when speaking with administrators in the office, their colleagues in the lunchroom, and their own children at home. This ability to shift speech styles is a mark of sociocultural competence. Using a particular register with a peer group is a way of signaling membership in a social group. The language of teens is a clear example of this. In the same way, in certain settings, competent bilinguals code-switch to signal that they are members of a particular discourse community (Gee 1990).

Two good friends talking might say, *"Oye,* should we tell María?" *"¿Por qué?* She is always *chismeando."* ("Hey, should we tell María?" "Why? She's always gossiping.") This speech style is one way of signaling that the two speakers are part of the same social group, a group of competent bilinguals. These examples show that people code-switch with those they know will understand both languages, and they code-switch spontaneously unless, of course, they are deliberately trying to obscure their meaning to a monolingual person who is listening!

For students learning a second language, inserting a word from the native language can serve as a strategy for communication when the speaker lacks linguistic resources. If a native English speaker is trying to express an idea in Spanish and comes to a point where he doesn't know the appropriate Spanish word, he may insert an English word into the sentence. This strategy keeps communication from breaking down. Even when the listener speaks little or no English, she can usually guess the meaning of the English word from the context. However, this strategy should not be confused with code-switching.

Teachers Collaborate to Plan and to Find Resources

Dual language teachers also need to understand curriculum, know how to plan, and collaborate with other teachers. We want to emphasize the word *collaborate,* because in effective dual language schools, teachers work well together. Many times teachers work in teams with an English-side and Spanish-side teacher. Even when one teacher provides instruction in two languages, the teacher must collaborate with other teachers at that grade level to provide a consistent curriculum. Teachers must also work with their colleagues across grade levels to ensure that the curriculum builds logically from one grade to the next.

At Runn Elementary School, teachers meet in grade-level teams to plan horizontally. Yvonne interviewed Ms. Maldonado, who explained that teachers at her grade level meet during work days and over lunch to coordinate themes and to make sure they are covering standards and teaching the state-required benchmarks. They also meet to solve particular problems at their grade level. Recently, as we mentioned earlier, third-grade teachers met to discuss how they could help raise the level of the academic Spanish their students were acquiring. They also met with the reading specialist to get further input and advice on how to implement new strategies.

In addition, teachers collaborate to plan across grade levels. Ms. Maldonado described how teachers plan vertically at her school. This year, the third-grade team will meet with second-grade teachers to discuss expectations for students in third grade and to help their colleagues plan their second-grade curriculum so that there will be articulation across the grade levels. In Chapter 6, we provide further discussion and an extended example of planning.

Teachers also collaborate to find resources. Especially in new programs, finding resources for teaching around themes and teaching content in the non-English language can be a problem. Although it is difficult to find resources in some languages, rich resources are available in Spanish. When teachers in dual language programs work together, the job of locating resources is not so overwhelming. The librarian can be a help, but if the program is new, the librarian may not be accustomed to looking for resources in languages other than English. Non-English resources can often be found at state and national bilingual conferences. If a few teachers from a school go to these conferences, one of their responsibilities can be to look for such materials. Teachers can also find resources by checking the Internet. Publishers have increased their production of books in a variety of languages because of the demand from dual language schools, and more materials are available each year.

One last point about collaboration, in general, and the sharing of resources must be made. In discussion with a two-way resource specialist working at a fairly well established school in the Midwest, Yvonne mentioned that one English-side teacher she had observed seemed to be especially effective. Yvonne had noticed that the teacher was passionate about her subject and used excellent materials and strategies. The specialist's response was somewhat lukewarm, so Yvonne probed. The specialist admitted the teacher was excellent but was not used to working with others and might be dropped from the program. The teacher seldom shared materials or her expertise with her fellow teachers. She was impatient with and antagonistic toward her Spanish-side team member, who was proficient in Spanish but still working on a teaching credential. Although she worked with two groups of students, this teacher favored her morning homeroom group and often neglected the children who came to her in the afternoon. She often refused to attend grade-level or across-level meetings. She claimed they were a waste of time for her. In reality, she did not understand the two-way program and its goals at all and did not see her role as any different than it had been when the school was an all-English school.

If program administrators can help teachers like this see how they can share their resources, knowledge, and skills, perhaps problems such as this one might not become serious. Proficient, experienced teachers are the best possible supports for newer teachers and teachers who are struggling. Part of their professional responsibility is to serve as a teacher of teachers. Above all, they need to view themselves as members of a collaborative team whose goal is to improve education for all students.

 ## Conclusion

In this chapter we presented essentials that apply to the whole school, to administrators, to administrators and teachers together, and to teachers. The effective dual language programs we have visited or read about have all or most of these essentials in mind, and teachers and administrators constantly work to improve their programs. In the following chapters we discuss curriculum essentials, including the importance of teaching language through content, using themes, and developing a meaningful literacy program. In the final chapter, we help readers consider how to plan both horizontally and vertically and we provide an example of an extended theme in a dual language setting. With the appropriate curriculum, dual language programs can help all students succeed.

 ## Learning Extensions

1. The first two whole-school essentials deal with understanding and supporting dual language and being flexible and open to change. Review the two examples provided. Can you see how these essentials are critical for the success of a dual language program? Are these essentials present in your dual language program or in a program that you know? Discuss this with a partner.

2. Equity is often listed as one of the positive outcomes of dual language education. In this chapter we discuss some equity issues for dual language. What are these concerns? Have you seen any of these issues in dual language programs you know about in your community? Discuss this, drawing on the programs you know about.

3. In discussing administrative and administrator and teacher essentials, we provided an extended example of one excellent principal, Ms. Gaona, who works with her staff to create an excellent program. Review the essentials and connect those essentials to what Ms. Gaona and others do at Runn Elementary School.

4. What kinds of things that are being done at Runn Elementary School would you like to see being done in the dual language program you know? If you do not know a dual language school, visit one and then use what you learn to answer the question.

5. Consider a dual language teacher you know. How does that teacher display the teacher essentials listed in this chapter? Write a short case study of the teacher and evaluate the teacher referring to each of the essentials.

Curriculum Essentials

As we have worked in and visited dual language schools across the country, we have observed that excellent schools have administrators and teachers who meet the guidelines we laid out as essential characteristics in Chapter 3. In this chapter we turn to what we have observed are essentials for the curriculum in successful programs. Many of the essentials are common sense, but just because they are logical does not mean they are always present. We have organized these curriculum essentials into four sections: curriculum essentials for overall organization, curriculum essentials for lesson delivery, curriculum essentials for assessment, and curriculum essentials for a meaningful literacy program. We consider the final curriculum essential so important that we have devoted an entire chapter to that topic. We encourage educators involved in dual language programs to consider each essential for their curriculum.

Curriculum Essentials for Overall Organization

The first three essentials are interconnected. Research on language acquisition has shown that language is best and most efficiently learned when taught through content (Brinton, Snow and Wesche 1989; Richard-Amato 1996; Snow and Brinton 1997). For second language learners, that content is made more comprehensible when teachers organize around themes. Themes are especially effective for second language learners because they provide students with an overall schema. Students always know what the topic is even if they do not understand everything that is being said in their new language. When teachers organize the themes using students' first and second languages appropriately, themes provide students with a constant and interwoven preview in the first language, view in the second, and review again in the first. Teachers can connect themes to students' lives. In addition, themes can easily be connected to required standards.

Curriculum Essentials for Overall Organization

- Teach language through sustained content to develop academic language and academic content knowledge.

- Ensure that all aspects of the curriculum are interrelated through thematic teaching to provide a continuous preview, view, and review.

- Organize curriculum around themes that connect to students' lives and meet content and language standards.

Teach language through sustained academic content

We have written elsewhere about the importance of teaching language through academic content (Freeman and Freeman 1998a, 2002). Teaching language through content differs from traditional approaches. Traditional language teaching focuses on the language itself. Teachers teach the grammar and vocabulary. As a result of traditional teaching, many students know something about the language, but they can't use the language effectively for communication or for learning academic subjects.

There are several benefits to teaching language through content. This approach is more efficient. Students learn language, and at the same time, they learn the important academic content they need. In addition, when teachers teach language through academic content, students acquire more than the everyday language they need for basic communication. They also acquire the academic vocabulary that is so necessary to read and interpret academic texts and tests. As students study content, they are exposed to the language of each academic subject area in a natural context. For example, students studying insects read interesting books about insects, bring in insects to observe, keep journals about insects, do experiments with insects, and talk about all they are learning. These kinds of activities provide an authentic context for students to develop the language of science. In addition, since they are learning interesting academic content, students have a real purpose for developing a second language. Research supports the importance of teaching language through content to develop language. In a comparative study of two-way immersion and developmental bilingual education programs, de Jong (2004) found that two-way immersion students did well in English reading and writing even though they had not formally studied English literacy primarily because they studied science and social content in English.

> TWI students are engaged in science and social studies in English from first grade onwards in the "English" side classroom with native English speakers . . . As a result, ELLs in TWI programs regularly spend time in print-rich and literature-rich English language environments . . . Reading and writing activities are naturally integrated into the science/social studies . . . Ells in TWI program have therefore more opportunities to take advantage of access to literacy in their second language and can develop their English literacy skills informally early on. (103)

Figure 4–1 lists the reasons for teaching language through sustained academic content.

We included the word *sustained* in connection with learning language through academic content because it is important to organize the content teaching over an extended period of time (Pally 2000). For example, it is not enough for teachers to teach the language of insects by reading one book about insects, showing some pictures, and doing one activity. For students to acquire the language and the content of science by studying insects, it is important that students read and discuss multiple books on the topic and be involved in a variety

| **1.** Students get *both* language and content. |
| **2.** Students learn the academic vocabulary of the content areas. |
| **3.** Language is kept in its natural context. |
| **4.** Students have reasons to use language for real purposes. |

FIG. 4–1 Reasons for Teaching Language Through Sustained Academic Content

of activities. In other words, the content teaching about insects is sustained over a period of time and, most effectively, integrated across several subject areas.

Ensure that all aspects of the curriculum are interrelated through thematic teaching

Sustained content teaching is best accomplished by organizing curriculum around integrated themes. When we suggest thematic teaching, we mean that teachers choose a topic and then organize lessons around that topic across subject areas. This avoids what has been called the cha, cha, cha curriculum. In a cha, cha, cha curriculum, students might study insects in science, different community workers in social studies, rhyming words in language arts, fractions in math, and *ea* words for spelling. The different content areas are not related. It is as though the teacher finishes one area, such as science, and then, cha cha cha, the teacher moves on to a new, unrelated subject. Second language learners often get lost in the transition, and by the time they figure out that the topic has moved from insects to community workers, cha cha cha, the teacher is moving on to a new subject.

In thematic teaching the different subject areas are connected. So, for example, students studying how insects affect people could read a poem about insects and create their own insect poems in language arts, study where different kinds of insects live for geography, learn about how insects serve people in social sciences, observe insects and keep insect journals in science, investigate how insects spread or prevent diseases in health, and calculate insect reproduction rates in math.

In the past, some teachers who moved away from the cha cha cha curriculum toward themes took what might be called the gummy bear approach (Kucer, Silva, and Delgado-Larocco 1995). They wanted to connect the different subject areas even when what they were studying across subjects didn't really relate very well. So, for example, they might read a book like *Ira Sleeps Over* (Waber 1972) and talk about how Ira is comforted by his stuffed bear. Then when the class studies math, they might stack up gummy bears to make a graph or do addition problems within bear shapes. There is an attempt to connect language arts and math by the common element of the bear, but the connection is not authentic. Students aren't developing a deep understanding of a topic.

We suggest organizing around themes that answer big questions. For example, a theme could investigate the relationships and interdependencies of insects and humans. Students could try to answer questions like How do insects depend on humans, and how do humans depend on insects? and How are humans and insects alike, and how are they different? The big questions help provide unity for the theme and ensure that the connections among subject areas are not simply token efforts, as in the gummy bear approach. Instead, as students move from one subject area to the next, they continue to gather information to help answer important questions.

Kucer, Silva, and Delgado-Larocco (1995) discuss how they moved away from the gummy bear approach to thematic teaching. They write, "Our earlier attempts at thematic instruction resulted in units that meshed a large number of loosely related materials and activities around a central topic" (28). They point out that the materials and activities should help students arrive at the big picture. For that reason, "students need a curriculum that supports them in making links and connections" (29).

To help teachers conceptualize an integrated curriculum that moves beyond the gummy bear approach, Kucer and his colleagues conceptualize curriculum as a hierarchy with facts at the bottom, concepts in the middle, and generalizations at the top. They observe that "one of the most important goals of the schools is to help students learn to construct generalizations from the concepts and facts developed across various learning experiences" (30). One way to ensure that curriculum helps students develop generalizations instead of focusing on isolated facts is to organize themes based on big questions. As students formulate answers to these questions, they arrive at generalizations that relate the key concepts and are supported by specific facts. The big question keeps both students and teachers focused on the big picture.

Why organize curriculum around themes for dual language instruction?

When teachers organize their curriculum around themes based on big questions, students in dual language programs benefit in several ways. Figure 4–2 lists the reasons for organizing curriculum around themes.

Themes provide a continuous preview, view, review in dual language ◆
Thematic teaching enhances the effective use of preview/view/review in the dual language classroom. In traditional bilingual education, preview/view/review is a strategy that allows teachers to preview content in students' first languages before they study the content further in the second language. Then the teacher reviews the content in the students' first languages. This is not to be confused with concurrent translation, an ineffective strategy. Concurrent translation occurs when a teacher says something in one language and immediately

1.	Themes provide a continuous preview/view/review in dual language classes.
2.	Students know what the topic is even when instruction is in their second language.
3.	Because the curriculum concepts are previewed and reviewed in the students' first language and viewed in the second language, students more easily learn the content.
4.	Because the same topics are studied across content areas and languages, students build academic concepts and vocabulary more easily.
5.	Knowledge and skills acquired during instruction in the first language naturally transfer to the second language during thematically based content study.
6.	Through themes, teachers can connect curriculum to students' lives and backgrounds and draw on their language strengths.
7.	When concepts are previewed in the first language, students can learn better when working in collaborative groups in the second language.
8.	Because the curriculum makes sense, second language students are more fully engaged and experience more success.
9.	Teachers can differentiate instruction to accommodate differences in language proficiency.

FIG. 4–2 Thematic Teaching in Dual Language Programs

translates it into the students' native language. The problem with this approach is that students listen only to the language they understand. Therefore, they do not acquire the second language. In contrast, preview/view/review allows teachers to make the second language more comprehensible by giving an introduction, or preview, in the students' first languages, then teaching the content in the second language using a number of techniques to make the input comprehensible, and finally reviewing after the lesson in the students' first languages (Freeman and Freeman 2000).

In dual language classrooms, thematic instruction provides preview/view/review for all students. The way this functions depends on the model that is used. For example, in a 50/50 dual language setting where students study different content areas in different languages, they might read poetry about insects in English during English language arts and in Spanish during Spanish language arts and write poetry in both languages. If they study social studies and science in Spanish, they would read about insects, investigate their migration habits on the Internet, plot their locations on a map, and observe insects and keep journals all in Spanish. During math in English, students would investigate where different insects are usually found and graph the kinds of insects by continent. For Spanish speakers, the study in Spanish serves as a preview and review for the poetry study in English language arts and for the math activity in English. For English speakers, the study in English functions as a preview and review for the Spanish language arts, social studies, and science lessons.

If the program uses a 50/50 model divided by time, with Spanish in the morning and English in the afternoon, then for Spanish speakers, the morning Spanish study provides a preview for the English study of the same topic in the afternoon. The next morning, as they study the same topic, Spanish speakers get a first language review. For English speakers, the effect would be the same. As long as the languages alternate, what is presented in a student's first language provides a preview and review for the lessons presented in the second language when the curriculum is organized around themes. It is important to remember that the content is not repeated in each language. Instead, what is taught in one language builds on the same concepts as the lesson taught in the other language.

Preview/view/review has less of an effect in a 90/10 model. However, even in this model, if the instruction in English and the instruction in Spanish are related, then students will always get a preview and review in their first language of the content they are studying in the second language. Especially since the English instruction time is so limited in a 90/10 model at the early grades, it is critical that teachers connect what they do in English with the content theme of the Spanish instruction. In addition, since every lesson in either language is the view lesson for some students, teachers make extra efforts to make the input comprehensible while still promoting high levels of academic concept development.

In summary, then, in dual language programs with integrated, thematic instruction, students preview and review content in their L1 and view content in their L2. Figure 4–3 illustrates how preview/view/review functions when the different content areas are thematically related.

Students know what the topic is ◆ A second benefit of thematic teaching is that students know what the topic is as they begin to study in a new content area, even when this new content is taught in their second language. They do not waste time trying to figure out what the lesson is about. Their focus across content areas remains on the significant questions they are investigating. If the big question is How do insects affect people?, students know that whether they are studying in language arts, social studies, math, or science, the topic will be

Teaching around a theme	Lesson activity or time 1	Lesson activity or time 2	Lesson activity or time 3	Lesson activity or time 4	Lesson activity or time 5
Language	Spanish	English	Spanish	English	Spanish
Spanish speaker	preview or review	view	preview or review	view	preview or review
English speaker	view	preview or review	view	preview or review	view

FIG. 4–3 Preview/View/Review with Thematic Instruction

insects. For example, after native English speakers read and write poetry in English language arts and graph insects living on each continent during math in English, they are not so lost when they are asked to investigate insect migration in Spanish or plot locations on a map.

Students more easily learn the content ◆ Teaching around themes helps students develop academic content. Because the concepts have been previewed and are later reviewed in the first language, students more easily learn those concepts during lessons in the second language. In addition, because the topic is the same across content areas and languages, the vocabulary is drawn from the same semantic field. Students studying insects can expect that the key concepts and vocabulary will connect to insects and that these same terms will come up in different subject areas. Integrated thematic instruction provides students with multiple opportunities to learn academic content.

Students need repeated exposure to academic vocabulary to acquire it. Nagy, Anderson, and Herman (1987) found that native speakers needed to see a word several times in meaningful contexts to acquire the word's meaning and function. During thematic teaching, all students see and hear the key words connected to the topic several times. For example, during the insect unit, students might hear and see words such as *colony, adaptation,* and *migration* repeatedly as they study. Since the same topic is studied in both languages, students are also more likely to recognize cognate words.

Knowledge and skills transfer across languages ◆ Cummins (2000) summarizes research that shows that what students learn in one language is available when they study in a second language. By organizing around themes, teachers facilitate transfer. In addition, by alternating language use and providing preview/view/review, teachers ensure that students can develop key academic knowledge and skills as they study in their first language. Then, when students study the same topic in the second language, they can draw on concepts they developed in their first language and apply them to what they are learning.

Students who study about ant colonies in their first language can extend their knowledge when they study ant communities in their second language since the concepts transfer. Although the vocabulary may be different, both Spanish and English share Latin and Greek roots, so many words are cognates. A Spanish speaker who knows the word *adaptación* can easily recognize the cognate word *adaptation* in English.

Teachers can connect curriculum to students' lives ◆ Themes also offer teachers in dual language classrooms more opportunities to connect curriculum to students' lives. One obvious way is the teacher's use of the students' first language for part of the instruction. In addition, during theme studies, teachers can draw on students' background knowledge and interests. In the insect example, the organizing big question might be How do insects affect people? A teacher can use this question to connect the curriculum to students' lives. David and Yvonne live in the Rio Grande Valley of Texas, where many people work in agriculture. In November, the entire valley is filled with butterflies. In a study of insects, some of Yvonne's student teachers working in a dual language program were easily able to connect to students' lives because students could walk outside and collect butterflies. As they studied butterflies, the students investigated whether the caterpillars from which the butterflies came were harmful to the crops that many of their parents worked hard to help plant and harvest. Later in this book we describe a unit on community. A theme on a topic such as community also has obvious links to students' lives. Students can begin by studying their families and then move to investigate their school and the local community. From there, they can examine communities in the nation and the world.

Students in small groups learn better in their second language ◆ When teachers teach around themes, students who are learning in their nonnative language can more easily understand what their teacher and their classmates are saying in the second language when the content has already been previewed in their first language. For example, if the English language arts teacher asks students to work in bilingual pairs to write a poem in English about insects, the Spanish speakers in each pair understand the topic and have ideas to contribute because they have already studied insects and written poetry in Spanish about them.

Students are more fully engaged ◆ When curriculum connects to students' lives and makes sense to them, they become more fully engaged in lessons. Often, students who are being instructed in a second language appear to have a short attention span. They don't seem to stay focused on the lesson activities. However, as anyone who has studied a second language knows, it takes a great deal of mental energy to try to understand what is being said in a language in which one has only limited proficiency. The natural tendency is to take a break and think about other things. Students studying in a second language don't have short attention spans; they are just doing what anyone does when a book or lecture is hard to follow. They work at it for a while, and then they take a mental break.

The key for teachers is to keep students engaged and to keep providing comprehensible input to all the students in a class, even when half of them are learning academic content in a second language. It is only when the input is comprehensible and the students are engaged that acquisition takes place. When curriculum has been previewed in the students' first language and is connected to students' lives, it is more comprehensible and more interesting. Students are motivated to pay attention and want to learn.

Thematic teaching allows for differentiated instruction ◆ For dual language, teaching around themes offers another advantage over more traditional approaches. In a traditional classroom, teachers expect all students to learn the same information and respond in the same way. When teachers teach around themes, there is more opportunity to differentiate instruction by organizing assignments and activities so that students, regardless of their proficiency, can participate. Spanish speakers asked to write and illustrate a poem in English language arts working with English-speaking partners might give their partners ideas and contribute by drawing. It would probably be the native English speaker who would be able to provide the exact words and/or edit the writing of the Spanish speaker. In this way, the nonnative speaker participates fully and learns but is not forced to work and produce alone. The teacher holds different expectations for students learning in their second language, at least in the beginning stages.

Connect themes to content and language standards

In choosing themes and planning curriculum, teachers should align the themes with state-mandated content standards. Sometimes, standards are regarded as a set of musts that someone else has imposed. Commonly heard musts include "Your curriculum must be aligned to the standards," "The tests are aligned to the standards, so we must teach to the standards," and "The lesson plans must explicitly state which grade-level standards you are teaching." We hear these musts in schools from administrators who fear their students will fail standardized tests and their schools will be sanctioned. We hear these musts from well-meaning colleagues in colleges of education who believe teacher educators aren't preparing future teachers for the real world of school. We hear the musts from politicians and the general public who are convinced that educators aren't doing their jobs and need specific guidance.

Rather than regarding standards as a set of musts that someone else has imposed, teachers can take the standards and use them as a guide that provides a starting point from which to creatively meet students' needs. Akhavan (2004) describes her school's journey from being sanctioned by the state as underperforming to being regarded as providing excellent education for all students. It is a school where teachers and students, including many English language learners, succeed by working together. Administrators and teachers use standards not as "a long list of bits of abstract information students are expected to know and understand during specific grade level years" but instead as a way to connect to student needs and help students construct knowledge. She explains:

> Standards based instruction, when implemented effectively, can empower teachers to focus on children and their educational needs without zapping the essence of teaching, the excitement of learning, or taking away the energy teachers need to create effective classrooms. (12)

Akhavan urges teachers to focus on the learner, not on the subject or content, and explains how performance descriptors in standards suggest to teachers that they need to make their students active participants in their learning with words like *analyze, compare, create, problem solve,* and *understand.* Teachers in Akhavan's school organize thematic units around content and performance standards in ways that connect to students' lives and empower them.

In dual language classes, all students are acquiring a second language, so teachers must consider language standards as well as content standards when they plan thematic curriculum. Recently, a consortium of nine states has developed the *English Language Proficiency Standards for English Language Learners in Kindergarten Through Grade 12* (Gottlieb 2004). These standards serve as a bridge between state language-proficiency standards and state academic-content standards. There are five standards. The first is "English language learners communicate in English for social and instructional purposes within the school setting." The remaining four standards apply to each of the content areas: "English language learners communicate information, ideas, and concepts necessary for academic success in the content area of language arts, mathematics, science, and social studies." In a dual language setting, these same standards could apply to students learning Spanish as a second language. The standards document provides model performance indicators for each standard in the areas of listening, speaking, reading, and writing for students at five language-proficiency levels clustered at different grade levels. For example, for reading with beginning level K–2 students in science, the performance indicator reads: "classify living organisms by using pictures or icons." The standards document is extremely useful and serves as a model that more states will follow. We discuss language standards in more detail in Chapter 6.

Curriculum Essentials Related to Lesson Delivery

The next four essentials all deal with lesson delivery. It is not enough to organize curriculum around themes. It is also important that teachers create a risk-free environment in their classrooms, one that encourages learning. One way to help make the environment comfortable for students in a dual language setting is to establish a daily routine that students can count on. Organizing students in different groupings so that they can support each other is another way to make the classroom risk-free.

Another important curriculum essential has to do with the language of instruction. Teachers must use the designated language of instruction without falling into the trap of translating. This is why it is so important to employ strategies to make the input comprehensible. Rather than translating, effective teachers use a variety of techniques to scaffold instruction because second language learners are always present in the classroom.

- Establish a classroom environment and daily routines that are conducive to language and content area development.

- Group students to promote optimum academic and linguistic development.

- Maintain the language of instruction without translation.

- Scaffold instruction to make the input comprehensible for all students at all times.

Establish a positive environment and predictable routines

It is interesting to think back to foreign language classes taken in high school or college. If the memories are negative, the chances are that the instructor did not make students feel as if they could take risks with the language. Yvonne remembers a French professor who would cringe every time she answered a question he posed. He made it clear that her background in Spanish was *terrible* for her French pronunciation. Needless to say, Yvonne is still self-conscious when she tries to speak French.

Perhaps a few readers might remember having fun in their foreign language classes. Most positive memories of a foreign language class go beyond studying grammar and vocabulary and repeating dialogues. Students enjoy language classes when they understand what is going on and when they feel successful in using the language. Usually, positive experiences include working on projects with peers, singing songs, doing skits, or discussing topics of interest.

When students understand and are successful, the environment in a dual language classroom is positive and productive. One way to help students understand and be willing to take risks is to create a daily and weekly routine. Students who know the routine are more likely to make sense of the instruction. In dual language classrooms in Nebraska, south Texas, and California, not only do teachers have a routine but it is posted, in both Spanish and English, in the classroom or on the classroom door. Though the formats may differ, the routines are visually displayed for students.

The kindergarten and third-grade schedules pictured in Figures 4–4a and 4–4b were taken in well-established dual language schools in south Texas. Many teachers post their schedules on the classroom door or in the classroom itself. The schedule tells students what to expect at what time. Of course, the schedule also provides important environmental print that children soon learn to read.

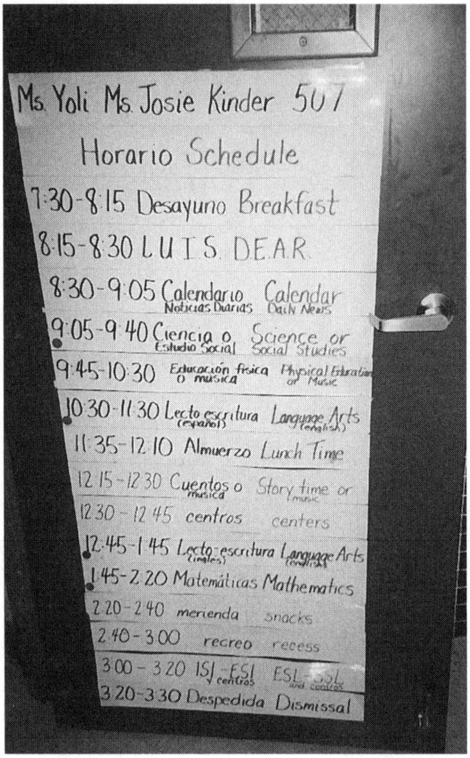

FIG. 4–4a Kindergarten Schedule

We recommend that there be a careful consideration of what to include in daily routines. The language of instruction and the order for the activities included in the routine will depend on the program model and grade level. Several activities that we think are essential for an effective dual language program are:

◆ daily news
◆ read-alouds
◆ writers workshop
◆ guided reading
◆ math concept development
◆ centers
◆ daily learning reflection

FIG. 4–4b Third-Grade Schedule

Daily news ◆ Daily News, sometimes called the morning message, is a gathering time in which students share and develop reading and writing skills. Daily News can also include math activities and announcements. For example, in many dual language schools in south Texas, teachers do the calendar, incorporating math concepts and special day celebrations, have students share, and involve students in a language experience morning message. A useful resource that shows how to use the morning message to teach different skills to beginning writers is the book *Getting the Most Out of Morning Message and Other Shared Writing,* by daCruz-Payne and Browning-Schulman (1998).

At Pharr Elementary School, a two-way school in Pharr, Texas, prekindergarten, kindergarten, and first-grade teachers use some unique techniques to assess student progress and support young writers as they develop reading and writing proficiency in two languages. The teacher has students gather at the rug and opens with the calendar activities, which might require students to count forward or backward by fives and tens. Students also do some addition and subtraction. Then the teacher moves to the large writing chart and with the students constructs a written greeting that includes a salutation, the day, and the date. Next a designated student shares some personal or class news, and the teacher writes the information on the chart. The teacher has the students help decide how to write the information. In this process, they work on different skills, including spelling of key words, capitalization, punctuation, and spacing. Usually, the teacher shares the pen and has students write a word, a short phrase, or even a sentence.

Because Pharr Elementary is a 50/50 program that alternates the language of the day, Daily News is done one day in Spanish and the next in English. During this time, teachers carefully monitor which students are contributing in each language. They also encourage all students to eventually contribute in both languages. The teacher writes the basic message with blue pen on English day and in red on Spanish day. The basic message includes the salutation, the date, and information about the weather. Then students volunteer news, which the teacher writes down. As she writes, she puts capital letters, punctuation marks, and tricky spellings in black pen. The teacher asks the children to identify key words that she has written. If a dominant Spanish-speaking child identifies a word, the child circles the word in red, and if a dominant English-speaking child reads a word, that child circles in blue. Sometimes students write parts of the news on the chart themselves. Spanish speakers write in red and English speakers write in blue.

A couple of examples help to clarify the process. Felipe, a Spanish-dominant child, contributes to the Daily News being done in English. He tells the teacher to start the word *Thursday* with *Th* and that the *T* must be a capital letter. The teacher writes the letters in black. When Andrea, an English-dominant girl, shares the pen on a day in which Daily News is done in Spanish and writes *Hoy* (Today) to begin the news, she uses a blue marker. Using the red and blue markers gives teachers a record of how many Spanish- and English-dominant children are contributing in each language during Daily News. This helps teachers see if they are calling only on Spanish speakers on Spanish day and English speakers on English day or if they are including speakers of both languages each day. Figure 4–5 shows Daily News charts from Pharr in both English and Spanish. Although teachers at Pharr Elementary use this format, teachers across the country also take advantage of a morning message but use different techniques.

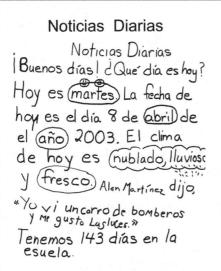

Noticias Diarias

Noticias Diarias
¡Buenos días! ¿Qué día es hoy?
Hoy es (martes) La fecha de
hoy es el día 8 de (abril) de
el (año) 2003. El clima
de hoy es (nublado, lluvioso
y (fresco.) Alan Martínez dijo,
"Yo vi un carro de bomberos
y me gusto Las luces."
Tenemos 143 días en la
esuela.

Daily News

Daily News
Good morning! What day (is)
it today? Today (is) (Monday.)
The date (is) (April 7,) 2003.
The (weather) (is) (cloudy)
and (foggy.) Arlen said,
"My dad bought me a
(little) Kitchen.
We have been in school
142 days.

The teacher writes capitals and punctuation in black and the basic text in red. The words *martes* and *abril* are identified by Spanish-dominant speakers and circled by them in red. The words *año* and *fresco* are identified by English-dominant speakers and circled in blue. A Spanish-dominant student writes his personal news in red.

Translation

Good morning! What day is today? Today is Tuesday. The date today is April 8, 2003. The weather today is cloudy, rainy, and cool. Alan Martínez said, I saw a firemen's car and I liked the lights. We have been in school 143 days.

The teacher writes capitals and punctuation in black and the basic text in blue. The words *is*, *Monday*, and *little* are identified by Spanish-dominant speakers and circled by them in red. The words *April*, *weather*, and *foggy* are identified by English-dominant speakers and circled in blue. A Spanish-dominant student gives personal news and writes her name in red. Dominant-English speakers write what she said in blue.

FIG. 4–5 Daily News

Read-alouds ◆ Read-alouds can be done anytime during the day but should be included at least once. It is better if teachers read to students several times throughout the day. The students may be gathered on the rug or be in their regular seats as long as all students can see and they all feel they are part of the reading experience. Weaver (2002) points out,

> By reading aloud, teachers demonstrate how to read with expression and how to portray characters' voices. They can read texts that are beyond the students' ability to read independently, thus introducing more complex situations, sentence structure, concepts, and vocabulary. (232)

The teacher introduces a book and reads it to the class. It is important to involve students so that they interact with the book. The teacher might ask children to predict what will happen or to respond to an event in the book. During the read-aloud, the teacher can model effective reading strategies. For example, the teacher might connect an event in the book to a personal experience and then invite students to do the same. A read-aloud should build upon students' prior knowledge and develop new concepts that students will use in other activities later on at the centers, during whole-class instruction, or during group projects. In this way, the book may be used as a preview to content vocabulary or key concepts of the theme to be studied.

Writers workshop ◆ The Language Experience Approach (LEA) is especially appropriate for use with second language learners. During LEA, the teacher guides students in the process of writing and helps them develop the skills needed to meet the writing standards for that specific grade level. LEA is similar to Daily News but is more extended. The students select a topic, usually one related to the theme of study. Students dictate the texts, and the teacher scribes on chart paper that all students can see. As students dictate, the teacher models a variety of writing skills, such as capitalization, paragraphing, and punctuation as well as sentence structure and story organization. All the students can contribute. The story may take several days to develop. Once a story is completed in one language, the class does writers workshop with a different story or content in the other language of instruction.

Of course, it is important that students have many opportunities to write on their own, too. Traditional writers workshop should also be incorporated into daily routines. When implemented well, writers workshop is a powerful tool for developing both reading and writing for second language learners (Akhavan 2004). There are different ways to set up writers workshop, and we encourage readers to look at the many resources available on this topic, including the classic work of Graves (1994, 1983).

Guided reading ◆ During guided reading, a teacher works with a small group of students on particular reading skills that these students need. The groups are flexible and change frequently. The students and the teacher work together through a complete story, preferably one related to the theme. For example, the teacher might begin by reading the story aloud as individual students follow along, tracking the words. Then the teacher might ask students to identify specific words. Often, teachers do word work, asking students to use plastic letters to form words from the story. Students might also write words. Then, students might take turns reading pages of the story aloud.

In dual language classes, guided reading is part of language arts instruction. If students are receiving literacy instruction in two languages, then they should do guided reading in each language. Guided reading affords teachers the opportunity to work with small groups of students on specific skills. Teachers can also informally assess students during this time and use that information to plan future lessons. Guided reading can be very effective. However, it is important that the reading groups not become permanent ability groups but rather that students be grouped and regrouped based on their need to work on specific skills. In addition, guided reading should not occupy too much instructional time during language arts because then the program becomes unbalanced. There needs to be time for read-alouds, shared reading, independent reading, and writing as well.

Often during guided reading, teachers use small books that have been leveled or organized to contain certain structures. These books can be useful if they contain attractive illustrations and interesting stories. In addition, though, it is important that these books be connected to the theme the students are studying if at all possible. In this way, students extend their knowledge of content as they work on reading strategies.

Math concept development ◆ During math time, it is logical that instruction and activities correspond with the content for the grade level. Whenever possible, this instruction should be connected to the theme. In other words, teachers should avoid the cha, cha, cha or gummy bear types of teaching with math. Although some teachers find it difficult to connect math content with language arts, science, and social studies, it is possible. When teachers really look carefully at the standards for math, there are a multitude of ways to integrate the required math concepts with a theme. During math time, teachers introduce the math concepts and skills that the students will apply as they study the theme.

Students can make graphs or charts, measure and record to compare and contrast, figure percents, and work with parts or fractions, using information related to the theme. Sometimes teachers have students use information from their thematic study to write story problems for their classmates to solve. For example, during a rain forest study, students learned how many plants, animals, and insects are affected by the cutting down one tree in the Amazon. Students took that data, wrote word problems, and asked peers to figure the effects of cutting down many trees.

Centers and projects ◆ Many teachers organize their classrooms with centers. These are areas where students can carry out specific activities working in small groups. In dual language classes, the language for the center will depend on the program model. For example, in a 50/50 alternate-day program, the center activity will be in Spanish one day and in English the next. This takes extra preparation, but it is important that the centers reflect the designated language of instruction.

In addition, the center activity should be based on the theme and serve to support the concepts that children are studying. Often teachers develop centers for different subject areas such as art, math, language arts, and science. During language arts, students might read a book and write in a journal. At a math center, students might solve a problem and graph the results. Centers are an excellent place to organize hands-on science and math activities.

During center time, some students may meet in small groups to complete projects related to the theme. These projects are often an extension of content studied in social studies or science. Individual students may also complete projects during the time allotted for centers. If students rotate through different centers, one or more of the centers may simply be areas where students can work together or alone on their projects. However, it is important that the projects and center activities all relate to the general theme of study.

Daily learning reflection ◆ Ideally, teachers should take time at the end of the day to reflect with students on what they have learned. This can be good for oral language development and/or for further language experience activities. Students can brainstorm as teachers write key concepts down and plan for the following day. This is an excellent time to assess what students have learned, to clarify concepts, and to help students connect new concepts with prior knowledge. However, the authors admit that this activity, though very important, is perhaps a luxury that most teachers do not find time for. Nevertheless, if reflection time becomes part of the daily routine, teachers and students benefit.

Routines are important for student learning, especially in dual language settings. Because they know the daily routine, students do not waste valuable time guessing what is going on. While routines differ in dual language schools, teachers who use routines provide students with better access to the curriculum.

Predictable physical environment—Mirroring the room ◆ Besides organizing around themes and using routines to help students understand what is happening during the day, teachers can also arrange their rooms in a way that allows for predictability. Two teachers in a two-way program in Omaha, Nebraska, produced an especially risk-free environment in their classrooms by creating a predictable physical environment in each room. These two first-grade teachers share the same students. One teaches the Spanish curriculum and the other the English. They plan their thematic units together carefully so the curriculum flows with the continual preview/view/review that we discussed earlier.

When students move from one classroom to the other, they can predict what will be in each part of the room they enter. The teachers have mirrored each other's classrooms. The bulletin board that has student artwork and other student projects in Spanish is located in the same place as the similar bulletin board in the English classroom. The calendar and rug for reading and language experience activities are in the same places in each room, and pocket charts, math graphs, and seasonal displays are located in the same area in each room. These teachers plan their lessons around one integrated theme, they use similar routines, and they have even set up their rooms in identical fashion. As a result, they create the optimal environment to promote learning for all their students.

Group students to promote optimum academic and linguistic development

Once teachers organize curriculum around themes and establish a predictable routine, they can turn their attention to how they group students for instruction. For some time, research has shown that second language learners are most apt to be engaged and learn when they work together cooperatively (Kagan 1986; Long and Porter 1985; McGroarty 1993; Holt 1993; Darling-Hammond, Ancess, and Falk 1995; Wells and Chang-Wells 1992). Because the idea of cooperative learning is to engage all students by giving each student responsibilities and drawing on his or her strengths, dual language classes are a natural setting for having students work together. There are always some students who have a greater command of the language of instruction than others. If teachers pair or group students so that each pair or group has some students with greater proficiency in one language and some with greater proficiency in the other, students can better help one another as they learn.

In two-way programs in which about half the students are native English speakers and half are native Spanish speakers, this type of grouping is easier to do. In these settings, teachers can pair native speakers of English with native speakers of Spanish. No matter which language is being used for instruction, students can always rely on their partners to help them comprehend the lesson. Of course, teachers also take into account other factors, such as personality variables, special skills, and academic background, in deciding how to organize students for an activity.

Deciding how to organize pairs or groups can be more complex in other settings. For example, in the Southwest the population of many schools is often almost 100 percent Latino. Sometimes the ELL population is as high as 90 percent, as in the example of Runn School, described in Chapter 3. Still, even in these schools, children come with various levels of proficiency in both English and Spanish. Some students speak mainly Spanish with very little English. Others understand but do not speak, read, or write English. Some are quite bilingual orally but lack literacy in both languages. Still others are much stronger in English than Spanish, though they may understand some Spanish and may be able to carry on basic communication in Spanish. Even in settings like these, teachers can use language strengths to group students so that they can help each other.

In south Texas, teachers write students' names on cards and put them up on a wall chart. They write names of students who are stronger in English in blue and those stronger in Spanish in red, arranging students in bilingual pairs, and changing the pairs weekly. Sometimes there are not enough strong students in one language, so some pairs have two names in the same color. In Figure 4–6, Jacob and John's names are both in blue. John is English-dominant but stronger in Spanish than Jacob. Brooke's name is in red. She is Spanish-dominant but stronger in English than Aaron.

A caveat about grouping students into bilingual pairs ◆ While grouping students into bilingual pairs provides good support for instruction, it is also important to consider the benefits of having students sometimes work in same-language pairs or groups. If at all times students are grouped with speakers of another language, they might never have the advantage of being challenged by their native language peers to develop more advanced vocabulary and syntax in their first language. In addition, when teachers have students in their classrooms who are not native speakers of the language of instruction, they are likely to simplify language rather than push all students to use advanced academic language.

De Jong (2002) describes how a two-way program in Florida decided to separate language arts instruction in fourth grade because Spanish-speaking students and some native English-speaking students were not at grade level in

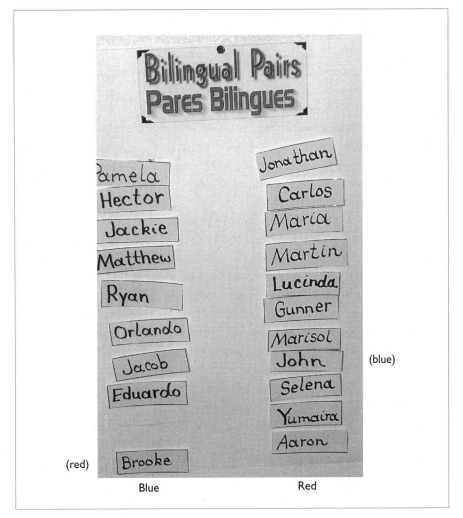

FIG. 4–6 Bilingual Pair Charts

Spanish, especially in oral language. Therefore, each group had English language arts and Spanish language arts separately for a period of time. "The native Spanish speakers were appropriately challenged with literacy activities and rich class discussion in Spanish. At the same time, the grouping by language reduced the range of Spanish language skills, and this allowed Spanish instruction for the native English speakers to be targeted to their proficiency level" (14). The results were positive for both groups. This study has implications for pairing or grouping students. It suggests that teachers should sometimes group students in same language groups to fully develop their language proficiency.

Nancy Commins (2004) has developed a model showing the dimensions of academic development and the effect of different grouping patterns for development. She argues that academic development includes oral communication, interactions with text, and conceptual development. In a two-way bilingual class, students can be grouped heterogeneously or homogeneously. For homogeneous groups, lessons can be given in the students' first language or their second language. In planning instruction, teachers should consider the opportunities and constraints each grouping combination offers. Figure 4–7 shows these opportunities and constraints.

When students work in heterogeneous pairs or groups, they have opportunities to help one another, since one student is always a native speaker of the language of instruction. In this situation, both students may develop greater conceptual understanding. Native speakers learn more as they explain ideas to their partner or group. Nonnative speakers understand lessons better because they receive help from peers. These interactions also lead to higher levels of proficiency in their second language. However, heterogeneous grouping also constrains teachers. While it is important not to water down the curriculum, it is also important not to instruct at a level that is beyond the abilities of the nonnative speakers. Thus, a teacher may limit vocabulary and syntax to ensure that the lesson is comprehensible, and, in the process, fail to provide the academic language that the native speakers need to fully develop their academic competence.

When students work together in homogeneous groups and the language of instruction is their native language, the teacher can use high levels of academic language. In addition, student anxiety levels may be reduced because they are being instructed in their native language. However, schools may find difficulty locating resources in the minority language, especially in the upper grades. Schools may also have difficulty finding teachers with high levels of proficiency in the minority language.

If the language of instruction is the students' second language, the teacher can modify the instruction to ensure that the language is comprehensible. Students may be less anxious because they are not competing with native speakers. As a result, they may take more risks in using their second language. The constraints for teachers in this situation are they must make the input comprehensible while still teaching high levels of academic content. At the same time, teachers must find ways to keep the second language learners engaged in lessons

Heterogeneous Groups	
Opportunities	**Constraints**
Native speakers learn as they teach their nonnative-speaking peers	Teacher must find ways to make input comprehensible for all students
Nonnative speakers learn from the native speakers	Teacher must try not to water down instruction
Nonnative speakers increase their second language proficiency because of interactions with native-speaking peers	
Students develop positive cross-cultural and/or cross-linguistic relationships	
Homogeneous Groups Working in Their First Language	
Opportunities	**Constraints**
Students can develop high levels of proficiency in their L1	Finding resources in the minority language, especially at upper grades
Students' anxiety levels are reduced	Finding teachers with high levels of academic proficiency in the minority language
	Students lose benefits of cross-cultural and cross-linguistic interactions
Homogeneous Groups Working in Their Second Language	
Opportunities	**Constraints**
Teachers can modify instruction to make the input comprehensible	Teachers must make input comprehensible and still teach high levels of academic content
Students are not competing with native speakers	Teachers must keep students engaged in activities
Students can take more risks	Students lose benefits of cross-cultural and cross-linguistic interactions

FIG. 4–7 Grouping Students

that may be difficult for them. A final constraint in homogenous grouping is that students lose the benefits of cross-cultural and cross-linguistic interactions.

In dual language classes, teachers face the challenge of helping students develop both linguistic and academic proficiency in two languages. It is important for teachers to consider carefully how they will group students for instruction to optimize both their language development and their conceptual development. While some time spent in homogeneous groups can be beneficial, in successful dual language programs students work in heterogenous groups for most of the day.

Issues of grouping students are complex. Students learn academic content better when working in bilingual pairs. The native-speaking partner can help make the input comprehensible. In addition, each member of the pair can participate in an activity and then respond in a form that is appropriate to his language proficiency level. For example, the native Spanish speaker might write a report in Spanish, and the native English speaker could provide the graphics to accompany the report. At the same time, for students to fully develop their language proficiency, they benefit from working in same-language pairs and groups. When students work in their native language, they can be challenged to use higher levels of academic language. When they work in their second language, teachers can adjust lessons to better meet their proficiency level. They key is for teachers to develop flexible grouping suited to student needs.

Maintain the language of instruction without translation

For some time, bilingual education studies have shown that concurrent translation is very ineffective for teaching students in a second language (Krashen 1996, 1992). Yet, the most natural thing for bilingual teachers to do when they see students are not understanding is to translate. Teachers want to help their students, and they don't like them to struggle. However, concurrent translation is very ineffective because students listen only to the language they understand and tune out the second language. Therefore, they do not acquire the second language.

Along many highways, the government has posted signs with both miles and kilometers. It is not clear whether the intent is to accommodate the background experiences of different drivers or if the hope is to have Americans learn the metric system. The signs certainly don't seem to be accomplishing that second objective. David and Yvonne seldom attend to the numbers representing kilometers. They just look at the miles because they have lived most of their lives in settings in which miles were the standard measure. Sandra, on the other hand, looks only at the numbers representing kilometers. She was brought up in Argentina, a country that uses the metric system. She disregards the numbers posted for miles. None of us is learning the other system. We are ignoring it, and that is what happens in classrooms when teachers provide the same information twice. Students focus on what is easiest to understand and ignore the rest.

David remembers a classroom example that helped him see how ineffectual it is to use concurrent translation. He was observing a student teacher who was teaching a social studies class with many English language learners. A bilingual aide sat in the back of the classroom. As the student teacher taught in English, using strategies to make himself understood, the aide, following her usual practice, translated everything the teacher was saying. Before long, the students in the class were not even looking at, let alone listening to, the student teacher. Instead, most of the students had actually turned their seats around to listen to the aide. They missed the opportunity to learn the academic English that the student teacher was working so hard to make comprehensible.

Our observations of dual language classrooms show us that something similar happens when teachers use too much translation. When a teacher who is supposed to teach in Spanish translates often to help the native English speakers in the classroom, soon those students depend upon that translation. They request translation when they are not given it and are unwilling to try to acquire Spanish on their own or even when working with their peers. This makes the situation worse, and soon the teacher complains that she must translate or students won't do the work. On the other hand, when teachers stay in the designated language for instruction, students develop effective strategies for making sense of their second language. They use all possible resources, including their peers and the previews provided through lessons taught in their primary language. These students develop the academic language they need to become bilingual and biliterate.

Scaffold instruction to make the input comprehensible

Teachers in dual language classrooms can help their students learn language and content by scaffolding instruction. Vygotsky (1962) explained that learning takes place in social interaction when an adult or more capable peer asks questions, points out aspects of a problem, or makes suggestions, working in a learner's Zone of Proximal Development (ZPD). He defines the ZPD as the difference between what a person can do independently and what the person can do with help. Bruner (1985) referred to this kind of help as a *scaffold*. A scaffold is an appropriate metaphor for the kind of assistance that supports learning. A scaffold supports a building during its construction and then is taken down once the building is completed.

Teachers in dual language classrooms often provide the support students need to understand and use their second language or to learn content in their second language. In addition to organizing bilingual pairs and collaborative activities, teachers use a number of other techniques to scaffold instruction. The teacher might ask a student who is writing a story in her second language some questions about what she has written to encourage a different choice of words or more details. The teacher's questions provide the scaffold that allows the writer to move beyond what she produced by working alone. Peers also provide scaffolds. For example, when students work in bilingual pairs, a native Spanish-speaking student can help his partner understand a lesson presented in Spanish. The native English speaker might help her partner at a center activity in English. The two students provide scaffolds for one another depending on the language of instruction.

Scaffolds are especially important for second language students. Gibbons (2002) points out that teachers should set high expectations for all students and engage them in challenging activities. At the same time, the teacher must organize instruction to provide the scaffolding needed for students to complete tasks successfully. She comments:

> Instead of simplifying the task (and ultimately risking a reductionist curriculum), we should instead reflect on the nature of the scaffolding that is being provided for learners to carry out that task. As far as possible, learners need to be engaged with authentic and cognitively challenging learning tasks; it is the nature of the support—support that is responsive to the particular demands made on children learning through the medium of a second language—that is critical for success. (10–11)

Gibbons discusses ways teachers can structure lessons to provide scaffolds for second language students as they read, write, talk, and listen in a new language.

For beginning readers, for example, scaffolding occurs when the teacher reads predictable stories and pauses to let the children fill in words using the language pattern. Graphic organizers provide visual scaffolds that give all learners, and especially second language students, support in understanding what they are learning. Dual language teachers often use Venn diagrams, webs, mapping, compare and contrast charts, sequencing charts, and other types of organizational charts to help their students access what they are studying and to help them connect concepts and vocabulary.

Hoyt's book *Make It Real: Strategies for Success with Informational Texts* (2002) provides many practical ideas teachers can use to help students comprehend content area books. Hoyt includes a large number of graphic organizers to use with different kinds of texts. This book is a good resource for any teacher working in a dual language setting because about half the students are learning in a second language at any time, and all the students benefit from the scaffolds that graphic organizers provide.

Soltero (2004) provides a helpful overview of graphic organizers for dual language teachers and suggests websites that provide valuable resources. Typing the words *graphic organizers* into an online search engine reveals many useful websites, including:

www.graphic.org/

www.writedesignonline.com/organizers

www.teachervision.fen.com/lesson-plans/lesson-6293.html?s2

www.educplace.com/graphicorganizer/ (a website that provides graphic organizers in Spanish)

Organizing curriculum around themes, following daily routines, having students work in bilingual pairs, and using graphic organizers are all ways that teachers can scaffold instruction in dual language classrooms. Rather than simplifying the curriculum to match the linguistic proficiency of students learning in their second language, teachers provide the scaffolds students need to engage in challenging academic instruction. Based on their observations of many dual language classrooms, Collier and Thomas (2004) support these curriculum essentials we propose when they write:

> In contrast to remedial programs that offer "watered-down" instruction in a "special" curriculum focused on one small step at a time, dual language enrichment models are the curricular mainstream taught through two languages. Teachers in these bilingual classes create the cognitive challenge through thematic units of the core academic curriculum, focused on real-world problem solving that stimulate students to make more than one year's progress every year, in both languages. With no translation and no repeated lessons in the other language, separation of the two languages is a key component of this model. Peer teaching and teachers using cooperative learning strategies to capitalize on this effect serve as an important stimulus for the cognitive challenge. (2)

Curriculum Essentials for Assessment

Assessment is absolutely critical in all classrooms. Teachers must be able to assess their students' progress in order to plan appropriate instruction. In the final chapter of this book we will discuss backward planning. Backward planning is based on the premise that teachers need to know where their students are before they plan for them. Planning must be informed first and foremost by analyzing students' strengths and needs.

In addition, planning should be guided by state and district standards. As teachers plan themes, they should review grade-level standards to be sure that the content of each standard is included in the theme. At some point, students will be assessed on these standards. However, it is important to distinguish between tests of standards and standardized tests. All schools give standardized, norm-referenced tests, such as the Iowa Test of Basic Skills. Such tests give teachers, administrators, and parents a measure of how their students are doing as compared with the group of students on whom the test was normed. Students' scores are based on how well they answer the questions in comparison with the norming group. Half the students who take a norm-referenced test must score below the norm and half must score above it.

In contrast, tests of standards are criterion-referenced. A student's score is based on the number of right answers, not on how well the student did compared with other students. All the students in a class could score 100 percent on a criterion-referenced test if they really understood the material. Teachers can only prepare students to score well on either kind of test by teaching the knowledge and skills the test measures. Unfortunately, testing pressure has led many teachers to try to shortcut the process and teach directly to the test. It is helpful to ensure that students understand the test format. But unless they know the test content, taking practice tests doesn't really help much.

Yvonne likes to use her preservice teachers as an example. When she first arrived in Texas, the upper administration of the university was putting pressure on the Department of Curriculum and Instruction. The administrators were very concerned that the test scores of the students on the state teachers exam were not high enough. Yvonne refused to panic or teach to the test. Instead, she read over the state teacher competencies and saw that most of what students were required to know fit well with her student-centered approach to literacy and biliteracy. She taught her course the first semester, involving the students in action research as they interviewed young children in English and Spanish about environmental print and their reading strategies. The future teachers also gathered writing samples and analyzed writing development in both Spanish and English. They read, wrote about, and discussed what they were learning. After students took the state exam at the end of the semester, several immediately e-mailed Yvonne and told her that they, and others too, believed that what they had learned in her class had really helped them on the exam. The activities they had done and discussed in class connected to the standards, and, because they had actually internalized the concepts, the questions were not too difficult to answer.

Teachers should use state or federal standards to determine what to teach. Curriculum should be informed by standards. Teachers can then assess the progress students are making toward those standards. Teachers should check regularly, using both formal and informal measures, to monitor student progress. They can then use the results of the assessment to guide teaching decisions. There are two curriculum essentials that relate to assessment:

Curriculum Essentials for Assessment

- Monitor students' academic and linguistic progress regularly.

- Adjust teaching in response to students' academic, linguistic, and social needs.

Earlier we discussed how the administrative team at Runn Elementary School had been concerned about ten third-grade students who had failed the standardized test in English. They were especially concerned because the records of some of those students showed that they had been designated as English-dominant since kindergarten. The principal took immediate action and asked ten teachers to each take one of the students for special tutoring. Ms. Sutti, the resource specialist, became involved when one of the teachers doing the tutoring brought her a writing sample from her student, Roberto. He had written:

Dere Mrs Garya
How or you donc.
I hop you ore din vana
My fert then to do is play
Footbool my fret tegn to eat
Is pizz. My fert tegn in school
Is math a raiten. I hop you
Rermdr me from kend. I was
Yer stnte. (Sutti 2003, 7)

Translation:
> Dear Mrs. Garay
> How are you doing?
> I hope you are doing fine
> My favorite thing to do is play
> Football my favorite thing to eat
> Is pizza. My favorite thing in school
> Is math and writing. I hope you
> Remember me from kinder. I was
> Your student.

Ms. Sutti went to Roberto's file and found he had entered prekindergarten as Spanish-dominant and had progressed well in both English and Spanish. He had gone from a Level 1 in oral language development in English to a Level 3. In Spanish he had begun as a Level 2 and gone to Level 5. However, despite the test results that showed he was more proficient orally in Spanish, his prekindergarten teacher, who no longer worked at the school, had placed him in a kindergarten class for English-dominant students. At that time at Runn students were given formal literacy instruction in kindergarten in their dominant language and literacy in the second language was added beginning in first grade. As a result, Roberto received literacy instruction only in English in kindergarten.

After reviewing his file, it was clear to Ms. Sutti that in first and second grade, Roberto's Spanish was much stronger than his English. He was beginning to show serious signs of academic struggle in both languages. He was considered for retention in first grade but passed a summer school program, so he was promoted to second grade. Reading test scores showed that Roberto really struggled in English despite the fact that he was considered English-dominant.

Having looked closely at Roberto's scores, Ms. Sutti and principal Ms. Gaona decided to take a closer look at all ten of the students who had failed. Their files suggested that these students had also been transitioned into English too quickly. A meeting was held with the principal, the kindergarten and first-grade teachers, and Ms. Sutti. Because everyone at the school was so concerned, the administrators called Yvonne and the regional bilingual director into the meeting. Ms. Sutti realized that although the student files were filled with various test results, all these results just obscured the big picture of the students' progress. She developed a one-page form that summarized all the information about each student and brought this form to the meeting. During the meeting the participants discussed how Roberto's early designation as English-dominant had affected his literacy development. Even in third grade he was still much more comfortable in Spanish than in English. At the end of the meeting, everyone decided that the key problem to be addressed was language assessment and placement in early grades. For some time the school had had three kindergarten classes, two in English and one in Spanish. Because there were two English classes and only one Spanish class, teachers had automatically been placing any child they thought could handle language arts in English into a kindergarten section for English-dominant students.

Everyone, including Ms. Gaona, was concerned. She reflected on the situation.

> What has happened I feel with the mistake we have made with the ten children that are in the third grade level is that not only I but the teachers on this campus still have a mentality of English is very important and let's shift to English as soon as possible . . . We have to be looking at what we're doing in a very open way because subconsciously we are making decisions that are still using the old philosophy of English is very important. This was an epiphany. (Sutti 2003, 12)

Because Ms. Sutti, Ms. Gaona, Ms. Garay, and the other teachers at Runn Elementary took a close look at Roberto and at the other struggling students, they were able to assess what the school had been doing and make significant changes. They decided that students were being moved into English too quickly, something that might typically happen in an early-exit bilingual program but should not happen at a dual language school. Too many students were being designated as English-dominant, especially for a school with a student population that is 99.7 percent Hispanic, and 90 percent testing as Limited English Proficient. As a result of this careful assessment and collaborative discussion, the administrators and teachers decided that students needed longer language arts blocks in their first language in first grade and that formal language arts instruction in a student's second language would not begin until second grade. In addition, there are now two sections of language arts in Spanish and one in English in kindergarten.

Guskey (2003) would support what administrators and teachers at Runn Elementary School have done. He explains that "assessment cannot be a one-shot, do-or-die experience for students. Instead assessments must be part of an ongoing effort to help students learn" (4). He goes on to explain that assessments must help teachers change instruction so that students "have a second chance to demonstrate their new level of competence and understanding" (4).

Guskey's conclusions fit well with what Ms. Gaona, Ms. Sutti, Ms. Garay, and the other teachers did:

> Assessments can be a vital component in our efforts to improve education. But as long as we use them only as a means to rank school and students, we miss their most powerful benefits . . . When teachers' classroom assessments become an integral part of the instructional process and a central ingredient in their efforts to help students learn, the benefits of assessment for both students and teachers will be boundless. (6)

Educators at Runn Elementary School made sure their students will have boundless benefits in the future. They took the information they had about their students and made critical changes that will help not only the ten students who failed the tests but many students in the years to come.

Assessment, then, can and should make a difference in curriculum decisions both at the school level and for classes and individuals. However, teachers need to know their students and know how to assess their progress in order to make important decisions. Both Ms. Sutti and Ms. Garay knew about spelling development in Spanish and English. They knew that Roberto comprehended little of what he read. They were aware of problems he had at home and how he was beginning to show serious signs of delinquency. These two educators were informed practitioners. They looked at Roberto as a whole, evaluating his academic, linguistic, and social situation because it is impossible to really help students without a full picture.

As the educators at Runn demonstrated, it is critical to be informed about theory and practice and to know the students. In Chicago those involved in dual language were so concerned about knowing how their students were progressing that the Chicago Public Schools gathered university experts and teachers to develop an assessment tool, the Dual Language Development Card, which helps teachers assess their students' listening, speaking, reading, and writing in both languages (Soltero and Moya-Leang 2002). Assessment instruments are especially helpful for those working in a dual language setting.

Teachers of second language learners need a variety of assessment tools at their fingertips so they can gather the information they need to make good decisions about how to teach their students. One very complete handbook that contains rubrics for assessing speaking, listening, reading, and writing skills for second language learners is produced by the Illinois State Board of Education and is available free online (www.isbe.net/assessment/pdfIMAGELangBook.htm). The handbook provides different rubrics teachers can use, a helpful discussion of caveats, forms to create student profiles, and definitions of assessment terms

(Gottlieb 1999). Several other useful resources for guidance in assessing students' oral and written language are also available (Ariza et al. 2002; Soltero 2004; García 1994; O'Malley and Valdez-Pierce 1996; Ekbatani and Pierson 2000). Though these assessments are for English Language Learners, they can be easily adapted to assess students' proficiency in acquiring any language.

Teachers can use a variety of formal and informal measures to monitor students' academic and linguistic progress. In dual language classes, this task is more challenging because assessment takes place in two languages. Dual language teachers need to understand a number of things to interpret assessments. They need to understand bilingual theory, the importance of developing students' first language, how bilingual children acquire a second language, and how biliteracy develops. Then they can use the results of assessments in two languages to adjust their teaching to meet the needs of all their students.

In this chapter, we have discussed a number of curriculum essentials. We began with essentials for overall organization. Next we considered essentials related to lesson delivery. We concluded by examining essentials for assessment.

In the following chapter we discuss the final curriculum essential for dual language: students in dual language programs must be provided with a meaning-centered literacy program. Since no student can succeed without literacy, we have devoted an entire chapter to this topic.

 Learning Extensions

1. We discussed how it is important in dual language to teach language through content. Think back about some of your own language learning experiences. How were you taught that language? Did you have traditional grammar and vocabulary instruction? Or did you learn the language through meaningful content? Be prepared to discuss this with your peers.

2. If you are teaching in a dual language setting, what is the content that you need to teach? Choose one content topic. What is some of the key vocabulary of that content topic that students would acquire when you teach that content?

3. We suggest teaching language through sustained content themes. Choose a grade level. Check the standards required by local schools. What could be a possible theme that would incorporate the standards? List some big questions that would encompass the theme.

4. In your classroom or in a classroom you observe, identify the daily routines. If there are no routines, what might be good to include in a routine? If there is a routine, does it seem effective? Does this chapter include ideas for routines that you think could be added to the routine you know? Which one(s)? Discuss this with a partner.

5. Consider the student population at a dual language school. How are students grouped within the classroom during instruction in each language? Considering what is discussed in this chapter, are there changes that might make the grouping more effective? Explain why you think the present grouping is or is not effective.

6. List at least ten ways you or other teachers can scaffold instruction in dual language classrooms. Bring your list to class to compile a class list.

7. What kinds of formal and informal assessment tools do you or others you know in a dual language program use? How are these assessments used to inform instruction?

Literacy Essentials

Developing a meaning-centered literacy program is the most important of the curriculum essentials. The development of reading proficiency is key to academic achievement in all content areas. State and national departments of education determine their evaluations of schools and programs, in great part, on standardized test scores in reading. In dual language, researchers use standardized reading test scores in English to prove that students, even though learning in two languages, do as well as or better than students studying only in English (Thomas and Collier 2002; Lindholm-Leary 2001). The fact is that reading test scores are often used as a measure of the effectiveness of different program models for English language learners (de Jong 2004). However, little research has been carried out in dual language programs to determine which approach to reading instruction best supports the development of high levels of literacy in two languages. In this chapter we will review key concepts about reading and present literacy essentials for dual language settings.

Teachers and administrators must develop a theory of reading and then match approaches to teaching reading with their beliefs about the reading process. The first two literacy essentials relate to an understanding of reading theory. Any theory of reading should center on making meaning. If meaning construction is not central, students, especially those reading in a second language, are likely to become good *word callers*, that is, they will learn to pronounce the words, but they may not understand what they read. We will begin our discussion of the first two reading essentials by examining some basic questions that must be taken into account when developing a program model:

◆ What theoretical model of reading best supports a meaning-centered literacy program?

◆ What does the research show about effective literacy instruction in dual language schools?

Dual language literacy instruction brings with it some very special considerations. After examining these basic questions, we turn to questions concerning the implementation of a successful literacy program in a dual language school. These questions include

◆ Which is the best language for initial literacy instruction?

◆ How can teachers help students transfer reading strategies to a second language?

◆ Should the same method be used to teach reading in each language, or do differences in the structures of the languages justify using different approaches to instruction?

◆ What is the difference between reading in the first language and reading in a second language?

At the end of this chapter, we will list our suggestions for a good literacy program for dual language, a model of reading instruction designed to help all students achieve high levels of biliteracy.

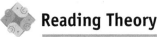 ## Reading Theory

Questions about the best method or methods for teaching reading can be answered only by considering the theory of reading that underlies the methods. For a program to be effective, there should be a good match between the theory of reading that teachers hold and the methods they choose. Further, for a literacy program to be meaning-centered, the theory of reading that informs the methods must center on meaning construction. There are two reading theory essentials.

<table>
<tr><td>Reading Theory Essentials</td></tr>
</table>

- Ensure a good match between the theory of reading and the teaching methods.

- Base methods on a theory that views reading as meaning construction.

Two Views of Reading

Two widely held theoretical models of reading are the word recognition model and the transactional, sociopsycholinguistic model. We have written extensively about the differences between these models elsewhere (Freeman and Freeman 2000, 2004). Briefly, the word recognition model views reading as a process of getting to meaning by recognizing words. Readers can recognize words by using various skills—phonics, sight words, structural analysis, and context clues. Vocabulary is pretaught and students build up a bank of sight words they cannot sound out. Readers use these skills to recode written language to oral language. When students change written marks to oral language, they are changing one code to another. They are recoding (Goodman 1993). In contrast, when readers get meaning from the written marks, they are decoding a message. Often, second language readers simply recode instead of decode. The belief of those who hold a word recognition view is that students can use all these skills—phonics, sight words, and structural analysis—to recognize words and then combine the meanings of individual words to get the meaning of a text.

Those who hold a word recognition view focus on skill development. *Put Reading First* (Armbruster and Osborn 2001), which offers a summary of the federally backed National Reading Panel report, presents reading as a process of recognizing words. This publication explains this approach to reading and lists suggestions for reading instructional methods for kindergarten through grade 3. The suggestions are all ways to help students build skills needed to recognize words. Reading skills begin with phonemic awareness and build to phonics. Students also need to build a bank of sight words. These are words like *of* or *one* that occur frequently but do not follow regular phonics patterns. Students also need to learn how to break down longer words, using structural analysis. For example, they could break down *transportation* into trans/port/ation and determine the meaning of the word by using the meanings of the parts. *Put Reading First* has been widely disseminated to schools and has served as the basis of school reading reform efforts. Despite criticism of both the National Reading Panel report and the summary (Coles 2000; Garan 2002), this book has shaped reading instruction in many dual language classes.

Proponents of a word recognition model argue that developing proficiency in written language is different from developing oral language proficiency. While children can acquire the ability to understand and produce oral language naturally, they must learn to read and write. Literacy development requires systematic, explicit teaching and learning. Teachers must teach the skills students need to translate written language into oral language that they understand. Literacy development depends on teaching and learning; it does not occur naturally as oral language development does. In addition, it is important for English language learners to develop oral language first, because that is the base on which knowledge of written language is built.

The model we advocate is a transactional, sociopsycholinguistic model. In this model, readers construct meaning as they transact with texts. Meaning is not in the text or in the reader (Rosenblatt 1978). Each text has a meaning potential, and readers use both cues from the text and their background knowledge to build meaning. Goodman (1984) explains that there are dual texts. There is the written text, but in addition, "the reader is constructing a text parallel and closely related to the published text. It becomes a different text for each reader" (97). The reason that this mental text is different for each reader is that readers differ in their background knowledge and their purposes for reading.

The concept of dual texts helps explain why we can read a text as an adult that we read years before as a child and get a very different meaning from the same written text. For David and Yvonne, the novel *Rain of Gold* (Villaseñor 1991), an epic romance story of two families from Mexico and the history of their coming to the United States, provides a clear example of Goodman's idea of dual texts. Their son-in-law, Francisco, came to this country at fourteen as an immigrant from El Salvador escaping poverty and war. *Rain of Gold* was for him "the best book I ever read! I could picture everything that was happening in my mind. It was like people I know and experiences I have had." When Yvonne read *Rain of Gold*, she was fascinated. She loved the book because it represented so many of the students she had taught and it helped her internalize the struggles, the passions, the contradictions she had encountered in the Mexican culture over the years. For one of Yvonne's Anglo students, whose family had little contact with immigrants, it was a long, tedious book with "way too many details." He read the book only because it was assigned to him by a university instructor teaching a class in cross-cultural understanding. Each person read the same book, the same words, but the mental text each reader constructed was completely different.

From a sociopsycholinguistic perspective, the reading process is both social and psychological. It is social because the meaning we construct depends on our purposes for reading and on the ideas we develop from interacting with others. In fact, the mental text we create keeps changing as we talk about a book with others. We interpret and reinterpret what we read in part based on our social interactions as we clarify or deepen concepts presented in the text.

Reading is also an individual psychological process. Readers use a series of strategies as they read. They sample the text, make predictions and inferences, confirm or disconfirm and correct their predictions, and integrate their new understanding with what they previously understood. Readers use their background knowledge and cues from three linguistic cueing systems—graphophonics, syntax, and semantics—as they transact with texts. Graphophonics refers to the letters and sounds; syntax involves the order of words in a sentence, and semantics has to do with the meanings of words. Readers use all three linguistic cueing systems simultaneously with a focus on building meaning from the text.

Proponents of a transactional, sociopsycholinguistic model argue that developing proficiency in written language is the same as developing proficiency in oral language. In each case, what is essential is that students receive comprehensible input, messages they understand (Krashen 2003). If the input is in written form, students will acquire the ability to read and write. Teachers can make the input comprehensible by reading to and with students, scaffolding instruction until students can read on their own.

Some researchers have characterized the word recognition model as a bottom-up model and the sociopsycholinguistic model as a top-down model. This characterization does seem to fit the word recognition model. Students start by mastering skills needed to recode words. Then they combine word meanings to get at the meaning of the text. They go from small parts (phonemes, graphemes, syllables, and words) to the whole (the meaning of a text). However, the sociopsycholinguistic model is not really top-down. Readers use their background knowledge and all the linguistic cueing systems simultaneously to build meaning as they transact with texts. They do not go from the whole (the meaning of the entire text) to the parts (recognition of words and letters). Instead, they use all their available resources to make sense of what they are reading.

Research Support for the Transactional Sociopsycholinguistic Model

Researchers who agree with a sociopsycholinguistic theory of reading argue that studies on eye movements during reading and research from miscue analysis lend support to the model. The eye movement studies conducted during the last one hundred years have shown that readers do not sample every letter of every word (Paulson and Freeman 2003). Instead, the brain directs the eyes to gather necessary information for making and confirming predictions during reading. When readers pause to fixate words, information is sent to the brain. When the eyes are moving between fixations, the brain receives no information. The eye movement studies show that readers fixate about two-thirds of the words in a text. No reader fixates every letter of every word. In addition, proficient readers fixate the important content words, especially the nouns and verbs that provide needed input for meaning construction, about twice as often as function words, such as conjunctions and prepositions. Eye movement data supports the assertion that readers selectively sample a text to get the information they need to make and confirm predictions.

Researchers who hold a word recognition theory of reading also argue that eye movement data supports their model. Stanovich (1998), for example, claims that there has been a "grand synthesis" of research that shows that proficient readers visually process nearly all the print and automatically recognize words. Poor readers, in contrast, rely heavily on context and do not make good use of the graphophonic cueing system. Publications such as *Put Reading First* use this interpretation of the data to advocate for reading programs that put a heavy emphasis on skills instruction in the areas of phonemic awareness and phonics to improve beginning readers' ability to recognize words rather than rely on context clues.

Kucer and Tuten (2003) conducted research to test the claim that less proficient readers rely more on context and that more proficient readers make better use of visual information to recognize words automatically. They examined the miscues of twenty-four proficient adult readers who were advanced graduate students. What they found was just the opposite of what Stanovich claimed. The proficient readers in the Kucer and Tuten study relied more on context and less on graphophonics than beginning readers do. Syntax was the most important cueing system for the adult readers. About 94 percent of their miscues were syntactically acceptable and 87 percent were semantically acceptable. That is, a very high percentage of the predictions they made fit with the grammar of the preceding context and made sense. However, only 35 percent of the miscues showed high graphic similarity to the word in the text and another 11 percent showed some similarity.

Kucer and Tuten conclude that "the readers relied most heavily on story and sentence meaning and syntax, made partial use of graphics and sounds and produced miscues that made sense" (290). In contrast, as other miscue data has shown, younger, less experienced readers rely more heavily on graphophonics and less on the other cueing systems. Kucer and Tuten's results caused them "to question early reading programs that rely heavily on the teaching of graphic and sound (phonic) strategies, especially in isolation, as well as programs that promote 'balance'" (290). The proficient adult readers did not make a balanced use of all three cueing systems. They relied more on syntax and semantics than on graphophonics. Since younger readers often overrely on graphophonics, instruction should help them use the other cueing systems.

A. Freeman (in press) analyzed bilingual students' eye movements and miscues during reading. All four of her bilingual readers made miscues that had high or some graphic similarity about 95 percent of the time. These same readers had much lower scores for syntax and semantics. Thus, this miscue data shows that these bilingual students, like the less experienced readers referred to in the Kucer and Tuten study, relied more heavily on graphophonics than on syntax and semantics.

In addition, the bilingual readers who Freeman analyzed were less proficient when reading in their second language, English, than in their first language, Spanish. Proficient readers fixate content words (nouns, verbs, adjectives, and adverbs) that provide key information more than function words (prepositions, conjunctions, articles). While the students in Freeman's study fixated content words more often than function words in both languages, their percentages were better in their first language. When reading in Spanish, they fixated 75 percent of the content words and 43 percent of the function words. In English they fixated 67 percent of the content words and 45 percent of the function words. These data suggest that the students had better control over Spanish syntax, and this subconscious knowledge helped them focus on the words that would provide key information as they read in that language. Students learning to read in a second language, like those in Freeman's study, need strategies that will help them focus on constructing meaning by relying more on syntactic and semantic cues than on graphophonic cues and by making greater use of the key content words in the text. To a great degree, though, these abilities develop through extensive reading in the new language with a focus on meaning.

Both models of reading have the goal of constructing meaning. However, methods based on the word recognition model focus on skills such as phonics and structural analysis of words. As a result, students may become more concerned with applying these skills to identify words than with making sense of texts. We have observed classes in which students read quite well orally. They were able to recode the written marks to oral language. Nevertheless, some students, especially second language readers, may sound better than they really are. Their comprehension may not match their oral production. The results show up in reading tests, particularly tests of comprehension in the intermediate grades.

The tendency of second language readers to regard reading as a process of word recognition is often reinforced by the kind of instruction they receive. In her review of the literature on second language reading instruction, Fitzgerald (1995) found that primary-grade teachers focused more on words and word recognition and less on comprehension when working with English language learners:

> Evidence from classroom observations of 20 to 250 students in bilingual programs in 21 schools suggested that, on average, primary-grade ESL reading instruction tended to focus mainly on word recognition, with an extraordinary emphasis on drill (about half of the total reading instruction time), with only about one-third of the total time spent on comprehension and very little time on vocabulary-meaning instruction . . . When comprehension was a focus, literal, factual information was emphasized . . . Further it appeared that the tendency to focus mainly on word recognition may have been even more heightened in lower reading groups. (128–29)

In contrast, methods based on the sociopsycholinguistic model keep the students focused on comprehension. Teachers provide strategies readers can use to increase and extend their comprehension of texts. They encourage readers to use their background knowledge and cues from all three linguistic systems to make sense of the text rather than rely on the graphophonic system to recognize words. Although the goal of the two models is the same, the route to the goals is quite different. As we examine other questions about how to develop a meaning-centered literacy program, it is important to keep the differences between these two theoretical models of reading and the implications for instruction in mind.

Reading Research in Dual Language Settings

Most of the research on dual language programs has used reading test results to assess the effectiveness of the program rather than focus on individual components, such as literacy instruction. For example, the Thomas and Collier studies

(2002, 1997; Collier 1995) compare different kinds of programs for English language learners, such as pullout ESL compared with transitional bilingual education or dual language. Although their research focuses on the models, Collier and Thomas chose schools or school systems in which the particular model was well implemented. Collier (1995) explains that well-implemented programs provide staff development that emphasizes whole language, natural language acquisition through all content areas, cooperative learning, interactive and discovery learning, and cognitive complexity for all proficiency levels. All of these elements are consistent with a sociopsycholinguistic view of reading.

Some research has specifically examined literacy programs in dual language settings. Calderón and Slavin (2001) describe the Success for All program at Hueco Elementary School in El Paso, Texas; Smith and Arnot-Hopffer (1998) analyze the Exito Bilingüe program at Davis Elementary in Tucson, Arizona; and Pérez (2004)discusses the literacy programs in two dual language schools in San Antonio, Texas. These descriptions offer insights into how different dual language schools have approached literacy instruction.

Success for All/Exito Para Todos—El Paso, Texas ◆ The Success for All/Exito Para Todos program was instituted at Hueco Elementary in El Paso. This school uses a 50/50 model of dual language instruction. Students are grouped by ability for a ninety-minute reading period each day. All students receive initial literacy instruction in their native language and then add reading in the second language at second grade. The program also includes individual tutoring for students who experience difficulty. There is a full-time facilitator, family support, and professional development for the teachers (Calderón and Slavin 2001).

During the first half year of kindergarten, the emphasis is on oral language development. Students are introduced to literacy through storytelling, shared book activities, and vocabulary exercises. They work on rhymes and letter investigations. During this time, students are instructed in Spanish for three days each week, followed by two days of English instruction. In the second half of kindergarten, they begin reading with a series of leveled books. By grade 1 the language of instruction alternates each week. The program includes listening comprehension and shared reading designed to build literacy skills. The program continues to follow an alternate-week schedule for grades 2 through 5. During these grades students read in English one week and in Spanish the next.

In the Success for All program, students are grouped by reading ability for instruction. Some teachers like this model because they work with students with similar reading abilities. A drawback of ability grouping is that older struggling readers are placed in the same class with younger students, and this is often discouraging for the older learners. In addition, students in low groups in ability tracking do not have access to more proficient peers. Another concern with this type of grouping is that because students move to different rooms at different grade levels for reading, it is difficult for teachers to develop integrated thematic units since at least some students are absent during the language arts period. A daily ninety-minute ability grouping takes time away from thematic content teaching.

Success for All is a scripted reading program. Teachers are given extensive training in the implementation of the program and follow strict guidelines. They use only the program materials. Materials are available in both Spanish and English. The books are leveled, and little authentic literature is incorporated. The approach to teaching reading is consistent with a word recognition model. Although the developers of Success for All have published reports showing that students in the program make great gains in literacy, research by investigators not connected with the program suggest that the results of Success for All are similar to the results for other reading programs (Pogrow 2000). We are especially concerned with the lack of authentic reading materials in the program. Bilingual students need authentic, culturally relevant materials to read.

Slavin and Cheung (2004) have published studies showing the effectiveness of Success for All for bilingual students. They conclude that the program is effective because it contains intensive systematic phonics. However, Krashen (2004) points out that the program involves students in extensive reading. Students read ninety minutes per day. In addition, in grades 2 through 5, students are expected to read at home for twenty minutes a day. Krashen suggests that gains second language students make in Success for All may be due to the extensive reading rather than to the phonics component. No studies compared the Success for All students with other students who read as much but didn't have the phonics so there is no clear evidence that it was the phonics that made the difference.

Exito Bilingüe—Tucson, Arizona ◆ At Davis Bilingual Magnet School in Tucson, Arizona, teachers implemented a Spanish literacy program, Exito Bilingüe (Bilingual Success). In this two-way program, students are instructed entirely in Spanish during kindergarten and first grade, except for a short period of kindergarten when some English is used to help native English speakers adapt to the school setting. By second grade, the school follows an 85/15 plan, and in third through fifth grade the model is 70/30. Because all instruction is in Spanish in kindergarten and grade 1, all students are taught to read first in Spanish, and English reading is introduced later.

The Davis literacy program was developed by teachers working with faculty from the nearby university. Teachers assessed students using running records with retellings. They then divided students into fourteen multiage reading groups. They provided reading instruction for one hour a day three days a week. The students at Davis were ability grouped for instruction. Ability grouping across grade levels brings with it the problems outlined earlier. However, the authors of the report on Davis comment that students were assessed and regrouped frequently. Teachers used a balanced approach to literacy that included read-alouds, shared reading, guided reading, and independent reading. Teachers were actively involved in the design and implementation of the program. They introduced the components of the balanced program gradually and continually reflected on their teaching. The program was not scripted, and teachers used a variety of resources to help students learn to read.

The students showed improvement in reading on both informal and formal assessments. Students made gains of three to four levels each year, as measured by running records. In addition, students in the program made gains on the English reading portion of the Stanford 9 test. Further, students were able to transfer their Spanish reading skills to English reading and writing. These results suggest that the program has lived up to its name, "Exito bilingüe." Smith and Arnot-Hopffer conclude that "contrary to the promises of commercially prepared, scripted reading curricula, dual language readers are best served by teachers working together to design literacy instruction to meet local conditions and learner needs" (1998, 261). The program Davis teachers developed reflects a sociopsycholinguistic model of reading.

Biliteracy in San Antonio, Texas ◆ In her book *Becoming Biliterate,* Pérez (2004) provides a detailed description of the curriculum in two dual language schools in San Antonio, Texas. Pérez gives specific classroom examples, including transcripts from reading lessons. Both schools used a 90/10 model of dual language. All children received initial literacy instruction in Spanish. English reading was introduced in third grade. However, Pérez explains that English literacy was evident before third grade.

> Although the teacher-directed reading and writing activities in these early grades were almost always conducted in Spanish, the children were exposed to English print and texts during the English language

development portion of the curriculum. Thus many children began to read and write in English before the formal teacher-directed English reading instruction began. (86)

It is interesting to note that one of the arguments for introducing reading in Spanish is that English is such a powerful and pervasive language that students will acquire English literacy naturally. This seems to be what happened in the schools Pérez describes.

The San Antonio schools used a balanced literacy framework that included read-alouds; shared reading; activities designed to develop phonemic aware-ness, letter knowledge, and phonics; and guided reading. While some students participated in guided reading groups, the other students circulated through lit-eracy centers designed to provide practice for the skills developed in guided reading. The program also stressed content area reading. By third grade an independent reading period was added to the schedule.

The literacy framework at the two dual language schools fits with either a word recognition or a sociopsycholinguistic view of reading. Individual teachers may have varied in their view of reading and in the way they implemented the program. However, pressures from testing may have led many teachers to focus on word recognition skills. Schools in Texas are assessed by student perfor-mance on the state-mandated test. As Pérez notes, it is this test "that the teach-ers and students feel dominates the curriculum and is what their performance will be judged by"(141). She goes on to comment:

Preparing for standardized or state tests has become a rite of spring in most schools. For the teachers and students in the two-way bilingual immersion program, this rite assumed major proportions. The pressures of testing . . . were a constant concern for the students and teachers. (142)

This concern led teachers to have students practice reading and writing pas-sages that were similar to those found on the test. Especially during the spring, almost all the literacy activities were strongly influenced by the test.

The descriptions of these three reading programs reflect the variety in approaches to literacy instruction in dual language classes. In the El Paso pro-gram, students learned to read in their first language and then added a second language. In the other two programs, all students began formal reading instruc-tion in Spanish. However, many students began to read in English even before formal instruction in English started. The El Paso school followed a scripted program brought in by outside experts. The reading program at Davis was developed and modified by the teachers working with local university faculty. Two of the programs used multiage ability grouping for reading. The El Paso program was more consistent with a word recognition model of reading than the other two. However, the San Antonio program was heavily influenced by pressures from testing, and those pressures led to an emphasis on word recognition skills. All three programs included many of the elements of a balanced reading program.

Balanced Reading Programs

Before we continue looking at literacy issues for dual language programs, it might be helpful to discuss balanced literacy briefly. As we have visited schools, we have always asked what approach to literacy the school is taking. Most administrators and teachers have told us that they have a balanced literacy program. However, our observations in those schools have shown us that balanced literacy can mean different things to different people. To some, balanced literacy simply means that teachers teach skills and phonics and also use basal reader stories and/or trade books during reading time. Others have told us that they have a balanced literacy program because they do guided and shared reading in addition to teaching phonics and phonemic awareness. Still other programs, which have a heavy emphasis on the direct teaching of skills, phonics, and phonemic awareness, claim that their literacy program is balanced because children read stories aloud during part of the instruction time.

The term *balanced literacy* arose around the time that whole language teachers were being criticized for not teaching phonics and other skills. Teachers, concerned about how to teach skills, phonics, grammar, and spelling, wanted to include those things along with literature in their reading instruction. Strickland (2004) encourages teaching through themes and incorporating skills in shared and guided reading. She suggests five rules of thumb that are useful for balanced dual language literacy programs:

1. Teach skills as a way to gain meaning. Skills are not ends in themselves.

2. Each day, include time for both guided instruction and independent work. Otherwise, students will never internalize skills and make them their own.

3. Avoid teaching children as if they were empty receptacles for knowledge. Instead, allow them to build knowledge in a process-oriented way.

4. Integrate print and electronic materials effectively. That way, your classroom will reflect the multimedia world in which students live.

5. Always consider standardized test scores in light of informal assessment data. Encourage parents to do the same. (4)

As more dual language programs are started, teachers and administrators should discuss their theoretical stance toward reading and then design a program that fits their view. As schools debate the best ways to help all students become bilingual and biliterate, they must address a series of questions related to the structure of the literacy program. In the following sections, we consider several of the issues that must be resolved.

Initial Literacy Instruction

The first issue is the choice of the language or languages for initial literacy instruction. This choice may depend on the model of the dual language program.

Literacy Program Essentials

- Consider the choice of language or languages for initial literacy instruction carefully because it has implications for the choice of program model.

- Choose an approach that is consistent with the theory of reading.

One of the first questions teachers and administrators designing a dual language program need to consider is whether formal literacy instruction should be introduced in the first language, in the second language, or in both languages simultaneously. This question must be addressed early because of the interrelationships between the program model and the way literacy is introduced. Dual language programs vary widely in how they approach initial literacy instruction.

One approach is to have all students learn to read first in their native language. A second approach is to have all students learn to read in both languages simultaneously. The third approach to initial literacy is to teach all students to read first in the minority language and then add reading in English later.

The first two approaches work best in a 50/50 model because then there is enough time for language arts in both Spanish and English. Students may be separated for language arts, with the English speakers getting English language arts and the Spanish speakers getting Spanish language arts, or all students may have a period of English language arts and a period of Spanish language arts.

In a 90/10 model there would be very limited time (only 10 percent of the day) for language arts in English for native English speakers. For that reason, a 90/10 model works best if all students have initial literacy instruction in the non-English language. In most 90/10 models there is no provision for English literacy development until second or third grade. Some schools that consider themselves to have a 90/10 model do provide literacy instruction for all students in their native language and then divide up the rest of the day 90/10. Although this model is often referred to as a 90/10 model, the actual amount of time in each language is probably closer to 70/30.

One reason for starting to teach reading in the non-English language has to do with the dominance of English for students living in an English-speaking country. English is the language of power. Important people speak English. If schools introduce reading in English, they just reinforce this domination. English language learners may conclude that their language, especially the written form, doesn't really count for much. On the other hand, instruction in Spanish sends the message that Spanish is also an important language. English speakers do not ever get the message that their language is not valued. They know that English is important, and there is no danger of their losing their heritage language. If reading is taught in Spanish, then English speakers regard this as an enrichment experience.

Further, many students may have already begun to read in English before starting school. Much of the environmental print, including print on television or the Internet, is in English. Children are surrounded by written English and begin to acquire the ability to read English. Results of standardized reading tests confirm that both native English speakers and English language learners in dual language programs can develop high levels of English reading proficiency even when they do not begin formal literacy in English until second or third grade (Lindholm-Leary 2001; de Jong 2004).

In addition, native English speakers in dual language programs are generally of a higher socioeconomic class than speakers of the non-English language, so they are more apt to have support for reading at home (García 2000). Many of these students have been given books and have been read to before they started school. Even if school reading instruction is in a non-English language, their parents may continue to read to and with them at home in English. As a result, native English speakers often acquire literacy in two languages simultaneously.

Little research has been conducted to answer questions about initial literacy. Students have succeeded in becoming biliterate in schools that introduce reading in two languages from the beginning as well as in schools that teach reading in one language first. Students have also succeeded when they learned to read first in their first language as well as when they learned to read first in a second language.

Two Views of Reading and Initial Literacy

From the perspective of the sociopsycholinguistic view of reading, there is no strong preference for teaching reading in one language or two from the beginning. If, in fact, written language can be acquired in the same way as oral language, then students could be expected to learn to read in two languages simultaneously in the same way that children brought up in bilingual households develop the ability to speak and understand two or more languages at the same time. As long as teachers make the written input comprehensible, students should be able to acquire the ability to read and write two or more languages at once. However, children could also acquire literacy in one language and then add a second language later. The sociopsycholinguistic model is consistent with teaching reading in both languages at once or one language at a time.

In contrast, the word recognition model of reading fits best when initial literacy instruction is provided in a student's first language. If reading is a process of recoding written marks into oral language, then it follows that comprehension depends on mastery of the oral language. Students who recognize that the letters *d o g* correspond to the phonemes /dag/ can make sense out of the word only if it is in their oral vocabulary. As a result, reading instruction should begin in a student's first language and build on the oral language knowledge he brings to school. For that reason, the word recognition model is only consistent with initial literacy in the first language.

Most programs introduce reading and writing in both languages or in the minority language only. This means that native Spanish speakers receive initial literacy instruction in Spanish. The assumption is that native English speakers, even when they begin formal instruction in a second language, will receive sufficient support for English literacy development from the home and the English-speaking environment outside of school.

One of the benefits of having native Spanish speakers learn to read in Spanish rather than in English is that they tend to receive instruction that is more focused on comprehension and is more cognitively challenging. Díaz, Moll, and Mehan (1986) found that the English language learners in a traditional bilingual class that they observed received very different kinds of literacy instruction when taught in English and Spanish. The same group of students received much more emphasis on comprehension when instructed in Spanish. These students were grouped for English reading instruction based on their oral English. Even though students' English reading levels exceeded their oral language levels, the teacher designed instruction suited to their limited oral language level in English.

Hudelson (1984) also conducted research with native Spanish speakers learning to read in English. Her research supports the idea that learning to read and write in a second language does not depend on achieving high levels of oral proficiency in that language. One of her findings was that "ESL learners are able to read English before they have complete oral control of the language" (224). She suggests that "ESL learners can (and should) write English before they have complete control over the oral and written systems of the language" (231). This research supports the idea that in dual language programs, students can learn to read and write in both languages at once even if they are not proficient in both orally.

Rather than seeing oral language development as a prerequisite for reading, teachers who take a sociopsycholinguistic view of reading regard all language encounters, oral or written, as feeding into a common data pool. Harste, Woodward, and Burke (1984) use this metaphor of a data pool to explain what happens as students use language. Every time a student reads, writes, speaks, or listens in any language, data is added to the pool, and the student can draw upon this data in subsequent oral or written language events. Hudelson (1984) applies this concept to a second language. Based on an examination of English learners' reading and writing, she concluded that "the processes of writing, reading, speaking, and listening in a second language are interrelated and interdependent" (234).

In the case of the students Díaz and his colleagues observed, the knowledge and skills they developed in Spanish reading could have been drawn on during English reading time, but the English teacher who gave the students low-level skills lessons did not access this resource. In addition, the researchers found that students could read at higher levels than their oral language performance indicated. Unfortunately, the English teacher thought that students' pronunciation problems were really decoding problems. As a result, the teacher spent a great deal of time on basic word recognition exercises.

This study (Díaz, Moll, and Mehan 1986) provides evidence that what counts is the way reading instruction is approached and the assumptions teachers make about students' abilities, not the particular language that is being used for instruction. When teachers regard students as capable learners and develop a meaning-centered literacy program, they provide instruction that is cognitively challenging and focuses on high levels of comprehension, and all students achieve higher levels of reading proficiency.

 ## Transfer of Knowledge and Skills to Reading in a Second Language

The next set of literacy essentials is based on research that shows that literacy knowledge that students develop in one language transfers to reading in a second language. This is true whether students are taught to read in one language at a time or two languages simultaneously.

Literacy Program Essentials
• Understand and trust in theory and research that shows that literacy transfers from one language to another.
• Use strategies to help students transfer literacy-related knowledge and skills from one language to the other.
• Understand differences and draw on similarities between languages to facilitate acquisition of literacy in two languages.

Teachers and administrators in dual language programs should understand how and why transfer occurs. Goodman (1984) points out, "Though written language processes appear to vary greatly as they are used in the wide range of functions and contexts they serve, reading and writing are actually unitary, psycholinguistic processes" (81). Whether students are reading in English, Spanish, Korean, or Arabic, they use the same cueing systems and the same strategies.

The teacher's job in a dual language classroom is to help students develop reading ability in two languages. The idea that what a student learns in one language is available in a second language has solid support. Teachers recognize that older English learners who enter school with high levels of reading proficiency in their native language learn to read and write in English much faster than students whose native language literacy is limited. They can transfer what they know about written language from their first language to a second language, even when the two languages use different writing systems.

Cummins (2000) has developed the linguistic interdependence principle to account for the ability to transfer knowledge and skills from one language to another. He contrasts two models of the relationship between the first and second languages. The separate underlying proficiency (SUP) model pictures the two languages as being located in different parts of the brain with no connection. The common underlying proficiency (CUP) model views the two languages as separate conduits feeding into one common area of the brain. Cummins reviews extensive research that supports the CUP model, which he describes using the metaphor of a dual iceberg. The surface features of the two languages differ. However, they are like the two tips of one large iceberg. At a deeper level, the proficiencies developed in the two languages form one unified entity.

Cummins (1994) states the linguistic interdependence hypothesis in this way:

> To the extent that instruction in Lx is effective in promoting proficiency in Lx, transfer of this proficiency to Ly will occur provided there is adequate exposure to Ly (either in school or in the environment) and adequate motivation to learn Ly. (19)

The interdependence principle states that what students learn in their first language (Lx) transfers to a second language (Ly) as long as students are exposed to the second language and motivated to learn it.

In dual language classes, students who learn to read in Spanish can transfer that knowledge to reading in English. However, as we discussed earlier, teachers and administrators at some schools do not trust that this transfer will take place. With the emphasis on standardized tests, even dual language schools begin to introduce English literacy earlier than necessary because they are not confident that the literacy knowledge and skills students develop in Spanish will transfer to English.

As Ms. Gaona at Runn Elementary School explained, students who were failing at third grade had been designated incorrectly as English-dominant in kindergarten and given literacy instruction in English when they needed to develop their literacy in Spanish. They were not ready for all-English literacy. Then teachers at third grade, worried about new high-stakes testing in their grade, emphasized English over Spanish in instruction and put too many children who were not ready into English testing. Ms. Gaona explained, "We still have a mentality at this school of English as being very important and 'Let's shift to English as soon as possible.'" Ms. Gaona and her staff realized what was wrong. They had not trusted that strong development in the first language would really transfer to the second.

Cummins (1989) hypothesizes that there is a certain threshold students must reach for transfer to occur. He writes:

> There may be a threshold level of proficiency in both languages which students must attain in order to avoid any negative academic consequences and a second, higher, threshold necessary to reap the linguistic and possibly intellectual benefits of bilingualism and biliteracy. (42)

One of the strengths of dual language programs is that students continue to study in two languages throughout the program. As a result, they develop the high levels of proficiency in both languages that lead to positive transfer, which can work in both directions in programs that teach reading in two languages from the beginning. In contrast, students in transitional bilingual programs often are transitioned into English before developing high levels of reading proficiency in their first language. As a result, they have not built an underlying proficiency that can transfer to the second language. Many students in transitional programs suffer from what Cummins refers to as "negative academic consequences."

In addition, Cummins states that CUP may be thought of as a central processing system consisting of memory, auditory discrimination, and abstract reasoning as well as specific conceptual and linguistic knowledge derived from experience and learning, such as vocabulary knowledge. He argues that the positive relationship between the first and second languages comes from three sources: (1) the application of the same cognitive and linguistic abilities and skills to literacy development in both languages, (2) the transfer of general concepts and knowledge of the world across languages, and (3) the transfer of specific linguistic features and skills across languages.

Readers use the same strategies and cueing systems to read in their first and second languages. They make predictions and inferences using graphophonic, syntactic, and semantic cues. They apply their background knowledge to construct meaning from a text. And, to the degree that the languages are similar, they transfer specific features and skills. For example, they know that they can read on and use context when they come to an unfamiliar word.

Cummins cites a number of studies to support his linguistic interdependence hypothesis. For example, Verhoeven (1991) found that literacy skills developed in one language strongly predict later development of these skills in a second language.

In her study of two dual language schools in Texas, Pérez (2004) documents evidence of the positive transfer of literacy skills and knowledge. She writes, "children first acquired literacy in Spanish and this had a positive consequence for the development of literacy in English" (108). She goes on to show, for example, that children used their knowledge of the Spanish alphabet to begin to encode and decode English even before they began formal instruction in English literacy. Students noticed differences between the written Spanish in their lessons and environmental print in English. One student asked the teacher why there were no accents in English. Pérez also notes that "Spanish graphophonic knowledge was used by many of the children in attempting to read and write English" (109).

Barnitz (1982) examined studies showing the transfer of knowledge from first to second language reading. He concluded that the studies of French immersion programs show positive effects of transfer in several ways:

> To summarize, the Canadian research implies that at least three linguistic factors facilitate a partial transfer of reading skills from French to English: (a) partial similarities of syntactic structure and vocabulary allow for common syntactic processing strategies and recognition of cognate vocabulary; (b) the alphabetic orthographies preserve the vocabulary similarities of the languages; and (c) the children learn to read the more simple spelling-to-sound code first (in French, the second language) and later tackle the more complex code in the native tongue, English. (564)

Barnitz also examined studies in which children were taught to read in two very different languages, such as Persian and English. Persian has a different syntactic structure than English. English follows a subject-verb-object pattern while the Persian pattern is verb-subject-object. The two languages have different orthographic systems with different characters. English is written left to right and Persian right to left. Barnitz argues that less transfer can occur when the two languages are different. Even in a case like Persian, though, some knowledge and skills transfer. Students know that there is a predictable syntactic pattern. Words are not arranged haphazardly. The characters represent sounds and are arranged in a consistent direction. Readers can use the graphic cues to make and confirm predictions with the goal of constructing meaning from the text. As Barnitz (1982) writes, "Meaning is the most important factor in reading instruction . . . teachers of English as a second language must help their students adjust to the new writing system in order to transfer meaningful literacy skills to English as their second language" (566).

August, Calderón, and Carlo (2000) analyzed the relationship between students' reading in Spanish at the end of second grade and their English reading at the end of third grade. They found that skills such as phonemic segmentation, letter identification, and word naming transferred from Spanish reading into English reading. Hudelson (1984) collected data from bilingual classrooms that showed that students taught to read in Spanish use this knowledge as they begin to write in English. In fact, studies have shown that students' reading and writing ability in their first language is a better predictor of second language reading than measures of their oral reading in the second language (Tregar and Wong 1984).

Edelsky (1982) studied the relationship between Spanish and English writing development in a bilingual program. Her data show that what students learned about writing in Spanish transferred to their writing in English. She concludes, "Data have been presented to support the perspective that what a young writer knows about writing in the first language forms the basis of new hypotheses rather than interferes with writing in another language" (227).

Traditional methods of second language teaching, such as the audiolingual method (ALM), were developed with the idea that the first language interferes with the second. For instance, Spanish speakers' pronunciation of English words is influenced by their Spanish pronunciation. In classes using ALM, teachers give students drills and exercises to help them overcome the negative effects of the first language. Differences between the two languages are emphasized with the aim of eliminating native language influence.

However, close examination of students' reading and writing, such as the study Edelsky conducted, shows that the first language is an asset, not a liability. Knowledge and skills developed in the first language do not interfere with the development of the second language. In dual language classes, teachers can facilitate transfer by focusing on similarities rather than differences.

Strategies That Faciliate Transfer

At one dual language school we observed in Texas, teachers use an alphabet chart designed by one of the teachers to capitalize on similarities between

English and Spanish. Often, the English alphabet chart uses one set of objects for the English letters (*b* is for *banana*) and the Spanish chart uses different objects (*b* is for *burro*). At this school the chart uses cognate words to represent the letters. For example, the letter *c* is associated with *castle* in English and with *castillo* in Spanish. Even though it is difficult to create a completely parallel chart because of the differences in sound-to-spelling correspondences between Spanish and English, the teacher who created this chart capitalized on the similarities, and this helps students transfer knowledge developed in Spanish to their English reading.

Teachers can also facilitate transfer by helping students recognize cognates. For example, teachers can put the page of a book on an overhead transparency and ask students to find cognates. In Spanish/English dual language classrooms, for example, students might come up with Spanish words like *historia* and *ciencias* in a reading and compare them with the English cognates, *history* and *science.* Then students can work in pairs to find cognates on other pages from their reading. They can use these to make a classroom cognate chart or to make individual cognate dictionaries. All these activities help students focus on similarities between the two languages (Williams 2001).

Transfer is also more likely to occur when teachers use similar methods to teach reading in each language. However, in some dual language programs, literacy instruction in Spanish looks very different from instruction in English. One of the problems that Díaz and his colleagues noted is that the Spanish and English reading teachers in their study did not communicate effectively. As a result, the same students were given very different kinds of instruction in their two languages. Instruction in English did not build on the strengths students had already developed in Spanish reading. Consequently, there was little transfer from Spanish reading to English reading.

Earlier we discussed two views of reading, the word recognition view and the sociopsycholinguistic view. Traditional methods of teaching reading in Spanish have been based on a word recognition view (Freeman and Freeman 1996, 1998b). Since Spanish has a more consistent set of sound-to-spelling correspondences than English does, instruction often begins with a focus on pronouncing syllables to help students decode words. In contrast, English reading may be introduced as a process of constructing meaning through making and confirming predictions using all three cueing systems.

Teachers may feel that the differences between Spanish and English justify using a different approach to teach reading in the two languages. This may make it difficult for a teacher, especially a new teacher, to use a consistent approach. A. Freeman (2001) tells of the challenges she faced when she started to work as a bilingual teacher:

> I have taught reading in both Spanish and English . . . I taught reading in both languages with an understanding that reading is a meaning making process . . . However, both co-teachers and teacher educators I worked with challenged my approach, especially my teaching in Spanish. They believed that I should use traditional methods of teaching reading in Spanish. (20–21)

When schools implement dual language programs and emphasize meaning-centered literacy instruction, some teachers who have used traditional methods of teaching reading in Spanish may find it difficult to change the way they teach reading. Pérez (2004) explains that in the two schools she studied, "one of the main reasons for teacher turnover cited by both teachers and administrators was differences in expectations, especially in the teaching of Spanish reading" (164). The district had adopted a balanced literacy model consistent with a sociopsycholinguistic theory of reading. However, "for some teachers, the adopted approach was too different from the more traditional Spanish literacy teaching philosophy" (164–65).

As a result, several teachers continued to insist on using traditional methods and materials. "They used an approach to teaching reading and writing that focused on syllabication, where reading instruction consisted of exercises in syllabication with controlled vocabulary" (165). Because of their strong beliefs that Spanish reading should be taught using a syllabic method, two teachers left one of the schools. Other teachers and administrators recognized that the development of an effective literacy program in two languages depended on using a consistent approach to teaching reading and writing in the two languages. By using a consistent approach, they facilitated transfer of Spanish reading skills to English reading.

How Are Spanish and English Reading Alike and Different?

The traditional teachers in the Pérez study used a different method for teaching reading in Spanish because of differences between the two languages. We believe that students learn to read better in a second language when teachers focus on similarities, not differences, and when they use the same method to teach reading in each language. Like Goodman (1984), we believe that reading is a unitary psycholinguistic process and that instruction should build on what is common to the two languages. Nevertheless, it is useful to examine the similarities and differences in reading in the two languages.

Smith (1985) argues that in reading, what is behind the eyes is more important than what is in front of the eyes. When we consider the differences in reading two languages, we often focus on what is in front of the eyes. This would include the characters in the writing system and the arrangement of words on the page. What is less obvious but more important is what is behind the eyes, the reader's knowledge of how letters relate to sound, how words are organized in patterns, and how words relate to things in the world. This knowledge can be applied to reading a new language.

All written languages place some sort of characters on a page. The characters used in writing vary from one system to another. The characters may represent ideas in languages such as Chinese, or they may represent sounds. If the characters represent sounds, they may stand for syllables, as in Japanese, or phonemes, as in English and Spanish. In addition, the characters may be arranged so that reading goes left to right, right to left, or top to bottom. It is clear that there may be differences in the shape, organization, and function of the characters on the page.

Despite the possible differences, when teachers help students focus on similarities and build on strengths, students can transfer knowledge and skills from first language reading to reading in the second language. In the case of Spanish and English, there are many similarities in the graphic display. Both languages are alphabetic. That is, in each language, letters represent phonemes, not syllables or ideas. Both languages use the same set of letters to represent sounds. Traditional Spanish alphabets included *ch, rr,* and *ll* as separate letters. However, currently these digraphs are not presented as distinct letters in the Spanish alphabet. In addition, Spanish includes *w* even though that letter appears only in words borrowed from other languages. As a result, students who learn the Spanish alphabet encounter the same letters in English.

In most cases, letters in Spanish represent the same sounds they do in English. There are some obvious exceptions. The letters *a, e, i, o,* and *u* each represent just one vowel sound in Spanish, and the same letters can represent different sounds in English. The letter *h* does not represent a sound in Spanish. In English it usually (but not always) corresponds to the /h/ phoneme. The *j* in Spanish is pronounced like the *h* in English. Despite these and other differences, there are many similar correspondences between spellings and sounds in Spanish and English.

In addition to similarities in the form and function of the graphic display, Spanish and English have similar, but not identical, syntactic structures. Both languages use a subject-verb-object pattern. Prepositions precede their objects. Articles precede nouns. Again, there are a few differences. Adjectives usually precede nouns in English, and they generally follow nouns in Spanish. English requires that the subject be a separate word, but in Spanish an inflection may be added to the verb to indicate the subject. Thus, the English *I have* may be written *tengo* in Spanish, with the *o* serving the function of the subject pronoun in English. Again, even though there are some differences, the syntactic structures of Spanish and English are similar.

Spanish and English also share semantic similarities. Semantic cues include word meanings, words that relate ideas, and words that go together. Most often we think of semantics as referring to lexical meanings of words. Lexical meanings are the objects and actions words refer to. One of the biggest challenges in reading a new language is building vocabulary in that language. Knowing that *perro* refers to a kind of four-legged animal does not help students when they encounter *dog* during their English reading. Fortunately, in the case of Spanish and English, there are a number of cognates students can draw on. A student who knows what *colonial* means in Spanish can apply that knowledge when reading *colonial* in English. Students can also rely on context to determine the meaning of new words. Moreover, readers can use nonlinguistic cues, such as pictures, to help figure out texts in a new language.

Semantics also refers to words that connect ideas. Words such as conjunctions and prepositions have a grammatical meaning rather than a lexical meaning. For example, *and* signals that the words or clauses being joined are similar, and *but* signals that the ideas that are joined are opposites. Conjunctions and prepositions occur in the same places in Spanish and English and signal similar relationships. In addition, semantic knowledge includes the knowledge that related words co-occur. A reader who knows that the word *golf* is likely to appear in a passage that contains related words such as *ball, tee,* and *green* can apply that knowledge to predict words that go together when reading a second language. Similarly, a discussion of *gimnasia* in Spanish brings with it words like *equilibrio, competencias, rutinas,* and *ejercicios.* Those who know gymnastics understand the meanings of *balance, competition, routines,* and *exercise,* which are words specific to that sport.

In addition to cues from graphophonics, syntax, and semantics, readers use their background knowledge to construct meaning from texts. It is easier to read a text in a second language if the topic or the story is familiar. Students who know a lot about the solar system can apply that knowledge when reading a second language. Readers can also more easily read a book that is similar to stories they have previously read or one that reflects life experiences they have had. We have written elsewhere of the importance of using culturally relevant texts for all students (Freeman and Freeman 2001, 2000). Culturally relevant texts are those in which the characters, events, settings, and ways of talking and interacting are similar to the ways people talk and act and to the places in which people live in the student's community. Teachers who use culturally relevant books provide texts students can more easily understand because of the match between the story and the students' lives. For students reading in a second language, it is especially important that at least some of the texts be culturally relevant.

How Are Spanish and English Writing Alike and Different?

As students begin to read in a second language, they also begin to write in that language. As in reading, students draw on what they have learned in their first language to write in a second language. Knowledge of first language writing serves as a valuable resource in second language writing. Much of what students learn in Spanish writing transfers to English. However, there are differences in the development of writing in Spanish and in English.

We have discussed Spanish and English writing development in detail elsewhere (Freeman and Freeman 1996, 1998b). Here we will point out a few key differences. The most notable difference is that students beginning to write in Spanish use vowels, and young writers of English begin with consonants. For example, Efraín started his story about a submarine by writing the letters *a, o, e, i, o, e, a, d, a, e, e, a, a*. This string of letters would have been totally unintelligible to his teacher, Carolina, if he hadn't drawn a picture and if she hadn't asked Efraín to read back to her what he had written. Efraín drew a picture of a boy swimming and a submarine in the ocean. Carolina wrote what he read aloud, placing the words under his letters. Here is the result.

    a   o e   i o e ada e   e   a   a
    cuando el niño estaba en el agua (when the boy was in the water)

Efraín's letters represented most of the vowels in the words.

Another of Carolina's students represented the words *Porque hay hielo* (because there is ice) with the letters *oeaelo*. By placing the letters over the words and considering the context of the story, Carolina could see the correspondences:

    o   e   a   elo
    porque hay hielo (because there is ice)

Like Efraín, this student relied on the vowels to express her message. With more experience, students writing in Spanish begin to fill in the consonants.

This pattern of vowels first can be perplexing for English-speaking teachers. It is almost impossible to figure out what a child has written by looking at a string of vowels like *oeaelo*. This is because consonants provide stronger clues for word identification than vowels do in both Spanish and English. Readers have little trouble filling in the vowels in a sequence such as l_ttl_ r_d r_d_ng h_ _d . The task is much easier than filling in the consonants in a sequence such as _ o _ _ i _ o _ _ _ a _ _ _ _ e _ _ _ ee _ ea _ _ .

Students learning to write in English usually begin with consonants. One student, for example, wrote *hs* for *house* and *ldbg* for *ladybug.* Teachers can often read beginning writing in English, but they may struggle to decipher beginning Spanish writing. Why do researchers consistently find this difference between early Spanish writing and early English writing?

As children begin to write, they move through several stages. At first, they don't realize that letters represent sounds. Instead, they assume that letters represent objects. For that reason, they may write several letters to represent something that is big, like a house, and only a few letters to represent something that is small, like a mosquito. At some point, students reach the understanding that letters represent sounds, not things. They often begin by writing one letter for each word in a sentence. At the next stage, their letters often represent syllables. Eventually, they grasp the alphabetic principle that each sound is represented by a letter.

Both Spanish and English writers go through this same progression. However, students writing in Spanish begin with vowels and add consonants while students who write in English begin with consonants and add vowels. The reason for this difference has to do with the differences in the consistency of sound-to-spelling correspondences between the two languages. Spanish has only five vowel phonemes, and these match up with the letters *a, e, i, o,* and *u.* These vowels are always pronounced the same way, and their sound is always represented by the same letter. When children begin to write Spanish, they naturally carefully sound out the syllables, but the sounds that are most salient to them, the sounds they most notice, are usually the vowels. Every syllable contains a vowel, and it is the vowel that is spelled most consistently in Spanish, so students use vowels to represent the words they wish to express. In some words, like *cuando,* in which two vowels occur together, students write the letter that represents the most salient sound, *a*. In most cases, though, each syllable in Spanish has just one vowel.

In English, there are about fourteen vowel phonemes, so English orthography relies on various combinations of letters to represent the sounds. There is not a one-to-one correspondence in English between vowel sounds and letters. In addition, the same vowel sound can be spelled different ways, as in *may, weigh, raid,* and *great.* Further, the same letters can represent different vowel sounds, as in *great, tea, bread,* and *idea.* On the other hand, consonants represent the same sounds quite consistently. The letter *p* usually represents the /p/ phoneme even though *ph* represents /f/ in some words. Letters like *c* and *g* have two different values depending on the following vowel. Nevertheless, there is a good match between sounds and spellings for English consonants, so it is not surprising that young writers use consonants to represent English words.

Aside from this initial difference, writing development in Spanish and English follows the same pattern. Students begin with single letters to represent words, and then they add more letters, spaces between words, and accents and punctuation marks as their writing matures. It should be noted that Spanish speakers living in the United States may use both consonants and vowels because of their exposure to environmental print in English. As with reading instruction, the key for teachers working with students writing in a second language is to emphasize similarities, build on strengths, and keep the focus on constructing a meaningful written message.

Developing a Meaning-Centered Literacy Program

Literacy Program Essential

- Organize a program that includes meaning-centered activities to foster literacy development in two languages.

In effective reading programs, teachers keep students focused on meaning as they read and write in their first and second languages. Teachers know that literacy knowledge and skills developed in one language will transfer to a second language as long as the similarities between the languages are emphasized and the instructional methods are consistent.

From a sociopsycholinguistic perspective, students acquire literacy in a first or second language when they receive comprehensible written input (Krashen 2003). Teachers can make the input from books comprehensible by scaffolding instruction. Weaver (2002) describes "the gradual release of responsibility model of instruction developed by Pearson and Gallagher" (326). Figure 5–1 shows the gradual release model.

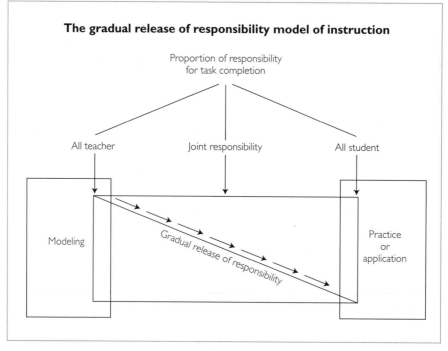

The gradual release of responsibility model of instruction

Proportion of responsibility
for task completion

All teacher   Joint responsibility   All student

Modeling

Gradual release of responsibility

Practice
or
application

FIG. 5–1 Gradual Release of Responsibility

As the model suggests, responsibility rests at first entirely with the teacher. During this period, the teacher models reading by reading books aloud. During the next stage, the teacher and students take joint responsibility for reading. The teacher conducts shared and guided reading sessions, gradually shifting more responsibility to the students. In the third stage, the students assume all responsibility as they do independent reading. The teacher continues to provide minilessons to help students develop the strategies needed to read different genres, but the goal of instruction is for the students to internalize the strategies so that they can read an increasing variety of texts independently.

Providence Schools in Rhode Island (2004) has published *Essential Components of a Balanced Literacy Program* on its website. The features of the program fit well with the Weaver model and gives schools a routine to follow that provides meaningful literacy instruction. The program focuses on three major areas: reading, writing and word study. The framework includes "reading to, with, and by children." In Figure 5–2 we list the Providence essentials with our own adaptations and additions.

Balanced Literacy

Daily Message

This is what we have described previously. Teachers and students work together to script a message, calling attention to concepts of print such as word spacing, capital letters, punctuation, and spelling. Topics for this activity may vary, including classroom news, an upcoming event, the theme being studied, or a summary of new learning.

Interactive Read-Aloud

Drawing on a variety of genres including fiction, nonfiction, poetry, biography, and informational texts, the teacher reads with the students. The teacher models reading, reading strategies, and thinking and questioning. This can include discussion and writing extensions.

Shared Reading

The teacher uses big books, poetry and songs on charts, and class-created books to read, reread, and problem solve together. Overheads and pocket charts can also be used with the students.

Word Work

The teacher provides students with opportunities to build phonemic awareness and phonics by reading poetry, songs, and chants and helping students understand how letters and words work. In upper grades, this time provides opportunities for word study such as finding cognates in texts.

Guided Reading

This includes specific time for the teaching of a reading strategy or skill, center time, and interactive writing.

- *Small-group lessons*—The teacher meets with small groups of students with similar reading needs to work on specific strategies. Students read new books and reread familiar books as the teacher monitors and supports their reading.
- *Literacy centers*—While the teacher works with small groups, other students work in centers with activities that reinforce what they have been learning in read-alouds, shared reading, word work, or guided reading. These may include activities such as buddy reading, reading the room, making books such as alphabet books, working at listening centers, writing in journals, and individual reading from the classroom library.
- *Interactive writing*—The teacher and students compose text together. This Language Experience activity can be scribed by the teacher, or the teacher can share the pen and have students do some writing. This can also include brainstorming connected to content learning, writing letters, writing stories, or writing reports.

Writers Workshop

Teachers support students in the writing process by helping them write in different genres. Teachers can model various stages of the writing process. Students brainstorm, do quickwrites to get ideas on paper, write drafts, read each other's drafts, revise, edit, and sometimes publish. During writers workshop, teachers can work on writing skills through individual conferences or minilessons.

FIG. 5–2 Adaptation of Providence Schools' Essential Components for Balanced Literacy

Balanced Literacy
Independent Reading The teacher provides time for students to read alone or quietly in pairs. Students choose their own books, sometimes with their teacher's guidance. At the end of this time, students may discuss their reading with their partners or share with the whole class.

FIG. 5–2 Adaptation of Providence Schools' Essential Components for Balanced Literacy (*continued*)

Having a meaningful routine is critical, but unless the materials support readers, and especially second language readers, it is difficult to have an effective program. We have developed a checklist to help educators choose books that have features that support beginning readers. Figure 5–3 is a checklist of characteristics of texts that help make written input comprehensible. Books that contain these characteristics provide the extra support beginning readers need to make sense of texts. These features provide scaffolds teachers can use to help students move from dependent to independent reading in two languages.

• Are the materials authentic? Authentic materials are written to inform or entertain, not to teach a grammar point or a letter-sound correspondence.
• Are the materials predictable? • Books are more predictable when students have background knowledge of the concepts, so teachers should activate or build background. • Books are more predictable when they follow certain patterns (repetitive, cumulative) or include certain devices (rhyme, rhythm, alliteration). • Books are more predictable when students are familiar with text structures (beginning, middle, end; main idea, details, examples, etc.). • Books are more predictable when students are familiar with text features (headings, subheadings, maps, labels, graphs, tables, indexes, etc.).
• Is there a good text-picture match? A good match provides nonlinguistic visual cues. Is the placement of the pictures predictable?
• Are the materials interesting and/or imaginative? Interesting, imaginative texts engage students.
• Do the situations and characters in the book represent the experiences and backgrounds of the students in the class? Culturally relevant texts engage students.

FIG. 5–3 Checklist: Characteristics of Texts That Support Reading

Conclusion

One of the most important components of an effective dual language program is meaning-centered literacy instruction. Two views of reading are the word recognition view and the sociopsycholinguistic view. The first holds that reading is a process of recognizing words to get to the meaning of a text. Word identification is accomplished through learning phonics rules and sight words and using structural analysis to unlock longer words. The second view is that readers use their background knowledge and cues from three linguistic cueing systems to construct meaning from a text. The focus of instruction is on helping students develop comprehension strategies for use in independent reading. Although both theories have meaning construction as a goal, only the sociopsycholinguistic model keeps meaning construction as both the means and end result of the reading process.

Even though evaluation of dual language programs is often based on reading test scores, only limited research has been carried out to determine the most effective model for literacy instruction in dual language settings. The balanced literacy approaches used in the schools described by Smith and Arnot-Hopffer (1998) and Pérez (2004) and the Providence Schools balanced literacy program essentials (2004) are most consistent with a sociopsycholinguistic model. All three programs scaffold instruction, gradually releasing responsibility for reading from the teacher to the students.

Research does not provide clear answers to questions about the best language for initial literacy instruction. Some dual language programs teach all students to read and write in their first language and then add second language literacy at second or third grade. Other programs start all students reading in the minority language and then add English literacy at about third grade. Most native English speakers score well on reading tests in English even when their initial instruction is in Spanish. This may be the result of the dominance of English in the U.S. context and the fact that many native English speakers in dual language programs receive support for English literacy from the home even before they begin to receive formal English literacy instruction at school.

What seems important about initial literacy instruction is that it continue long enough for students to develop high levels of proficiency in the language. Pressures from testing have led some schools to transition students into English reading early, even in dual language programs. However, Cummins' (2000) research suggests that students need to develop a certain threshold level of proficiency to gain the benefits of biliteracy. Students who can read and write well in one language transfer their knowledge and skills to reading in a second language. Teachers can facilitate transfer by focusing on similarities between the languages and by adopting similar approaches to teaching reading in the two languages.

In effective dual language schools, teachers keep the focus of instruction on constructing meaning. They provide scaffolded instruction to ensure that written input is comprehensible for all students. In these schools all students can become bilingual and biliterate.

 ## Learning Extensions

1. Consider the reading programs in both languages in your dual language classroom, at your dual language school, or in a dual language school you know. What is the daily routine for literacy instruction and what are the key activities? From this information, do you believe the school takes a word recognition or a sociopsycholinguistic view of reading?

2. Review the dual language literacy programs described at the beginning of the chapter (Success for All in El Paso, Texas; Exito Bilingüe in Tucson, Arizona; and the dual language literacy programs in San Antonio, Texas). What are the strengths of each program and what concerns you about each program? How can those programs inform your own?

3. We discussed balanced literacy in this chapter. Balanced literacy looks different in different places. If your classroom and/or school is taking a balanced literacy approach, is it consistent with a sociopsycholinguistic view? In what ways?

4. One approach to balanced literacy would be to emphasize all three cueing systems equally. At your school, how much instructional time in reading is focused on each of the three systems? What does that tell you about how balanced the program is?

5. In what language or languages is initial literacy instruction taught in your dual language program? What is the rationale for this decision? How is it working?

6. Look at the literacy instruction in both languages at your school. Is the approach to literacy the same for both languages? After reading this chapter, what changes, if any, do you think should be made?

7. A key premise of bilingual education maintains that what is learned in one language transfers to the second language. Even in dual language schools, sometimes English is promoted more strongly than the second language. What is happening at your dual language site? How equally are both languages developed? Does everyone believe that transfer can and will happen?

8. What are some key differences in how initial writing develops in Spanish and English? What are some of the similarities? What is the best way to support beginning writers in a dual language setting?

9. At the end of the chapter we described the Providence program. What activities and routines are the same in your program? Which activities and routines would you like to incorporate in the literacy program in your classroom and school?

Planning Essentials

One of the key curriculum essentials is to teach language through content organized around integrated themes. In this chapter, we explain how teachers in dual language settings can plan for thematic curriculum. We begin by considering essentials for overall planning. Next, we discuss essentials for long- and short-term planning. In our discussion of both long- and short-term planning, we describe in detail a theme that exemplifies effective teaching in a dual language classroom.

Overall Planning Essentials
• Develop a student profile.
• Identify key concepts in the content and language standards.
• Consider how the students will be assessed on the standards.
• Do both long-term and short-term planning.
• Engage students in challenging, theme-based instruction.
• Continually assess, reflect, and adjust instruction.

Backward Planning

Teachers face the challenge of planning meaningful instruction for all of their students. Traditionally, teachers have followed a procedure that might be referred to as forward planning. They start with the established grade-level curriculum and the teacher's guides. Teachers also consider the available materials and resources in each language. For example, third-grade teachers often teach about the solar system, and books, charts, graphs, and science activities are usually available for the solar system unit. With the grade-level expectations and the resources in mind, teachers may begin by planning short units. Teachers who integrate instruction across subjects usually start with one subject, choose a unifying theme, and then decide how to connect other subject areas to the theme. Because there is never enough time, teachers quickly focus on immediate, short-term plans. After all, they have to be ready when the kids come in Monday morning. Forward planning begins with grade-level curriculum expectations and moves toward specific daily plans. What students can do and what they need to learn are not central to a forward-planning model.

Akhavan (2004) writes, "Plan backward from the standard performance (or what students should learn to do and understand) to meet the individual needs of the children. If we don't plan our instruction well, we could end up anywhere" (17). The approach to planning we suggest for dual language classes is based on what several experts in curriculum design refer to as backward planning (Wiggins and McTighe 2000; McTighe and Wiggins 1999; Guskey 2003). The process begins and ends with the students. Teachers carry out formal and informal assessments to develop a class profile. They identify the key concepts in both content and language standards. They consider how the students will be assessed on the standards. They develop long- and short-term plans. They engage students in challenging, theme-based curriculum. As they teach, they continually assess students, reflect, and adjust instruction. The goal is to help students develop the understandings they need to meet the content and language standards. Figure 6–1 illustrates the cyclical nature of backward planning.

Determine What Students Know and Can Do

Akhavan (2004) states that although standards are important, planning must always start with the student. She offers three important reminders: "Teach the child, not the standard. Teach the writer, not the writing. Teach the reader, not the book" (18).

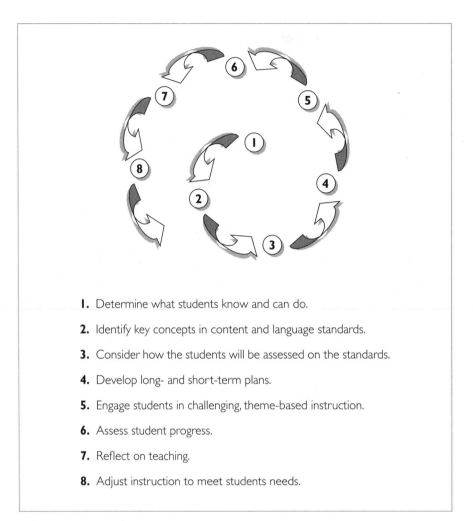

1. Determine what students know and can do.

2. Identify key concepts in content and language standards.

3. Consider how the students will be assessed on the standards.

4. Develop long- and short-term plans.

5. Engage students in challenging, theme-based instruction.

6. Assess student progress.

7. Reflect on teaching.

8. Adjust instruction to meet students needs.

FIG. 6–1 The Planning Cycle

Teachers need to know their students' current level of knowledge and skills. Rather than rely on what all third graders are supposed to have learned, effective teachers review student records and conduct formal and informal assessments to determine what individual students know and have learned. Most teachers have access to required assessment results that they can use for decision making. In addition, teachers can conduct informal assessments. They can ask third graders to read a story and write a summary of it. By observing students as they engage in this activity and by reading the summaries, a teacher can get a great deal of information about each student's current literacy development. Follow-up assessments might include Cloze procedures or miscue analyses. Dual language teachers need to assess both content knowledge and oral and written language proficiency in two languages.

The administrative and teacher team at Runn Elementary used both formal and informal assessments when they were concerned about poor student performance of the ten third-grade students mentioned earlier. They not only looked at standardized test scores but also conducted informal assessments to gather more information that helped them make decisions about the instruction these students needed.

Content and Language Standards

Curriculum should connect to both content and language standards and should be centered on key concepts. As they review the standards for each subject area, teachers identify key concepts and turn them into big questions. For example, in the area of science, a teacher might identify concepts such as plant growth and nutrition and ask questions such as "Where does food come from?" and "What happens to food in your body?" The important thing is for teachers to familiarize themselves with the standards before deciding what concepts each standard requires. Wiggins and McTighe (2000) refers to this process as "unpacking the standards."

Content standards define what the students should learn and be able to do at the end of each grade level. Most schools establish benchmarks that identify the understandings and skills students need to develop for each content area at their grade level. In addition, schools develop performance indicators that describe the level students need to achieve to meet the content standards. It is important for teachers to review both benchmarks and performance standards and consider how students will be assessed before making teaching plans.

In dual language classes, students should meet two sets of standards. First, they need to meet grade-level standards in each content subject area. In addition, since all students are learning or further developing a second language, they also need to meet language standards. The Teachers of English to Speakers of Other Languages (TESOL) organization has developed a useful set of standards that dual language schools can use to gauge the development of students' proficiency in two languages (1997).

The TESOL booklet explains and illustrates the standards clearly. The same standards apply to students at different grade levels, preK–12. The TESOL document states:

> The standards described in this document specify the language competencies ESOL [English to speakers of other languages] students in elementary and secondary schools need to become fully proficient in English, to have unrestricted access to grade-appropriate instruction in challenging academic subjects, and ultimately to lead rich and productive lives. (10)

The document also emphasizes the importance of distinguishing between content and language standards for ESOL learners:

> Content standards do not provide educators the directions and strategies they need to assist ESOL learners to attain these standards because they assume student understanding of and ability to use English to engage with content. Many of the content standards do not acknowledge the central role of language in the achievement of content. (10)

The standards are organized around three goals: (1) use English to communicate in social settings, (2) use English to achieve academically in all content areas, and (3) use English in socially and culturally appropriate ways. The TESOL document uses the term *English*, so these language standards are appropriate for the English language learners in a dual language class. For native English speakers, the same goals and standards apply to the second language. For example, the first goal for native English speakers in a Spanish/English program would be restated as "use Spanish to communicate in social settings."

The goals reflect the importance of students' developing both communicative and academic language and using language that is appropriate to the social context. The TESOL booklet lists descriptors and sample progress indicators for each standard. For example, for Goal 1, Standard 1, "to use English to communicate in social settings," the book lists descriptors such as "sharing and requesting information," "expressing needs, feelings, and ideas," and "using nonverbal communication in social settings." Sample progress indicators include such things as "engage listener's attention verbally or nonverbally" and "elicit information and ask clarification questions" (31).

The book also provides vignettes showing how teachers have put the standards into action in a variety of settings with English language learners. The vignettes are divided into preK–3, 4–8, and 9–12. Following each vignette is a brief discussion that explains how the teacher followed the standard. There is a vignette for each standard at each of the three levels.

A helpful overview chart is included. It lists vignettes for some of the standards at each grade level and outlines the sample progress indicators a teacher would use for students with different levels of English proficiency—beginning, intermediate, advanced, and limited-formal schooling. For example, the second-grade vignette for Goal 1, Standard 2, "to use English to communicate in social settings," describes students in the library selecting books to take home. The chart lists "Ask 'wh' questions about types of books and story lines from peers" for intermediate students. The indicator for advanced students is "Post 'what if' questions to peers and teachers about alternate endings to stories read" (23). It is important for teachers to keep in mind how students will be assessed on language standards as well as on content standards. *ESL Standards for Pre-K–12 Students* is an invaluable resource for language standards. Figure 6–2 lists the TESOL goals and standards.

Goal I—To use English to communicate in social settings

- Standard I— Students will use English to participate in social interactions.
- Standard 2— Students will interact in, through, and with spoken and written English for personal expression and enjoyment.
- Standard 3— Students will use learning strategies to extend their communicative competence.

Goal 2—To use English to achieve academically in all content areas

- Standard I— Students will use English to interact in the classroom.
- Standard 2— Students will use English to obtain, process, construct, and provide subject matter information in spoken and written form.
- Standard 3— Students will use appropriate learning strategies to construct and apply academic knowledge.

Goal 3—To use English in socially and culturally appropriate ways

- Standard I— Students will use appropriate language variety, register, and genre according to audience, purpose, and setting.
- Standard 2— Students will use nonverbal communication appropriate to audience, purpose, and setting.
- Standard 3— Students will use appropriate learning strategies to extend their socio-linguistic and sociocultural competence.

FIG. 6–2 TESOL Goals and Standards

Long-Term and Short-Term Planning

Once teachers have reviewed the language and content standards and decided how to assess student knowledge and skills, the next step in backward planning is to make both long- and short-term plans that will engage students in challenging, theme-based curriculum. Throughout the unit, teachers use both informal and formal assessments to evaluate student progress. They use this information to reflect on their teaching and to adjust their instruction to help students develop deeper understandings of key concepts.

Long-Term and Short-Term Planning Essentials
• Plan collaboratively to ensure a unified approach to curriculum.
• Do both horizontal and vertical planning.
• Develop long-term themes based on big questions.
• Develop short-term units within each theme.

Collaborative Horizontal and Vertical Planning

Both long- and short-term plans are shaped by student needs and content and language standards. In dual language settings, teachers need to plan collaboratively. One of the administrative essentials we discussed earlier was the need to provide time for teachers to plan together. If teachers work in teams with an English-side teacher and a Spanish-side teacher, these two should spend time together on a regular basis to do all their long- and short-term planning.

In addition, grade-level teams can meet to review curriculum within the grade level. This is referred to as horizontal planning because teachers are looking at lessons at the same grade level. Since all the students at each grade must meet the same content standards, it makes sense for teachers to discuss how they plan to help students meet those standards. When teachers meet to share ideas and resources, students benefit. If the materials are limited, teachers might need to decide how to organize to optimize the use of available resources. For example, if all the teachers plan to do a unit on the solar system, they might decide to teach the unit at different times so that each teacher would have access to charts, videos, or books, or they might teach different parts of the unit at different times.

Planning should be vertical as well as horizontal. Teachers from different grade levels should meet several times each year to review the articulation across grade levels. During these meetings, teachers can discuss the ways that content taught in one grade provides the background students need to build on in the next grade. At the same time, teachers can monitor to see if students are developing appropriate content knowledge and literacy skills in each language. These vertical planning meetings serve as important checkpoints to ensure that curriculum is articulated and that students are making the expected progress.

Some districts have developed and published resource books for teachers that reflect effective horizontal and vertical planning. An excellent resource designed specifically for dual language teachers is *Think Themes* (Collier et al. 2002), developed by Chicago teachers for use in prekindergarten through third grade. The guide contains materials and resources for four units: plants, magnets, insects, and simple machines. The opening pages of the resource guide contain graphics showing how each unit is part of a general theme. For example, plants and insects are part of the change theme, and magnets and simple machines are part of the form and function theme.

The description for each unit includes a list of the Chicago content standards and a list of language standards the unit meets. For each language standard, the book also lists student performance indicators. Following this, there are pages that outline a series of activities. Each activity is described, and then materials, strategies, and resources are listed. The following pages in each unit contain blackline masters in English and Spanish that could be used during the activities as well as a series of assessment activities. *Think Themes* is a useful guide for Chicago dual language teachers. Other districts could draw on this resource as they develop their own plans for thematic teaching.

Another helpful resource is a book and software for planning developed by Jacobs (1997). She has written extensively about curriculum mapping, a procedure teachers can use to collect and organize a database of the curriculum in a school or a district. This database contains all of the content, skills, and assessments that the school uses. The maps enable administrators and teachers to examine their curriculum carefully to see what standards are being included and which ones have been left out. It also helps school personnel discover gaps and overlaps in the curriculum. Some standards may be covered several times and others not at all. Atlas, a web-based application, can be used to facilitate curriculum mapping. The website for this useful software can be found at www.rubicon.com.

Long-Term Planning

Working individually, in pairs, or in grade-level teams, teachers make long-term plans to teach integrated, thematic curriculum. After reviewing the standards and identifying key concepts, they develop three or four themes that will serve as the focus of instruction for the year. This approach ensures that students move beyond learning facts and concepts to forming generalizations (Kucer, Silva, and Delgado-Larocco 1995). These generalizations become the basis for big questions that students can investigate. For example, one theme might involve food and health. To answer the question "Why is agriculture important?," students study three interrelated units: plants and seeds; from the field to the table; and nutrition. The questions for these units might be: "How do plants grow from seeds?" "Where does food come from?" and "What is a healthful diet?" When teachers organize around big questions, curriculum becomes a process of investigation in which students learn how the different academic content areas provide the tools to answer important questions. Figure 6–3 is a model for long-term planning.

As Figure 6–3 shows, teachers organize three or four themes each year. Gloria, for example, developed a theme on self-identity. Her big question was "Who

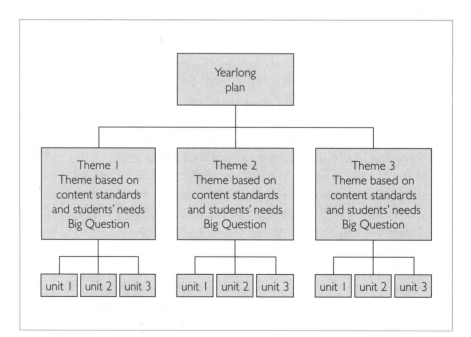

FIG. 6–3 Long-Term Planning

am I?" Gloria then planned three interrelated units designed to explore this big question. During each of these units, students investigated a related big question: "What are my roots?" "Who are the people who have influenced me?" and "What are my goals?" As the theme study progressed, students moved from one related unit to the next. Each unit examined one aspect of the bigger question. Each of these units lasted one to four weeks.

Long-term planning also involves decisions about which content areas to focus on. Some themes lend themselves naturally to science. Others fit better with social studies or language arts. For example, the self-identity theme lends itself to language arts. As teachers make yearlong plans, they should choose themes that fit with different content areas. The first theme might be centered on language arts, the second on science, and the third on social studies. What is important is to balance the content areas, so that each of the academic subjects serves as the primary area of investigation during part of the year.

The subject area most central to a theme serves as a sort of umbrella. Then teachers can decide how to bring in the other subject areas under that umbrella. For instance, if students are studying a theme based on the big question "Who am I?" they would read biographies and autobiographies in language arts and social studies, they would study human development in science, and they would do activities to graph growth during math. Teachers should ensure that all subject areas are integrated into the curriculum even though one content area is primary for a particular theme.

From Long-Term to Short-Term Planning

In this chapter we have explained a process dual language teachers can use to plan integrated, thematic curriculum. The process begins with backward planning, a series of steps that starts and ends with a focus on students and their needs as well as on content and language standards. Teachers then move to long-term planning, often working with others at their grade level and across grade levels. Long-term planning involves identifying themes and developing units. These themes are presented in the form of big questions that students can investigate using tools from the different academic content areas. For each theme, one of the content areas serves as the umbrella. The other content areas are then integrated into the theme study.

From long-term planning, teachers move to short-term planning. They begin by designing units of one to four weeks within each theme. They introduce each unit, organize lessons within the unit, and then conclude the unit with an activity that serves as a transition to the next unit. This model of planning takes into account differences in language proficiency that dual language students have in each language. Lesson plans follow school or district formats. Themes, units, and lessons are all based on both content and language standards.

Figure 6–4 shows the relationship between the long-term planning of a theme that might extend for two to four months and the short-term planning of units within that theme.

Short-Term Planning

Once teachers have carefully developed long-term plans, they move to planning units and individual lessons. Each theme is divided into units of study that last from one to four weeks. Figure 6–5 provides a close-up view of the structure for units.

Teachers begin the unit with an introductory activity. For example, for a unit on plant growth, Sandra had her students ask parents, all of whom worked in agriculture, to contribute seeds for the study. The parents labeled the seeds and answered interview questions about the seeds, such as When is it planted? What kind of care does the plant need? When is it harvested? and What products come from the plant? This activity drew on the backgrounds of students and parents and involved all the parents in the unit study. The seeds the students brought in then served as materials that they used in subsequent activities.

The introductory activity is followed by a series of lessons in each language. The format for individual lessons is usually prescribed by the school or district. In a dual language setting, lesson plans must take into account the fact that about half the class is studying in a second language. Lessons should be based on standards and have both content and language objectives. They should be interrelated across subject areas. In planning their lessons, teachers should follow the curriculum essentials we described in previous chapters, keeping these guidelines in mind:

- ◆ Assess students' background knowledge in the subject area to be studied.
- ◆ Draw on this background knowledge by having students work with and learn from one another.
- ◆ Select the academic concepts and skills to be taught in each lesson.
- ◆ Select the language skills to be developed through the lessons.
- ◆ Help students connect what they are learning in school with their experiences outside school.
- ◆ Organize lessons so that all students can participate actively, even when their language proficiency is limited.

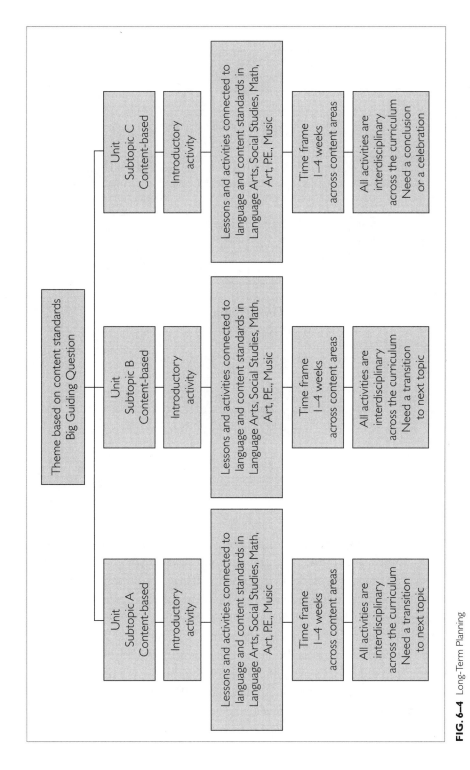

FIG. 6–4 Long-Term Planning

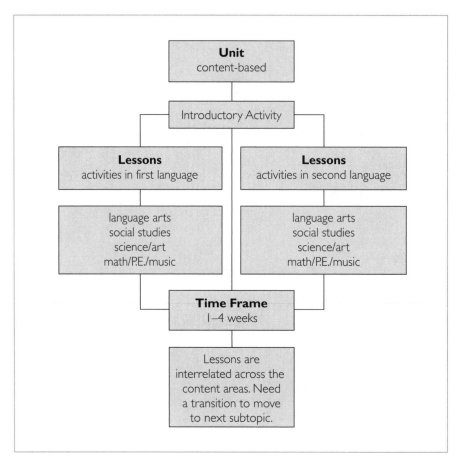

FIG. 6–5 Short-Term Planning

The final activity in each unit serves two purposes. It brings closure to the unit, and it provides a transition to the next unit. Teachers might conclude by reading a book, engaging students in a science activity, or having students do an art activity. For example, students who complete a unit on plants and seeds could dramatize the book *Just One Seed/Una semilla nada más* (Ada 1990a, 1990b), they could present the results of a science project on how plants absorb water, or they could create a classroom art gallery to display their collages made of different leaves and stems of plants. The book could serve as a transition from plant growth to products that come from plants. At the end of *Just One Seed/Una semilla nada más*, all the products of a sunflower are listed. Students then could read *The Tortilla Factory/La tortillería* (Paulsen 1995a, 1995b), a cycle book that describes and beautifully illustrates how people till the earth, plant corn seeds, harvest corn, grind corn to make dough, make tortillas from the dough, and eat the tortillas for strength to plant more seeds. This book illustrates the products that come from corn seeds.

The final activity provides the teacher with an opportunity for informal assessment of student learning. It also serves as the springboard for introducing the next unit. Students should see clear connections among the units in each theme. The closing activity for the last unit in a theme should help students make generalizations about the concepts they have learned, and it should help them celebrate their learning. The celebration might involve a presentation of student work for other classes or for parents.

Long-Term and Short-Term Planning—María

María teaches second grade in a 50/50 dual language program in a small city in central California. One theme that the second-grade teachers at María's school selected was community. They chose What makes a community? as the big question that would guide their study. During a meeting with teachers of other grade levels, the second-grade teachers reviewed what students had learned about community during first grade and what they would study in third grade. By teaching about community, the second-grade teachers could meet several of the content standards for social studies, so the teachers used social studies as the umbrella content area for the units within this theme. María developed three units for this theme: diversity in community, the place where we live, and citizens of today. Figure 6–6 shows her plan for the theme, including the topics for each unit.

Through this theme study, María hoped to increase her students' understanding of community. Her goals included having students compare aspects of familiar communities with characteristics of communities in other cultures and at other times. Students would also examine relationships among ways of living, the physical environment, and traditions. They would be introduced to problems confronting communities and explore possible solutions. Students would also gain understanding about citizenship and the lives of families and children in different settings.

María began her planning by identifying the knowledge and skills students would develop during the study of community that she would assess formally and informally during each of the units of study. By the time they finished this

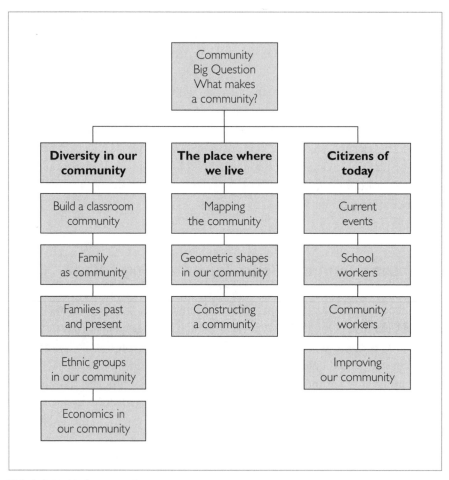

FIG. 6–6 María's Community Plan

theme study, María expected that her students would understand what makes a community. They would be able to identify the kinds of people who reside in a community, where they live, why they are important, how they contribute to the community, and how communities grow or cease to exist. María also wanted her students to be able to discuss in depth the idea of community and the impact community has in shaping character. At the end of the study, she hoped students would be able to present the idea of community by describing a community's customs, its physical environment, and its human traditions.

In the following sections we describe each unit of the community theme in detail. We include a description of the lessons, the content and language standards that the lessons meet, and the assessments María used. We refer to literature in Spanish and English that María read, but beyond that we don't specify the language of instruction for each lesson or set of lessons because we realize that teachers wishing to use any of these ideas would need to adapt them to fit the dual language model their school is implementing, whether it be 90/10, 50/50 by time, 50/50 by content area, or any of the many possible variations on these basic models. The resources and children's literature titles mentioned in this discussion are listed in Figure 6–7, shown on page 202.

Diversity in Our Community

The first unit in María's community theme was designed to increase students' awareness of the different groups that live in the school's predominantly Latino community. Students would explore the strengths of each group and how each group enriches the larger community. She had read Banks (1989) and hoped to move beyond the Contributions Approach, where the focus is only on heroes, holidays, and a sharing of cultural artifacts. In addition, María realized that before they could investigate the different groups within the community, students needed to begin to develop the concept of community.

Building a classroom community ◆ María planned an introductory activity that would help her students understand that people form communities so that they can work together toward common goals. To begin the unit, she divided the class into groups of five. She gave each group a bag that contained a variety of items used in school, such as a ruler, a box of crayons, a book, and a pencil. All the bags had the same kinds of items. She then asked which group could join the objects together to make the longest chain. The challenge was to accomplish this without talking to one another.

The umbrella content area for this theme was social studies. As they worked together, students began to form an important social studies concept: community. In addition, they began to recognize the importance of helping each other and using communication for common, productive action. Since the students were not allowed to talk, they had to find other means of communication. This introductory activity also met several math standards. For example, students had to estimate whether an object was longer in one position than in another. The members of each group had to measure their complete chain of objects to compare theirs with the results of other groups.

After the students completed the activity, María discussed with them what helped them work together and what hindered them. Students began to understand that communities are made up of groups of people who can work together productively. To help students connect the activity to the concept of building community, she read limited-text books in Spanish for discussion. Some books were about children in school working together to make friends, including *Para algo son los amigos* (*That's What Friends Are For*) (Canetti 1997) and *El primer día de clase* (*The First Day of School*) (McVeity 1997), and she read *El dólar* (Zimelman 2000), about a child solving the problem of sharing his one dollar with friends. During English instruction she read similar books about friends and cooperation at school, like *The First Day of School* (Parkes 2004) and *We Can Be Helpers* (Almada 2004b).

In communities, people play different roles. María asked her students to look at their chains of objects and to think about how each person in a community is like one of the objects in the chain. Each one is different, but each plays a role and contributes to the entire community. If one object is removed from the chain, the community must be reformed, but in the process it shrinks.

To help students understand how one individual, working with others and drawing on other members of the community, can create positive change, María read *Making a Difference* (Almada 2004a). This story tells how children who wanted to skate or use skateboards gathered support to have the city build a specific place for skating. The book shows children moving to Bank's Level 4, the Social Action Approach, where they take action to change something in their community (Banks 1989).

At the end of the activity, María gave the students an overview of the unit, and she asked them to brainstorm some of the different communities they were part of. Students realized they were part of a local community, a school community, and a family. Some students were also part of a religious community. Others were members of a sports team.

Family as community ◆ The next area that students studied in the diversity unit focused on family as community. María wanted her students to extend their concept of community to include family as a particular type of community. To transition to this next series of lessons, María read parts of the book *In My Family: En mi familia* by Carmen Lomas Garza (1996) in English during English time and other parts in Spanish during Spanish time. The author of this bilingual book recounts familiar events of Latinos growing up in Texas. She tells of cleaning *nopales* (cacti), coloring Easter eggs, bringing in the *curandera* (healer), and having backyard barbeques. Garza accompanies the short reflections with beautiful illustrations. María knew that her students would connect with this culturally relevant book since many of the activities described were ones students had experienced with their immediate and extended families. She used this book and others such as *Los padres* (*Parents*) (Vendrell and Parramón 1987), *Los abuelos* (*Grandparents*) (Vendrell and Parramón 1987), *Con mi familia* (*With My Family*) (Romero 1996), *¡Qué semana, Luchito!* (*What a Week, Luchito!*) (Cumpiano 1991), *Room for One More* (Jacobs 2004), *Let's Eat* (Zamorano 1996), and *My Very Own Room: Mi propio cuartito* (Pérez 2000)—all books about families living and working together and supporting each other—to help students think about how a family forms a community. She had students work in groups to complete Venn diagrams that compared characteristics of a family with the ideas about community they had previously discussed.

María also used these books to introduce an interview activity. She gave students a questionnaire that they would use to interview family members. Students would use data from the interview to write a family history paper. Students asked family members about their past experiences and their own family memories and also collected photographs and special objects the family had kept over time.

After conducting the interviews, students discussed interesting discoveries that they had made and shared pictures and artifacts. They talked about the places where their parents and grandparents had lived. They also talked about differences between how their families live now and how they had lived in the past. María read them the limited-text book *Hoy y hace cien años* (Reynoldson and Shuter 1993), which shows homes and places in schools today and a hundred years ago. The English version of the book, *Today and One Hundred Years Ago* (Reynoldson and Shuter 1991), was also available in the room. This reading and class discussion helped students clarify ideas for their writing assignment. Writing their family histories took several days. The students wrote drafts, conferred, revised, and edited, going through all the stages of the writing process.

These activities met several content standards. These included two social studies standards: "Students will trace the history of the family through the use of primary and secondary sources including artifacts, photographs and interviews," and "Students will compare and contrast their daily lives with those of their parents and grandparents." The lessons also met several TESOL language standards. As they interacted nonverbally in the opening activity, they met the following standard: "Students will use nonverbal communication appropriate to audience, purpose, and setting." During the brainstorming, they "use[d] English (or Spanish) to interact in the classroom." And as they completed the Venn diagram, they "use[d] English (or Spanish) to obtain, process, construct, and provide subject matter information in spoken and written form." María informally assessed her students' writing as she met with them one-on-one to edit their papers. She also used a rubric to grade the final pieces after the students had published them.

For the next assignment in this unit, María first paired each student with a classmate. She asked the students to share their papers and what they had learned about their families as communities and about their heritage. This activity helped students develop oral language and helped them start to think about differences within families and communities.

Families past and present ◆ After the family history sharing time, the students went to the computer lab to do a Web quest. With the help of the teacher and the computer lab assistant, they were guided to specific websites that allowed them to explore the communities where their families had originated. They collected information to compare and contrast those communities with the community where they lived now. For students from Mexico, a key resource site was one developed by the Universidad de Guadalajara (http://mexico.udg.mx), which included information about the history, geography, economy, art, and politics of different parts of the country. Since the website is in Spanish, this was an excellent resource for reading in Spanish. For this assignment, María asked students to answer three questions: (1) How did people in communities in the past take care of one another? (2) Who were key members of these communities? and (3) What did community members do?

Once the students found this information, they divided into groups to create Venn diagrams that compared and contrasted the early communities of students from different groups. Since María's dual language class was made up primarily of students from Anglo and Mexican backgrounds, this exercise allowed students to compare and contrast traditional urban and rural communities in the United States and Mexico. The groups presented their completed diagrams to the class.

This lesson built on the previous lessons in the unit and helped students further expand their concept of community. The lesson met the following social studies standard: "Students will compare and contrast their daily lives with those of their parents, grandparents, or guardians." It also met two TESOL language standards. As they shared their family histories, students "use[d] English (or Spanish) to interact in the classroom," and in completing the Web quest and constructing the Venn diagrams, students "use[d] English (or Spanish) to obtain, process, construct, and provide subject matter information in spoken and written form." In addition, they "use[d] appropriate learning strategies to construct and apply academic knowledge."

María assessed the students informally by observing and taking anecdotal records as they engaged in oral discussion in groups. She also assessed students' ability to work in a group. In addition, she used the Venn diagram each group presented to the class and the students' individual Web quest printouts for more formal assessments of their development of concepts and skills.

Ethnic groups in our community ◆ The next lessons engaged students in studying the different groups in their own community. Besides students native to the United States and to Mexico, María had students in her dual language class from El Salvador, Laos, and China. One student's ancestors were Native Americans. Students used the information they had already gathered to begin this investigation. María invited volunteers to read their family histories to the class. As the students read, María pointed out characteristics common to a specific group. Working with the students, María placed these ideas on a T-chart. On one side of the chart, she listed the name of the ethnic group, and on the other side, she listed common characteristics taken from the student papers. She then led the students in a discussion about the variety of ethnic groups represented in their classroom community. They also talked about how the variety of groups in their classroom community mirrored the variety of groups in their city.

As a follow-up to this activity, María introduced the concept of graphing and showed students some different types of graphs. She modeled how to read each of these graphs. One type was a bar graph. María showed the students how they could create a bar graph with one column for each ethnic group represented in their classroom community. Next, she gave each student a Post-it. Students came up and placed their Post-its on the bar graph to create columns that showed how many members of each ethnic community were in the class. Students counted the Post-its in each column and discussed which groups had the greatest representation and which groups had the least.

During English time, María read to her students *Our Journey* (García and García 2004), the story of a migrant family, now living in Texas, who had lived in many other parts of the United States. This family history included a time line. As a homework assignment, María asked her students to work with their parents to each make a time line that would show the major events in their family history. She sent home packets with instructions in both Spanish and English along with construction paper, scissors, and crayons for families to use to make their time lines. Time lines are another kind of graph. María wanted to help her students understand that there are different ways to present information, and the family history papers and the family time lines were two ways to represent what they had learned about their families.

The next day, María divided students into small groups so that they could compare their time lines. As students worked together, María circulated around the room, giving extra assistance to students who needed more help with their time lines. After the students shared, they posted their time lines on bulletin boards around the room. Then María provided time for the students to walk around the room to observe and appreciate the work done by classmates. The students enjoyed reading the details from their classmates' time lines.

This series of lessons within the unit addressed one of the social studies standards: "Students will place important events in their lives in the order in which they occur." It also met language arts standards because it involved students in speaking and listening to solve problems as they worked in groups. In addition, the time line lesson met a math standard: "Students will collect numerical data and record, organize, display and interpret the data on bar graphs and other representations." María was careful to note in her plans the different content standards she was addressing during the unit. These units met two TESOL language standards of Goal 2, "To use English (or Spanish) to achieve academically in all content areas." For example, by reading their family histories to the class, students "use[d] English (or Spanish) to interact in the classroom"; as they completed the T-chart, the graphing activity, and the time lines, they "use[d] English (or Spanish) to obtain, process, construct, and provide subject matter information in spoken and written form." In addition, during all their interviews, oral presentations, and group work, students met the first standard of Goal 3, "To use English (or Spanish) in socially and culturally appropriate ways" because they "use[d] appropriate language variety, register, and genre according to audience, purpose, and setting."

María assessed her students in a number of ways during these lessons. She took anecdotal notes as students presented their family histories to the class. She also observed their participation as they created the bar graph. María discussed with the students a rubric she would use to evaluate their time lines. She knew that if she made her expectations clear, students would produce better work. Then she applied the rubric to each student's finished project.

Economics in our community ◆ The end of one unit in a theme should serve as a transition to the next unit. María planned the next series of lessons to develop concepts of money and calculation. First, she reminded the students that in their community, school, and homes, there were diverse people. She then read *Una ciudad, una escuela, muchas comidas,* which also comes in the English version *One City, One School, Many Foods* (Palacios 1997b, 1997a). The class discussed the foods the children from different backgrounds ate at home. María brought magazines to the class and had students work in groups to find pictures of all kinds of different foods. She also asked students to look for pictures of the ingredients in those foods. For example, if students found a picture of tacos, they also looked for a picture of corn, tomatoes, and lettuce. Students cut out their pictures. María also contributed pictures she had gathered.

The students grouped the pictures into collages so that different dishes, such as spaghetti, were placed with their ingredients, like pasta, tomatoes, onions, and garlic. Then everyone put the collages up around the room. Students walked around the room to look closely at each cluster of pictures. Then María called all of them to the first cluster and asked them to describe each dish and its ingredients, and together the teacher and students labeled them.

Next, María asked each group to decide how much the food in one of the picture clusters might be worth. She brought in grocery store ads that students could refer to. Students discussed with one another the value of the ingredients in a dish of spaghetti or a bowl of soup. Then they attached prices on Post-its to the pictures to show the cost of each item.

María wanted to help her students develop concepts about money, including how coins and bills represent different values. She read them *The Story of Money* (Ward 2004b) and students discussed it. The book shows pictures of money from different countries, including Mexico. María brought in some bills and coins from Mexico, and she and the students converted the value of the Mexican money into U.S. dollars and cents.

To continue with money and math, María next divided students into groups and gave each student some play money. She organized an activity in which students exchanged money. The goal was to trade coins and bills and still keep the same total amount. Students learned that they could swap five one-dollar bills for a five dollar bill or ten pennies for a dime. Students enjoyed playing with the money and started to develop some important math concepts. As a final activity for the day, María put students in bilingual pairs and each pair decided which foods around the room they wanted and then they "bought" that food with their play money.

These final lessons in the unit introduced concepts from an additional social studies standard: "Students will understand the role and interdependence of buyers (consumers) and sellers (producers) of goods and services." These lessons addressed a math standard: "Students will model and solve problems by representing, adding and subtracting amounts of money." The lessons met language arts standards because they involved students in speaking and listening as well as in writing. In addition, the activities met a visual arts standard through the making of the collages: "Students will apply artistic processes and skills, using a variety of media to communicate meaning and intent in original works of art."

The lessons met TESOL language standards as well as content standards. For example, as they created and displayed their collages, students "use[d] appropriate learning strategies to construct and apply academic knowledge." Throughout the unit, María organized activities that helped all her students develop strategies for obtaining and presenting academic information. The money exchange activity gave students the chance to "use English (or Spanish) to interact in the classroom" and to "use appropriate language variety, register, and genre according to audience, purpose, and setting."

María assessed students both informally and formally during this series of lessons. She took anecdotal records as students worked on their collages and traded money. To further help them develop the concepts of money, she and the students read together from a big book, class collection of readings, *Golden Opportunities* (Rigby 2004). This book contains readings about free enterprise, stories of children starting small businesses, and wise buying tips. In addition, María read *But I Want It!* (Washington 2004), another book on wise buying. María then asked students to construct a menu for a restaurant of their choice. Working in bilingual pairs, students discussed what kind of food they wanted to serve, where the restaurant would be located, and why they thought the restaurant would be successful. They considered who would probably come to the restaurant and how much their customers could afford. Though their knowledge of economics was limited, this gave students an opportunity to begin to consider the value of money and products.

We have specified the TESOL language standards that students met during the different activities in this unit. María focused on Goal 2, the development of academic language. She ensured that all three standards were met, including the use of appropriate learning strategies. Although her emphasis was on academic language development, María also planned activities that helped students develop social language. In her planning, María noted the content and language standards each lesson or series of lessons met. In this way, she could show that she was providing the standards-based instruction the district required.

As we describe the other two units in this theme, we continue to list the content standards each series of lessons met. However, we do not include the language standards because we think that the examples in this first unit demonstrate how teachers can meet the language standards. It is important, though, for teachers to keep in mind both content and language standards as they plan, remembering that there are always second language learners in a dual language classroom and that the same language standards apply for the non-English language as well as for English.

The Place Where We Live

María used another book to transition to the next unit in her theme on community. In this unit, she wanted to focus on the location of communities and of important places within a community. She began by doing a shared reading of *Somewhere in the Universe* (Drew 1997), a predictable big book. Each page asks students to find a specific location within an area, starting with the universe and moving to the Milky Way galaxy, planet Earth, the United States, particular states and towns, all the way to Jason's house. After the interactive reading, María showed students the page with the United States and asked them to find their state. Then she helped students see where their town was located. She next read to the students *Siguiendo direcciones* (Boyle 1993c). The English version, *Following Directions* (Boyle 1991b), was also available. She pointed out to the students the picture of the compass rose on the maps on each page and asked them to use the compass rose on the large map to find the different directions. Students decided their state was in the southwest part of the United States.

After this, María asked students to find the names of the countries and towns their families had come from. Students looked back at their family histories to locate the information. Once they had this information, students were ready for the next activity. María gathered all the students and held up a Styrofoam ball. "Who knows what this is?" María asked.

Students answered, "It's a ball."

María showed the students the page from *Somewhere in the Universe* that shows Earth as a globe, and she explained that they would make their own globes using Styrofoam balls.

Looking at the page from the book and two globes María had brought in, students worked in pairs to cut colored paper into the shapes of the continents and pin the continents on their globes. They labeled each continent and also labeled the oceans. Finally, working together and with their teacher's help, the students put pushpins in the globes to represent the places their families had come from. Students proudly displayed their final art projects around the room.

Mapping the community ◆ María read *La ciudad* (*The City*) (Rius and Parramón 1986). This is a story about two girls who use a map as they tour a city. They observe people and places, such as a busy street, a park, a movie theatre, and a church. As a homework assignment, María asked students to walk around their own neighborhood with a friend, parent, or other family member and write down the names of streets and notice the locations of interesting or important buildings and places. The next day, students shared with the class what they had observed on their walks as María listed what they said.

Then María read *Mirando mapas* (Boyle 1993b), which shows map drawings of neighborhoods and a small city. The English version, *Looking at Maps* (Boyle 1991c), was also available. María also showed the class some different maps of cities and towns, including the one in *Somewhere in the Universe* (Drew 1997), which has a simple grid drawing of a neighborhood with a key to the locations. Students then divided themselves into groups according to where they lived. María gave each group a small book version of *Somewhere in the Universe* and a large piece of butcher paper. Referring to the sample map in the little book, students worked to make maps of their neighborhood areas, drawing in the streets and labeling key places such as restaurants, doctors' offices, post offices, and parks. Each map included a key. When the students were finished, each group posted its map on the bulletin board.

These introductory activities met parts of several social studies standards: "Students will locate on a map where their ancestors live(d), telling when the family moved to the local community and how and why they made the trip," "Students will label a map of the North American continent, including countries, oceans, major rivers and mountains," "Students will identify the essential map elements: title, legend, directional indicator and date," and "Students will locate in a simple letter-number grid system the specific locations and geographic features of their neighborhood or community." The activities also met language arts standards involving listening and speaking, giving and following directions, and responding appropriately to oral communication.

María continued to assess her students' language development and content knowledge informally by taking notes as they worked in groups. She also used the Styrofoam globe and the neighborhood grid projects to measure students' understanding of concepts and development of new skills in social studies. In the next activity, María brought in several math concepts.

Geometric shapes in our community ◆ To introduce geometric figures, María read two books, *Las figuras geométricas* (*Geometric Figures*) (Flores, Castro, and Hernández 1993) and *Ruedas y más ruedas* (*Wheels and More Wheels*) (Espinosa 1997), which reinforced the idea that there are geometrical shapes in the environment. She put large colored geometric shapes up on the whiteboard. She asked students to look at the shapes and think of something each shape reminded them of. Juan said that the triangle reminded him of an upside-down ice-cream cone. As the students shared their ideas, María checked that they knew the names of the different geometric shapes.

To connect this activity with the unit of study, María asked students to talk in pairs about where they had seen shapes like these as they walked through their neighborhoods. Students quickly realized that these shapes were everywhere on the road signs. At this point, María read *¡Puedo leer dondequiera!* (*I Can Read Everywhere!*) (Avalos 1991), a big book showing several pages of different signs in a community. She next showed the students two big posters with road signs, one she had requested from the local motor vehicle department and another labeled *Letreros* (*Signs*) (Ives 1997). Students identified the shape of each sign. The yield sign, livestock crossing, and men working signs, for example, were triangles, the railroad crossing sign was a circle, and the hospital sign was a square. Since many signs showed symbols, but not words, María wrote the names of the shapes and the meanings of the signs on the board. Then María divided students into groups and gave each group a bag with cutouts of the geometric shapes. Students worked together to label each shape with an appropriate road sign. Each student chose one sign, held it up, and explained to the class the shape and the kind of sign it was.

To further connect the idea of geometric shapes with community, María read three books that helped students think about the shapes of buildings and important structures such as the pyramids: *Dallas Shapes Up* (Hirsch 2004), *Shapes Around the World* (Ward 2004a), and *Los edificios de Nueva York* (*The Buildings of New York*) (Mace 1997).

The work with geometric shapes addressed one of the second-grade math standards: "Students will describe and classify plane and solid geometric shapes (e.g., circle, triangle, square, rectangle and polygon, cube, sphere, rectangular prism) according to the number and shape of faces, edges and vertices." It also met language arts standards: "Students will interpret information from diagrams, charts, and graphs" and "Students will organize presentations to maintain a clear focus." The activity also met a visual arts standard: "Students will apply artistic processes and skills, using a variety of media to communicate meaning and intent in original works of art." María informally assessed her second graders as they interacted with one another and gave their brief oral presentations. Her formal assessment was based on how well students could label the geometric shapes as they made their signs.

Constructing a community ◆ María planned a culminating activity for this unit that involved parents. She had students write notes to their parents asking them to save old cans, cartons, and other items, including Popsicle sticks. During several weeks, with reminders, students brought in clean, used containers from home. María arranged for several parent volunteers to come in during afternoons over the three days needed to complete the project.

On the first day of the project, María divided her class into groups of four with one parent volunteer as a group leader. As much as possible, each group consisted of students and a parent from the same neighborhood. María gave each group a set of materials and written instructions. Then she explained to the students what they were to do. They would construct a model of their neighborhood. She showed them a model of her own neighborhood that she had created. She asked the groups to look at the materials they had and decide how to use them to complete the project.

The construction involved students in cutting out model buildings from boxes and other cardboard and using other materials to represent their neighborhood. María reminded them of the signs they had made earlier. Students included the signs in the models they made. The construction took three afternoons to complete. Students had to find different ways to measure materials to create buildings and public areas that were roughly to scale. As the students and parents worked together, María circulated around the room and offered help. When all the groups had finished, they displayed their models on tables around the room. Then they invited the other second-grade classes to come and tour their room. As students from the other classes looked at the models, students from each group explained all the parts of the neighborhood community they had constructed.

This project met several content standards. It expanded on the social studies standard: "Students will demonstrate map skills by describing the absolute and relative location of people, places and environments." It met three language arts standards: "Students will paraphrase information that has been shared orally by others," "Students will follow two-step written instructions," and "Students will report on a topic with supportive facts and details." It also met a visual arts standards: "Students will apply artistic processes and skills, using a variety of media to communicate meaning and intent in original works of art." María informally assessed the students during their class discussion, their group work, and the oral presentations of the projects. She also formally assessed them with a rubric to evaluate the students' knowledge, understanding of new concepts, and development of skills as shown by the completed models.

Citizens of Today

Current events ◆ The third unit of the community theme built on the first two and expanded students' understanding of community. María distributed copies of the local newspaper to students sitting in small groups. They leafed through the pages and discussed what they noticed. Then she asked students how newspapers were different from big books and how they were the same. During Spanish time the students also looked at newspapers published in Spanish and read the book *El periódico* (*The Newspaper*) (Solano-Flores 1987).

As students volunteered answers, María wrote them on a Venn diagram on the board. Students noticed that newspapers and big books are about the same size and shape but that newspapers usually have more pages. They also pointed out that newspapers are divided into sections. María asked them to decide what each section in their papers contained. They listed these section headings on the board. Students also observed that the headlines in newspapers are like the titles of books because both use big fonts. One difference they noticed is that some newspaper stories start on one page and continue on a later page with other things in between. Also, there were many stories in the newspaper and usually only one in a big book. On the other hand, both the newspaper and a big book had a table of contents.

After this introductory activity designed to familiarize students with newspapers, María drew a chart with three columns on the board. She wrote the headings "International," "National," and "Local" over the columns. Then she asked students what they thought each of these words meant. After they discussed the labels, María pointed to a story on the front page of her newspaper about a United Nations meeting in Brussels. She asked the students whether they thought this article was about an international, national, or local event. The students recognized that this meeting was international. María then went on to show how other stories were about national or local events. She pointed out that many of the international and national events were in the front section, and most of the local events were in the second section. She wrote "UN meeting" under the first column on the board and headlines for the national and local articles under the next two columns.

Next, she asked students to work in pairs to locate three or four articles for each column. She gave each pair a three-column chart and asked them to fill in headlines for the articles following the model on the board. As the students worked, María circulated around the room to help pairs who were having difficulty placing articles on their charts. When all the students had completed their charts, María asked them to look again at the chart on the board. She called on the pairs one at a time to come up to the board and add one item to one of the columns. After students added an item, their classmastes discussed whether they agreed that it was in the right column. By the time each pair had added one event, the chart was full.

María collected the individual charts and then engaged the students in a math exercise. She asked students, working in pairs, to count the number of events in each column and then use the graph paper she handed out to represent the events as a bar graph. Once students completed their graphs, María asked them questions using key mathematical vocabulary: *more than* and *fewer than*. Students concluded that there were more local and national events than international events in their paper and fewer international events than national events.

María then put a transparency of one article on the overhead projector. First, she read the article to the students. Then she led them through an analysis by asking the key questions Who? What? When? Where? and Why? She underlined the parts of the article that answered each question. Then she asked students to choose an article and identify the parts that answered each of the five questions. When the students completed this task, she asked them to write short summaries of the articles they had read, using the key information they had identified and trying to say it in their own words. Students helped one another to complete this writing assignment.

Next, María asked the students to look at the headlines of the articles they had listed under the heading "National." She asked students to pick out articles that had anything to do with the government and make a list of names and roles that were listed in those articles. For example, students found the president and different senators named. María then read *Working for the Government* (Crum 2004), which describes how the United States government works and who the key players in the government are. Students talked about how those who work in the national government are a community that serves the whole country.

Analyzing the kinds of articles in a newspaper, identifying the parts of an article, identifying articles about the government, and writing a summary increased students' awareness of the kinds of events that occur in different communities locally, nationally, and internationally and their awareness of the roles different people play in these communities. The students started to understand the similarities and differences among communities. This lesson built the knowledge students needed to meet social studies standards related to governmental institutions and practices in the United States and other countries. It also met two math standards: "Students will represent the same data in more than one way" and "Students will identify features of a data set." In addition, the activity met the language arts standard "Students will use titles, table of contents and headings to locate information in expository texts." María used the three-column chart as a summative assessment tool. Students demonstrated their understanding of the concepts of international, national, and local communities. She also used their summaries of the articles to assess their developing reading and writing abilities.

School workers ◆ To help students begin to understand the roles different members play in a community, María involved her students in a variety of activities. First, she reminded the students of the story she had read earlier, *Making a Difference* (Alamada 2004a), in which the main character and his friends talked to several community members, including the librarian, the park keeper, his parents, city council members, and a reporter, to accomplish what they wanted, the creation of a skate park. She had the students get together with their bilingual partners. Then María gave each pair a slip of paper with the name of a part of the community and two characters. For example, for the home, the characters were a mother and child talking at bedtime; for the school, a child and a teacher in the hall; for the local community, a customer and a clerk in a store; and for the hospital, a nurse and a patient. She told the students that they would create dialogue and develop short skits that would show how these characters interact in each community setting.

To help the students, María led the class in a language experience activity. She wrote the word *home* on a piece of butcher paper and then listed two characters, a brother and a sister. She asked students to think about what these characters might say to one another. As students volunteered ideas, she wrote the dialogue on the chart paper. When they finished, she asked two students to read back the parts. Then she gave students time to work in their pairs to create their own short skits. As students worked, María circulated around the room and helped pairs who were having trouble writing their skits.

When all the students had finished, each pair presented its dialogue. After each skit, the students and María briefly discussed what kind of community this was and how people acted in this community. María then posed several questions for class discussion: What is a community? What do people in a community do? What does a good community look like? After this discussion, María gave each student three Post-it Notes. María tacked up a piece of butcher paper with the word *Community* written in the middle. Then she asked students to think back over the skits, the class reading, and the discussion and write down one thing a community member does on each Post-it. She called on students to come up and place their Post-its on the butcher paper. As they put up their Post-its, students explained what they had written. For example, one student wrote, "Nurses help sick people." After this, María asked the students to look at all the Post-its on the chart. With María's help the students clustered together Post-its that reflected similar activities. This lesson helped students summarize the information they had been learning. At the end of this clustering activity, María asked the students, "What do all these communities we have studied have in common?" She told students to think about this question and make a list of ideas to share the next day in class.

By having students perform and analyze their skits, María addressed some theatre standards: "Students will perform in group improvisational theatrical games that develop cooperative skills and concentration," "Students will use improvisation to portray such concepts as friendship or hunger," and "Students will identify the message or moral of a work of theater."

María used her observations of students during the class discussion time and the short skits as an initial assessment. She wanted to know answers to the following questions: Do students clearly understand what a community is? Are they able to see the connection between this new information and what they have been learning throughout these two units? María also used the students' Post-it Note contributions to the Community chart as an informal summative assessment.

When teachers organize curriculum around themes, students get involved. One of María's students, Susan, told her she had a book about community. The next day Susan brought in *First Day, Hooray!* (Poydar 2000) for María to read. The students gathered on the rug for the read-aloud. *First Day, Hooray!* tells how different school employees get ready for the first day of school. María used the book to help students begin to think about their school community. After reading the book, María asked her students to brainstorm a list of all the people who worked at their school and what each one did. As the students gave ideas, María wrote them on butcher paper. She listed each employee and that person's duties. During Spanish time, she read *La clase* (Sánchez and Bordoy 1991), which describes how different members of the classroom community interact.

Then María told her students they were going to take a short field trip. They were going to take a walking trip around the school to see where the different people worked. She also explained that she would bring a digital camera and students could help her take pictures of people in the places where they worked. The students enjoyed their field trip. They visited the library, the main office, the cafeteria, the custodian's room, and the area where the buses were kept. At each stop, they took pictures of the people and places.

When the students returned to their classroom, María read *En mi escuela* (Boyle 1993a) (English version: *Around My School* [Boyle 1991a]), which describes areas in a school. Next, she showed them a map of their school that she had enlarged. She asked students to label some of the areas on the map. Students began by identifying their classroom and the classrooms near them. They put the teacher's name and the grade level for each room. They also found the library, office, cafeteria, resource room, gym, and custodian's area on the map. This activity helped students understand more about the physical aspects of their school community.

Next María suggested that the class invite some of the school employees to come and tell them more about their jobs. The students liked this idea, so María explained that they should write some letters of invitation. She modeled a letter by writing on the whiteboard as students gave ideas. She asked the students how the letter should start, what should go next, and how the letter should end. Once the class letter was completed, María divided the students into groups and asked each group to compose a letter to one of the people on their brainstorming list. She collected the finished letters and told the students she would deliver them that afternoon.

The next day the children were excited as they eagerly awaited the guest speakers. One of the school custodians, the vice principal, the school nurse, one of the secretaries, the librarian, and a cafeteria worker all made their appearance one by one and gave ten-minute talks about what they did for the school. The students listened attentively. After each presentation, students had a few minutes to ask questions. They also took notes on key ideas they were learning about each school job.

After all the speakers had finished, María introduced a writing assignment. She told the students that they would each be writing about one of the speakers. Using the overhead projector, she modeled how to write the short report. She did a think-aloud so that students could better understand her composing process. She started by saying, "I think I will write about the librarian. I enjoy going to the library, and I was surprised at all the things she does." Together they brainstormed a list of things the librarian had said. She showed the students how to write a short report with good paragraphs that had a topic sentence and supporting details. As she wrote the report, she asked students to give ideas about the librarian using information from the class brainstorming list.

Then María divided the students into pairs and asked each pair to choose one of the other speakers to write about. Each pair picked their favorite speaker, made a list of details they had learned about this person's job, and then wrote a short report about this employee. As a final step, María helped the students arrange the reports into a class book titled *Important People and Places in Our School Community*. She put a copy of the labeled map in the front. Then, on each page, she put a picture of one of the areas in the school, which students helped her label. The pictures showed both the places and the employees who worked there. If students had written a report about one of the employees, that report was also included. Students enjoyed reading through the completed class book. They especially liked the page that had their class picture.

The activities addressed several language arts standards: "Students will paraphrase information that has been shared orally by others," "Students will write clear and coherent sentences and paragraphs that develop a central idea. Their writing will show they consider audience and purpose," "Students will create readable documents with legible handwriting," and "Students will restate facts and details in the text to clarify and organize ideas." María informally assessed students as she checked for comprehension during and after reading the books. She noted which students participated in the brainstorming activity and which students could label parts of a map. She used the report writing activity as a summative formal assessment.

Community workers ◆ The students had studied the kinds of work people at their school did and the work people in their families did. María wanted to help students expand their concept of roles people have in the larger community. She reminded students of the models they had built of their community. She explained that now they were going to study the kinds of work different people in the community do.

To begin this series of lessons, she read *A Worker's Tools* (Hughes 1998) and *Community Helpers from A to Z* (Kalman and Walker 1997). She also read books in Spanish that talked about roles of people in the community, including the big book *¿Quién usa ésto?* (*Who Uses This?*) (Miller 1990) as well as *Oficios y más oficios* (*Occupations and More Occupations*) (Bennett 1991), *Yo quiero ser* (*I Would Like to Be*) (Kratky 1995), *El mercado* (*The Market*) (Solano-Flores 1986), and *Los adultos* (*Adults*) (Solano-Flores 1990). After the reading, María put a T-chart on the board. On one side, she wrote "Community helpers," and on the other side, "Work they do." Then she asked students to recall the different people from the books and their jobs. As students responded, María placed the information on the chart. When they had finished with all the characters from the books, María asked if they could think of any other community workers, and she added their names and jobs to the chart.

The stories and follow-up activity served as a bridge for the next lessons. María asked students to think of some places in their community and the people who worked there. The class made a list of these places and people. Then, the class and María chose some different jobs they were interested in knowing more about. Following the model they had used to invite school employees to visit them, students worked in small groups to write invitations to a worker at a fast-food restaurant, a grocery store cashier, a police officer, a gardener, and a doctor. Students delivered the invitations in person, and María made arrangements for the speakers to come in to the class over the next few weeks. The guests spoke about their jobs and what they liked and disliked about them and then answered questions the students had.

After all the speakers had finished, María led a writing activity. She asked students to remember the information about the cashier. María listed the details they gave her on the board. Then she worked with the students to show them how to use this information to write a paragraph about the cashier. With the completed paragraph up on chart paper for students to see, María divided the students into groups of three and gave each group books the class had read together and others that told about different jobs. The students in each group looked through the books and drew a picture of a community worker in the workplace. Then they used the books as a resource and wrote a paragraph describing the community worker's job. They used the model paragraph on the board as a guide. María helped students assemble the pages from each group into a class book that they titled *The Community Helper Book*. They added the book to their classroom library.

One occupation that fascinated all of the children was firefighter. María arranged for a class field trip to a nearby fire station. Before going, she read

Firefighters! (Banks 1999). After reading the book, the students brainstormed some questions they wanted to ask the firefighters on their field trip. At the fire station, the fire captain welcomed the children. Two firefighters gave them a tour of the station, showed them their equipment, and let them try on some of the firefighters' clothes. The students also got to hold some of the equipment the firefighters used. The children had a chance to ask the firefighters many questions about their work. When they returned to school, María asked the children to write in their journals all the things they could remember about their field trip. Then María asked the students to use the ideas from their journals to make a class list of all that they had learned about firefighters.

Listening to María read, writing a class book, and going on the field trip were all good learning experiences that increased students' understanding of community. These activities met several content standards. They addressed the following language arts standards: "Students will paraphrase information that has been shared orally by others," "Students will report on a topic with supportive facts and details," "Students will write clear and coherent sentences and paragraphs that develop a central idea," and "Their writing will show they consider the audience and purpose." The lessons also met the social studies standard "Students will explore the lives of actual people that make a difference in their everyday lives." María assessed the students in different ways during these activities. She kept anecdotal records of the students' interactions and questions in class and during the field trip. In addition to these informal assessments, María used the pages of the class community helper book as a summative final assessment.

María knew that her students had made great gains in their understanding of community through the many activities they had engaged in during the unit of study. To help the students synthesize their learning, María asked them to do a quickwrite. She instructed them to write for two minutes on each of these questions: What has been most interesting to you during this unit? and What did you learn the most about? Students wrote busily and then María asked them each to share their writing with two other people. Next she asked each group to share two ideas with the whole class—one thing that they had found interesting and one thing that they had learned the most about. María wrote the key ideas down under the two categories "Most Interesting" and "Learned Most About."

Improving our community ◆ María wanted to move her students from an understanding of social studies concepts to social action (Banks 1989). She reminded them of the book *Making a Difference* (Almada 2004a), in which children had convinced community members to help them build a skating park. She also read *La calle es libre* (*The Streets Are Free*) (Kurusa 1983), a story about how children in a poor *barrio*, with the help of the adults in their community, got city officials to give them land to build a park. Then, the entire *barrio* community cleaned the land and built a park. She also read them *The Treasure on Gold Street: El tesoro en la calle de oro* (Byrd 2003), the story of how another *barrio* community cared for a mentally handicapped adult who lived among them.

The students discussed the books and then talked about things in their community and school that needed improvement or ways they could help others. The class made a list of things that could be improved, including cleaning up a vacant lot near the school, making the yard of a home for senior citizens look better, visiting senior citizens who were lonely, and helping neighbors who could not afford to hire people to make repairs. The class discussed how to do something specific and wrote a commitment to improve the community in one of the ways listed.

María knew that her students had come away from this unit with a deeper understanding of community. Through reading, writing, discussion, field trips, and various projects, the students, as a community, had learned. They had learned about the people that make up communities and the work they do. Perhaps most importantly, they realized that they were members of several communities and their actions could positively impact the lives of others in their communities. They continued to expand their understanding of community during their study of the other themes in their yearlong integrated curriculum. Figure 6–7 is a bibliography of some of the books María used in her community unit.

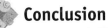 ## Conclusion

María's theme exemplifies effective planning. Because of the pressures they are under, teachers often start their planning by thinking about what they will do the next day or week. Then, if they are planning an integrated curriculum, they try to plan lessons that bring in the different subject areas. They also begin thinking about how each lesson might fit into a longer unit of a week or two. Finally, teachers might look at the district or state standards to see how the lessons connect with the standards.

Rather than engaging in this traditional forward planning that starts with a lesson and ends with the standards, María used backward planning. This approach begins with a careful assessment of students. Teachers assess how well students have developed the knowledge and skills associated with national, state, or district language and content standards expected of them to that point. Then

Ada, A. F. 1990a. *Just One Seed*. Carmel, CA: Hampton-Brown.

———. 1990b. *Una semilla nada más*. Carmel, CA: Hampton-Brown.

Almada, P. 2004a. *Making a Difference*. Barrington, IL: Rigby.

———. 2004b. *We Can Be Helpers*. Barrington, IL: Rigby.

Avalos, C. 1991. *¡Puedo leer dondequiera!* Cleveland: Modern Curriculum Press.

Banks, M. 1999. *Firefighters!* Boston: Houghton Mifflin.

Bennett, B. 1991. *Oficios y más oficios*. México, D.F.: Editorial Patria.

Boyle, B. 1991a. *Around My School*. Barrington, IL: Rigby.

———. 1991b. *Following Directions*. Barrington, IL: Rigby.

———. 1991c. *Looking at Maps*. Barrington, IL: Rigby.

———. 1993a. *En mi escuela*. Trans. M. Cappellini. Barrington, IL: Rigby.

———. 1993b. *Mirando mapas*. Trans. P. Almada. Barrington, IL: Rigby.

———. 1993c. *Siguiendo direcciones*. Trans. M. Cappellini. Barrington, IL: Rigby.

Byrd, L. 2003. *The Treasure on Gold Street: El tesoro en la calle de oro*. El Paso, TX: Cinco Puntos Press.

Canetti, Y. 1997. *Para algo son los amigos*. Boston: Houghton Mifflin.

Crum, M. B. 2004. *Working for the Government*. Barrington, IL: Rigby.

Cumpiano, I. 1991. *¡Qué semana, Luchito!* Carmel, CA: Hampton-Brown.

Drew, D. 1997. *Somewhere in the Universe*. Crystal Lake, IL: Rigby.

Espinosa, S. 1997. *Ruedas y más ruedas*. Boston: Houghton Mifflin.

Flores, B., E. Castro, and E. Hernández. 1993. *Figuras geométricas*. Miami: DDL Books.

García, A., and A. C. García. 2004. *Our Journey*. Barrington, IL: Rigby.

Garza, C. L. 1996. *In My Family: En mi familia*. San Francisco: Children's Book Press.

Hirsch, C. 2004. *Dallas Shapes Up*. Barrington, IL: Rigby.

Hughes, M. 1998. *A Worker's Tools*. Crystal Lake, IL: Rigby.

Ives, T., illus. 1997. *Letreros*. Boston: Houghton Mifflin.

Jacobs, R. 2004. *Room for One More*. Crystal Lake, IL: Rigby.

Kalman, B., and N. Walker. 1997. *Community Helpers from A to Z*. New York: Crabtree.

Kratky, L. J. 1995. *Yo quiero ser*. Carmel, CA: Hampton-Brown.

Kurusa. 1983. *La calle es libre*. Caracas, Venezuela: Ediciones Ekaré-Banco del Libro.

Mace, A. 1997. *Los edificios de Nueva York*. Katonah, NY: Richard C. Owen.

McVeity, J. 1997. *El primer día de clase*. Boston: Hougton Mifflin.

Miller, M. 1990. *¿Quién usa ésto?* New York: Scholastic.

Palacios, A. 1997a. *One City, One School, Many Foods*. Crystal Lake, IL: Rigby.

———. 1997b. *Una ciudad, una escuela, muchas comidas*. Crystal Lake, IL: Rigby.

Parkes, B. 2004. *The First Day of School*. Barrington, IL: Rigby.

FIG. 6–7 Community Theme Books

Paulsen, G. 1995a. *La tortillería*. Trans. G. D. Andújar. Orlando, FL: Harcourt Brace.

———. 1995b. *The Tortilla Factory*. New York: Harcourt Brace.

Pérez, A. I. 2000. *My Very Own Room: Mi propio cuartito*. San Francisco: Children's Book Press.

Poydar, N. 2000. *First Day, Hooray!* New York: Holiday House.

Reynoldson, F., and J. Shuter. 1991. *Today and One Hundred Years Ago*. Barrington, IL: Rigby.

———. 1993. *Hoy y hace cien años*. Trans. M. Cappellini. Barrington, IL: Rigby.

Rigby. 2004. *Golden Opportunities*. Barrington, IL: Rigby.

Rius, M., and J. M. Parramón. 1986. *La ciudad*. Woodbury, NY: Barron's.

———. 1987. *Los abuelos*. Woodbury, NY: Barron's.

Romero, O. 1996. *Con mi familia*. Carmel, CA: Hampton-Brown.

Sánchez, I., and I. Bordoy. 1991. *La clase*. Bogotá, Colombia: Parramón.

Solano-Flores, G. 1986. *El mercado*. México, D.F.: Trillas.

———. 1987. *El periódico*. México, D.F.: Trillas.

———. 1990. *Los adultos*. México, D.F.: Trillas.

Vendrell, C. S., and J. M. Parramón. 1987. *Los padres*. Woodbury, NY: Barron's.

Ward, B. 2004a. *Shapes Around the World*. Barrington, IL: Rigby.

———. 2004b. *The Story of Money*. Barrington, IL: Rigby.

Washington, L. 2004. *But I Want It!* Barrington, IL: Rigby.

Zamorano, A. 1996. *Let's Eat*. New York: Scholastic.

Zimelman, N. 2000. *El dólar*. Katonah, NY: Richard C. Owen.

FIG. 6–7 Community Theme Books (*continued*)

teachers consider the standards for the coming year. They refer to the benchmarks and performance standards that have been established for students at their grade level as they decide how they will assess their students. With the assessments firmly in mind, they turn to long- and short-term planning.

María met with other teachers at her grade level for her long-term planning. The other second-grade teachers shared useful ideas for lessons and resources. In some cases, they adjusted plans so that limited resources could be better utilized. By planning collaboratively, they ensured a unified approach to the second-grade curriculum. The second-grade teachers also met with first- and third-grade teachers to discuss how their community theme fit with what students already had studied and what they would be studying the following year. By doing this kind of vertical planning, the teachers were able to make plans that built on and extended students' knowledge while preparing students for the following year.

In their second-grade group, the teachers decided on a long-term theme and three units. As they planned, they kept both content and language standards in mind. In addition, they checked that their lessons were consistent with the curriculum essentials outlined in the previous chapters. As a result of their careful planning, María and the other teachers at her dual language school provided the best possible curriculum for all of their students.

Learning Extensions

1. Consider a theme you have taught or have seen someone else teach. Was forward or backward planning used? How might you improve your approach to planning?

2. If you are not presently doing both horizontal and vertical planning with your colleagues, how might you get that started? What might be some reasons you could give them for doing this?

3. Choose a theme you have taught or would like to teach. Look at the standards you need to follow. Choose at least two content standards from each subject area and two TESOL language standards that you could connect to that theme. List some activities that would involve students in the theme and help them achieve what the standards call for.

4. Think back over María's unit. What are two activities that she did that you could adapt and use in a unit you are teaching?

5. María used books to help students develop the concepts she was trying to teach. Choose two books she read and explain how those books were effective.

6. María constantly wove reading, writing, speaking, and listening into her unit. In a dual language classroom, there are always second language learners. How did María support the students' language and content learning? List some general strategies she used as well as a couple of specific examples.

7. María's unit did not include science activities. With a partner, consider science activities that would fit this theme. What science content standards would these activities meet?

8. Backward planning requires that teachers assess what their students know before planning. María consistently assessed her students. List some different ways she found out what they had learned and what they still needed to learn.

Afterword

Dual language programs are springing up in school districts all across the country. Their popularity stems from a variety of sources. All students in the programs score well on standardized tests in two languages. The programs offer enrichment education for all students. Dual language programs result in improved social relationships among students from different linguistic and ethnic backgrounds. Parents of native English speakers like the programs because their children learn a second language. In the introduction, we discussed the features that all dual language programs share.

Common Characteristics of Dual Language Education Programs
• Students include native English speakers and native speakers of another language.
• Students are integrated during most content instruction.
• Instruction is provided in two languages.
• Students become proficient in two languages.
• Student achievement in English for all students is equal to or exceeds that of students learning in English only.

Although dual language programs share certain core characteristics, they vary considerably. This variation is reflected in the different labels used to refer to the programs. In addition, dual language programs have been implemented following a variety of models. Even though the most common models are the 90/10 and the 50/50, programs around the country show considerable variety.

In Chapter 1 we reviewed different kinds of bilingual programs. We began by describing programs we had been involved with in Latin America. We also discussed bilingual schools in Europe. We listed the various program models and the academic results for students in different kinds of programs. We concluded by describing the development and growth of dual language programs in the United States.

In Chapter 2 we gave brief descriptions of several dual language programs from around the United States. These descriptions highlighted the great variety among dual language programs. In addition, we analyzed the different kinds of students and teachers in dual language programs. For each type of student or teacher, we listed characteristics and needs.

Although dual language programs vary greatly, successful programs are based on a set of essential elements. Beginning with Chapter 3 we listed and illustrated these essentials. We began with whole-school essentials. These are essentials for all school personnel in effective dual language schools.

Whole School Essentials
• Understand and support the goals and benefits of the program.
• Be flexible and open to change.
• Be committed to academic and social equity and the promotion of equal status for both languages.

Effective dual language programs have strong leadership. The leadership team often consists of the principal and a language specialist. Certain essentials apply specifically to administrators in dual language programs.

Administrative Essentials

- Monitor to ensure consistent planning, curriculum implementation, and classroom organization.
- Provide and participate in ongoing professional development for teachers through consultants, school visits, and conferences.
- Provide necessary funding for rich and varied materials in both languages in all content areas.
- Provide time for teachers to plan and problem-solve together.
- Provide positive feedback to encourage students, teachers, and other staff and make them feel appreciated.

The next set of essentials applies to both administrators and teachers. For programs to succeed, these essentials need to be in place.

Administrator and Teacher Essentials

- Collaborate on the development and implementation of all aspects of the program.
- Understand that academic competence in two languages takes time to develop.
- Work for consistency in program planning, classroom organization, and literacy instruction across and within grade levels.
- Respond to parental concerns and needs.
- Include parents from both language groups in program planning and implementation.
- Promote and explain the dual language program to parents, the school board, and the community.
- Display a passion for the program, the students, and their families.

Some essentials apply specifically to teachers in a dual language program. Without effective teachers, no program can succeed.

Teacher Essentials
• Develop high levels of proficiency in two languages or proficiency in one language and a receptive knowledge of the second language.
• Recognize and appreciate language variation but model conventional oral and written language when providing instruction in either language.
• Collaborate to articulate curriculum within and across grade levels.
• Collaborate for both short- and long-term planning.
• Collaborate to locate resources in both languages.

In Chapter 4 we discussed curriculum in dual language programs. We began with the overall organization of the curriculum and then turned to lesson delivery and assessment.

Curriculum Essentials for Overall Organization
• Teach language through sustained content to develop academic language and academic content knowledge.
• Ensure that all aspects of the curriculum are interrelated through thematic teaching to provide a continuous preview, view, and review.
• Organize curriculum around themes that connect to students' lives and meet content and language standards.

The first set of essentials applies to the approach to curriculum. The following essentials focus on daily lessons.

Curriculum Essentials for Lesson Delivery
• Establish a classroom environment and daily routines that are conducive to language and content area development.
• Group students to promote optimum academic and linguistic development.
• Maintain the language of instruction without translation.
• Scaffold instruction to make the input comprehensible for all students at all times.

Assessment informs curriculum. Effective teachers use formal and informal assessment to plan their lessons.

Curriculum Essentials for Assessment

- Monitor students' academic and linguistic progress regularly.

- Adjust teaching in response to students' academic, linguistic, and social needs.

In Chapter 5 we discussed literacy in dual language programs. A goal is that all students become bilingual and biliterate. For all students to become proficient readers and writers in two languages, an effective literacy program must be established. Since tests of reading are often used to evaluate programs, student progress in reading is crucial. The first set of essentials focuses on the relationship between theory and practice.

Reading Theory Essentials

- Ensure a good match between the theory of reading and the teaching methods.

- Base methods on a theory that views reading as meaning construction.

Students in some dual language programs learn to read and write in their native language first and then add literacy in the second language. In other programs all students learn to read in the non-English language and then add English literacy later. Both of these approaches have proven successful. Program planners must make careful choices in order to create an effective literacy program.

Literacy Program Essentials

- Consider the choice of language or languages for initial literacy instruction carefully because it has implications for the choice of program model.

- Choose an approach that is consistent with the theory of reading.

Whether students all learn to read and write first in their native language or learn in one language and then add a second, it is important for administrators and teachers to have an understanding of how literacy knowledge and skills transfer across languages.

Literacy Program Essentials

- Understand and trust in theory and research that shows that literacy transfers from one language to another.

- Use strategies to help students transfer literacy-related knowledge and skills from one language to the other.

- Understand differences and draw on similarities between languages to facilitate acquisition of literacy in two languages.

To ensure that students develop high levels of proficiency in reading and writing in two languages, administrators and teachers focus on meaning.

Literacy Program Essential

- Organize a program that includes meaning-centered activities to foster literacy development in two languages.

In Chapter 6 we considered planning in more detail. We advocated a process, known as backward planning, that begins with assessment and connects to standards.

Overall Planning Essentials

- Develop a student profile.

- Identify key concepts in the content and language standards.

- Consider how the students will be assessed on the standards.

- Do both long-term and short-term planning.

- Engage students in challenging, theme-based instruction.

- Continually assess, reflect, and adjust instruction.

In dual language programs, teachers collaborate on long- and short-term planning to develop effective integrated, thematic curriculum.

Long-Term and Short-Term Planning Essentials

- Plan collaboratively to ensure a unified approach to curriculum.

- Do both horizontal and vertical planning.

- Develop long-term themes based on big questions.

- Develop short-term units within the themes.

Dual language programs offer great promise. In these enrichment programs, all students can become bilingual and biliterate. All students can achieve high levels of academic and linguistic proficiency. Intergroup relationships improve as well. Students in many current programs are attaining these benefits:

- ◆ true bilingualism and biliteracy
- ◆ more opportunities for economic success
- ◆ improved intercultural relationships in the school and community
- ◆ intercultural friendships
- ◆ cognitive flexibility that also leads to higher-order thinking skills and better problem-solving abilities

For English language learners, there are additional benefits:

- ◆ pride in the native language and culture, which improves self-esteem
- ◆ ability to communicate with extended family
- ◆ improved academic performance in English
- ◆ higher academic aspirations

Because dual language programs offer so many benefits, the danger is that some schools may jump on the dual language bandwagon without sufficient preparation or resources. They might choose a model that does not fit with their teachers or students. They might implement some aspects of the program well but struggle in other areas.

We have read the research on dual language, visited many dual language schools, and talked to teachers and administrators across the country. Based on this reading, the visits, and the conversations, we have developed these lists of essentials. Our hope is that these lists will prove useful to teachers and administrators working in dual language schools or planning to start a program. A complete list of these essentials can be found at the end of the book. We have seen many examples of exciting education in dual language programs. Both native English speakers and English language learners benefit as they become bilingual and biliterate. We are convinced that schools that follow the essentials we list here will offer all students the kind of education they richly deserve.

Dual Language Essentials

Whole School Essentials

- Understand and support the goals and benefits of the program.

- Be flexible and open to change.

- Be committed to academic and social equity and the promotion of equal status for both languages.

Administrative Essentials

- Monitor to ensure consistent planning, curriculum implementation, and classroom organization.

- Provide and participate in ongoing professional development for teachers through consultants, school visits, and conferences.

- Provide necessary funding for rich and varied materials in both languages in all content areas.

- Provide time for teachers to plan and problem-solve together.

- Provide positive feedback to encourage students, teachers, and other staff and make them feel appreciated.

Administrator and Teacher Essentials

- Collaborate on the development and implementation of all aspects of the program.

- Understand that academic competence in two languages takes time to develop.

- Work for consistency in program planning, classroom organization, and literacy instruction across and within grade levels.

- Respond to parental concerns and needs.

- Include parents from both language groups in program planning and implementation.

- Promote and explain the dual language program to parents, the school board, and the community.

- Display a passion for the program, the students, and the families.

Teacher Essentials

- Develop high levels of proficiency in two languages or proficiency in one language and a receptive knowledge of the second language.

- Recognize and appreciate language variation, but model conventional oral and written language when providing instruction in either language.

- Collaborate to articulate curriculum within and across grade levels.

- Collaborate for both short- and long-term planning.

- Collaborate to locate resources in both languages.

Curriculum Essentials for Overall Organization

- Teach language through sustained content to develop academic language and academic content knowledge.

- Ensure that all aspects of the curriculum are interrelated through thematic teaching to provide a continuous preview, view, and review.

- Organize curriculum around themes that connect to students' lives and meet content and language standards.

Curriculum Essentials for Lesson Delivery

- Establish a classroom environment and daily routines that are conducive to language and content area development.

- Group students to promote optimum academic and linguistic development.

- Maintain the language of instruction without translation.

- Scaffold instruction to make the input comprehensible for all students at all times.

Curriculum Essentials for Assessment

- Monitor students' academic and linguistic progress regularly.

- Adjust teaching in response to students' academic, linguistic, and social needs.

Reading Theory Essentials

- Ensure a good match between the theory of reading and the teaching methods.

- Base methods on a theory that views reading as meaning construction.

Literacy Program Essentials

- Consider the choice of language or languages for initial literacy instruction carefully because it has implications for the choice of program model.

- Choose an approach that is consistent with the theory of reading.

- Understand and trust in theory and research that shows that literacy transfers from one language to another.

- Use strategies to help students transfer literacy-related knowledge and skills from one language to the other.

- Understand differences and draw on similarities between languages to facilitate acquisition of literacy in two languages.

- Organize a program that includes meaning-centered activities to foster literacy development in two languages.

Overall Planning Essentials

- Develop a student profile.

- Identify key concepts in the content and language standards.

- Consider how the students will be assessed on the standards.

- Do both long-term and short-term planning.

- Engage students in challenging, theme-based instruction.

- Continually assess, reflect, and adjust instruction.

Long-Term and Short-Term Planning Essentials

- Plan collaboratively to ensure a unified approach to curriculum.

- Do both horizontal and vertical planning.

- Develop long-term themes based on big questions.

- Develop short-term units within the themes.

Key Terms and Acronyms

American Hispanic Educators Association of Dade (AHEAD)

Audiolingual Method (ALM)

Center for Applied Linguistics (CAL)

Center for Research on the Education of Students Placed at Risk (CRESPAR)

Common Underlying Proficiency (CUP)

Developmental Bilingual Education (DBE)

Dual Immersion (DI)

Dual Language Education (DLE)

English as a Foreign Language (EFL)

English as a Second Language (ESL)

English Language Learner (ELL)

English Only (EO)

English to Speakers of Other Languages (ESOL)

Enriched Education (EE)

First or Native Language (L1)

Fully English Proficient (FEP)

La Secretaría de la Educación Pública (SEP)

Language Assessment Scales (LAS)

Language Experience Approach (LEA)

Lectura en Español–Reading In Spanish (LEE)

Limited English Proficient (LEP)

National Assessment of Educational Progress (NAEP)

National Association of Bilingual Education (NABE)

National Defense Education Act (NDEA)

Native English Speakers (NES)

Non Native English Speakers (NNES)

Office of English Language Acquisition (OELA)

Second Language (L2)

Separate Underlying Proficiency (SUP)

Spanish American League Against Discrimination (SALAD)

Structured English Immersion (SEI)

Sustained Silent Reading (SSR)

Teachers of English to Speakers of Other Languages (TESOL)

Texas Assessment of Academic Skills (TASS)

Texas Essential Knowledge and Skills (TEKS)

Texas Primary Reading Inventory (TPRI)

Transitional Bilingual Education (TBE)

Two-Way Bilingual Education (TWBE)

Two-Way Immersion (TWI)

Zone of Proximal Development (ZPD)

References

Ajuira, Alejandra. 1994. "An Exploration of Classroom Activity and Student Success in a Two-Way Bilingual and a Mainstream Program." Ph.D. diss., College of Education, Boston College.

Akhavan, Nancy L. 2004. *How to Triumph with the Standards: Tailor-Fit Instruction to Meet Your Students' Diverse Needs*. Portsmouth, NH: Heinemann.

Alanís, Iliana. 2000. "A Texas Two Way Bilingual Program: Its Effects on Linguistic and Academic Achievement." *Bilingual Research Journal* 24 (3): 225–48.

Amrein, Audrey, and Robert A. Peña. 2000. "Asymmetry in Dual Language Practice: Assessing Imbalance in a Program Promoting Equality." *Education Policy Analysis Archives* 8 (8): 1–17.

Ariza, Eileen, Carmen Morales-Jones, Noorchaya Yahya, and Hanizah Zainuddin. 2002. *Why TESOL? Theories and Issues in Teaching English as a Second Language for K–12 Teachers*. Dubuque, IA: Kendall/Hunt.

Armbruster, Bonnie, and Jean Osborn. 2001. *Put Reading First: The Building Blocks for Teaching Children to Read*. Washington, DC: U.S. Department of Education.

Associated Press. 2004. *Texas Elementary School Feels Northerner's Warmth*. Star-Telegram.com 2003 [retrieved 5 January 2004]. Available from *www.dfw.com /mld/starlegram/news/state/7337646.htm?template=contentModules/printstory.jsp.*

August, Diane, Margarita Calderón, and María Carlo. 2000. "Transfer of Skills from Spanish to English: A Study of Young Learners." Paper presented at the Preliminary Report to the Office of Bilingual Education and Minority Affairs, U.S. Department of Education, Washington, DC.

Banks, James. 1989. *Multicultural Education: Issues and Perspectives*. Boston: Allyn and Bacon.

Barnitz, John. 1982. "Orthographies, Bilingualism, and Learning to Read English as a Second Language." *The Reading Teacher:* 560–67.

Beardsmore, Hugo. 1995. "The European School Experience in Multilingual Education." In *Multilingualism for All*, ed. Tove Skutnabb-Kangas. Lisse, the Netherlands: Swets & Zeitlinger.

Bourdieu, Pierre, and J. Claude Passeron. 1977. *Reproduction in Education, Society and Culture*. London: Sage.

Brecht, Richard D., and Catherine W. Ingold. 1998. *Tapping a National Resource: Heritage Languages in the United States*. Washington, DC: Center for Applied Linguistics.

Brinton, Donna, Marguerite Snow, et al. 1989. *Content-Based Second Language Instruction*. Boston: Heinle and Heinle.

Bruner, Jerome. 1985. "Models of the Learner." *Educational Researcher* 14 (6): 5–8.

Cabezón, Mary, Elena Nicoladis, and Wallace E. Lambert. 1998. *Becoming Bilingual in the Amigos Two-Way Immersion Program*. Washington, DC: CREDE.

———. 2003. *Two-Way Bilingual Education: A Progress Report on the Amigos Program* [electronic]. National Center for Research on Cultural Diversity and Second Language Learning 1999 [retrieved 25 September 2003]. Available from *www.cal.org/crede/pubs/research/rr3.hml*.

Calderón, Margarita, and Robert Slavin. 2001. "Success for All in a Two-Way Immersion School." In *Bilingual Education*, ed. D. Christian and F. Genesee. Alexandria, VA: TESOL.

Center for Applied Linguistics. 2004. *Directory of Two-Way Bilingual Programs in the U.S.* [retrieved 9 April 2004]. Available from *www.cal.org/twi/directory*.

Christian, Donna. 1994. *Two-Way Bilingual Education: Students Learning Through Two Languages*. Washington, DC: Office of Educational Research and Improvement.

Christian, Donna, Elizabeth R. Howard, and Michael I. Loeb. 2000. "Bilingualism for All: Two-Way Immersion Education in the United States." *Theory into Practice* 39 (4): 258–66.

Christian, Donna, Christopher L. Montone, et al. 1997. *Profiles in Two-Way Immersion Education*. Washington, DC: Center for Applied Linguistics.

Cloud, Nancy, Fred Genesee, and Else Hamayan. 2000. *Dual Language Instruction: A Handbook for Enriched Education*. Boston: Heinle and Heinle.

Coles, Gerald. 2000. *Misreading Reading: The Bad Science That Hurts Children*. Portsmouth, NH: Heinemann.

Collier, Demetrya, Irma Hernandez, et al. 2002. *Think Themes*. Chicago: Chicago Public Schools.

Collier, Virginia. 1989. "How Long? A Synthesis of Research on Academic Achievement in a Second Language." *TESOL Quarterly* 23 (3): 509–32.

———. 1995. "Acquiring a Second Language for School." *Directions in Language and Education* 1 (4).

Collier, Virginia P., and Wayne P. Thomas. 1996. "Effectiveness in Bilingual Education." Paper read at National Association of Bilingual Education, Orlando, Florida.

———. 2004. "The Astounding Effectiveness of Dual Language Education for All." *NABE Journal of Research and Practice* 2 (1): 1–19.

Commins, Nancy. 2004. "Instructional Planning with Language and Social Context in Mind." Paper presented at the National Association for Bilingual Education conference, February, Albuquerque, NM.

Consortium of Texas Two-Way Dual Language Programs. 2004. *Directory of Texas Two-Way Programs* [retrieved 9 April 2004]. Available from *www.texastwoway.org*.

Crawford, James. 1997. Unz Initiative. Available from *http://ourworld.compuserve.com/homepages/jwcrawford/unz.htm*.

———. 2003. *Redesignation Rates*. [retrieved 29 April 2003]. Available from *http://ourworld.compuserve.com/homepages/JWCRAWFORD/castats.htm*.

———. 2004. *Educating English Learners: Language Diversity in the Classroom*. 5th ed. Los Angeles: Bilingual Educational Services.

Cummins, Jim. 1981. "The Role of Primary Language Development in Promoting Educational Success for Language Minority Students." In *Schooling and Language Minority Students: A Theoretical Framework*. Los Angeles: Evaluation, Dissemination and Assessment Center, California State University, Los Angeles.

———. 1989. *Empowering Minority Students*. Sacramento: CABE.

———. 1994. "The Role of Primary Language Development in Promoting Educational Success for Language Minority Students." In *Schooling and Language Minority Students: A Theoretical Framework*. Los Angeles: Evaluation, Dissemination and Assessment Center, California State University, Los Angeles.

———. 1996. *Negotiating Identities: Education for Empowerment in a Diverse Society.* Ontario, CA: California Association of Bilingual Education.

———. 2000. *Language, Power, and Pedagogy: Bilingual Children in the Crossfire.* Tonawanda, NY: Multilingual Matters.

daCruz-Payne, Carleen, and Mary Browning-Schulman. 1998. *Getting the Most Out of Morning Message and Other Shared Writing*. New York: Scholastic.

Darling-Hammond, Linda, Jacqueline Ancess, and Beverly Falk. 1995. "Collaborative Learning and Assessment at International High School." In *Authentic Assessment in Action: Studies of Schools and Students at Work*. New York: Teachers College Press.

de Jong, Ester. 2002a. "Developing a Successful Elementary Two-Way Bilingual Program." *Sunshine State TESOL Journal*: 8–17.

———. 2002b. "Effective Bilingual Education: From Theory to Academic Achievement in a Two-Way Bilingual Program." *Bilingual Research Journal* 26 (1): 1–15.

———. 2004. "L2 Proficiency Development in a Two-Way and a Developmental Bilingual Program." *NABE Journal of Research and Practice* 2 (1): 77–108.

Delgado-Larroco, Esther I. 1998. "Classroom Processes in a Two-Way Immersion Kindergarten Classroom." Diss., Division of Education, University of California–Davis.

Díaz, Stephen, Luis Moll, and Hugh Mehan. 1986. "Sociocultural Resources in Instruction: A Context-Specific Approach." In *Beyond Language: Social and Cultural Factors in Schooling Language Minority Students*. Los Angeles: Evaluation, Dissemination and Assessment Center, California State University, Los Angeles.

Dolson, David, and Kathryn Lindholm. 1995. "World Class Education for Children in California: A Comparison of the Two-Way Bilingual Immersion and European Schools Model." In *Multilingualism for All*, ed. T. Skutnabb-Kangas. Lisse, the Netherlands: Swets & Zeitlinger.

Edelsky, Carole. 1982. "Writing in a Bilingual Program: The Relation of L1 and L2 Texts." *TESOL Quarterly* 16 (2): 211–28.

Ekbatani, Glayol, and Herbert Pierson. 2000. *Learner Directed Assessment in ESL*. Mahwah, NJ: Lawrence Erlbaum.

Elley, Warwick. 1991. "Acquiring Literacy in a Second Language: The Effect of Book-Based Programs." *Language Learning* 41 (2): 403–39.

———. 1998. *Raising Literacy Levels in Third World Countries: A Method That Works*. Culver City, CA: Language Education Associates.

Feinberg, Rosa Castro. 1999. "Adminstration of Two-Way Bilingual Elementary Schools: Building on Strength." *Bilingual Research Journal* 23 (1): 47–68.

Fern, Veronica. 1995. "Oyster School Stands the Test of Time." *The Bilingual Research Journal* 19 (3 and 4): 497–512.

Fitzgerald, Jill. 1995. "English-as-a-Second-Language Reading Instruction in the United States: A Research Review." *Journal of Reading Behavior* 27 (2): 115–52.

———. 2000. "How Will Bilingual/ESL Programs in Literacy Change in the Next Millennium?" *Reading Research Quarterly* 35 (4): 520–23.

Freeman, Ann. 2001. "The Eyes Have It: Oral Miscue and Eye Movement Analyses of the Reading of Fourth Grade Spanish/English Bilinguals." Diss., Language, Reading and Culture, University of Arizona.

———. In press. "What Eye Movement and Miscue Analysis Reveal About the Reading Process of Young Bilinguals." In *Scientific Realism in Studies of Reading*, ed. A. Flurkey, E. Paulson, and K. Goodman. Mahwah, NJ: Lawrence Erlbaum.

Freeman, David E., and Yvonne S. Freeman. 2000. *Teaching Reading in Multilingual Classrooms*. Portsmouth, NH: Heinemann.

———. 2001. *Between Worlds: Access to Second Language Acquisition*. 2d ed. Portsmouth, NH: Heinemann.

———. 2004. *Essential Linguistics: What You Need to Know to Teach Reading, ESL, Spelling, Phonics, and Grammar*. Portsmouth, NH: Heinemann.

Freeman, Rebecca D. 1995. "Equal Educational Opportunity for Language Minority Students: From Policy to Practice at Oyster Bilingual School." *Issues in Applied Linguistics* 6 (1): 39–63.

———. 1996. "Dual-Language Planning at Oyster Bilingual School: 'It's Much More Than Language.'" *TESOL Quarterly* 30 (3): 557–82.

———. 1998. *Bilingual Education and Social Change*. Clevedon, England: Multilingual Matters.

———. 2004. *Building on Community Bilingualism: Promoting Multilingualism Through Schooling*. Philadelphia: Caslon.

Freeman, Yvonne S., and David E. Freeman. 1996. *Teaching Reading and Writing in Spanish in the Bilingual Classroom*. Portsmouth, NH: Heinemann.

———. 1998a. *ESL/EFL Teaching: Principles for Success*. Portsmouth, NH: Heinemann.

———. 1998b. *La enseñanza de la lectura y la escritura en español en el aula bilingüe*. Portsmouth, NH: Heinemann.

———. 2000. "Preview, View, Review: An Important Strategy in Multilingual Classrooms." *NABE News* 24 (2): 20–21.

———. 2002. *Closing the Achievement Gap: How to Reach Limited-Formal-Schooling and Long-Term English Learners*. Portsmouth, NH: Heinemann.

Freire, Paulo. 1970. *Pedagogy of the Oppressed*. New York: Continuum.

Garan, Elaine. 2002. *Resisting Reading Mandates*. Portsmouth, NH: Heinemann.

García, Georgia. 1994. "Assessing the Literacy Development of Second-Language Students: A Focus on Authentic Assessment." In *Kids Come in All Languages: Reading Instruction for ESL Students*, ed. K. Spangenberg-Urbschat and R. Pritchard. Newark, DE: International Reading Association.

Garía, Gilbert. 2000. *Lessons from Research: What Is the Length of Time It Takes Limited English Proficient Students to Acquire English and Succeed in an All-English Classroom?* Washington, DC: National Clearinghouse for Bilingual Education.

Gee, James. 1990. *Social Linguistics and Literacies: Ideology in Discourses.* Bristol, PA: Falmer.

Genesee, Fred. 1987. *Learning Through Two Languages.* Rowley, MA: Newbury House.

Genesee, Fred, and Patricia Gándara. 1999. "Bilingual Education Programs: A Cross National Perspective." *Journal of Social Issues* 55: 665–85.

Gibbons, Pauline. 2002. *Scaffolding Language: Scaffolding Learning.* Portsmouth, NH: Heinemann.

Gómez, Leo. 2003. "Dual Language Education: A Successful 50-50 Model." *TABE News* 22 (3): 10–13.

Goodman, Kenneth. 1984. "Unity in Reading." In *Becoming Readers in a Complex Society: Eighty-Third Yearbook of the National Society for the Study of Education,* ed. A. Purves and O. Niles. Chicago: University of Chicago Press.

———. 1993. *Phonics Phacts.* Portsmouth, NH: Heinemann.

Gottlieb, Margo. 1999. *The Language Proficiency Handbook.* Springfield, IL: Ilinois State Board of Education. Available from *www.isbe.net/assessment /pdfIMAGELangBook.htm.*

———. 2004. *English Language Proficiency Standards for English Language Learners in Kindergarten Through Grade 12.* Madison, WI: Wisconsin Department of Education.

Graves, Donald. 1983. *Writing: Teachers and Children at Work.* Portsmouth, NH: Heinemann.

———. 1994. *A Fresh Look at Writing.* Portsmouth, NH: Heinemann.

Greene, Jay. 1998. *A Meta-Analysis of the Effectiveness of Bilingual Education.* Claremont, CA: Tomas Rivera Policy Institute.

Griego-Jones, Toni. 1994. "Assessing Students' Perceptions of Biliteracy in Two Way Bilingual Classrooms." *The Journal of Educational Issues of Language Minority Students* 13: 79–93.

Guskey, Thomas. 2001. "JSD Forum: The Backward Approach." *Journal of Staff Development* [retrieved 7 April 04]. Available from *www.NSDC.org/library /publications/JSD/Guskey223.cfm?printPage=1@.*

———. 2003. "How Classroom Assessments Improve Learning" [retrieved 10 April 2004]. Available from *www.ascd.org/publications/ed_lead/200302/Guskey.html.*

Harste, Jerome C., Virginia A. Woodward, and Carolyn Burke. 1984. *Language Stories and Literacy Lessons.* Portsmouth, NH: Heinemann.

Holt, Daniel, ed. 1993. *Cooperative Learning: A Response to Linguistic and Cultural Diversity.* Washington, DC: Center for Applied Linguistics.

Howard, Elizabeth R., and Donna Christian. 2002. *Two-Way Immersion 101: Designing and Implementing a Two-Way Immersion Education Program at the Elementary Level.* Santa Cruz: Center for Research on Education, Diversity and Excellence, University of California, Santa Cruz.

Howard, Elizabeth R., Donna Christian, et al. 2004. *The Development of Bilingualism and Biliteracy from Grade 3 to 5: A Summary of Findings from the CAL/CREDE Study of Two-Way Immersion Education.* Santa Cruz: Center for Research on Education, Diversity, and Excellence.

Howard, Elizabeth R., and Michael I. Loeb. 1998. *In Their Own Words: Two-Way Immersion Teachers Talk About Their Professional Experiences.* ERIC.

Howard, Elizabeth R., Natalie Olague, et al. 2003. *The Dual Language Program Planner: A Guide for Designing and Implementing Dual Language Programs.* Santa Cruz: Center for Research on Education, Diversity, and Excellence.

Howard, Elizabeth R., Julie Sugarman, and Donna Christian. 2003. *Trends in Two Way Immersion Education: A Review of the Research.* Baltimore: Center for Research on the Education of Students Placed at Risk.

Hoyt, Linda. 2002. *Make It Real: Strategies for Success with Informational Texts.* Portsmouth, NH: Heinemann.

Hudelson, Sarah. 1984. "Kan yu ret an rayt en ingles: Children Become Literate in English as a Second Language." *TESOL Quarterly* 18 (2): 221–37.

Jacobs, Heidi. 1997. *Mapping the Big Picture: Integrating Curriculum and Assessment K–12.* Alexandria, VA: Association for Supervision and Curriculum Design.

Kagan, Spencer. 1986. "Cooperative Learning and Sociocultural Factors in Schooling." In *Beyond Language: Social and Cultural Factors in Schooling Language Minority Students.* Los Angeles: Evaluation, Dissemination and Assessment Center.

Krashen, Stephen D. 1992. *Fundamentals of Language Education.* Torrance, CA: Laredo.

———. 1996. *Under Attack: The Case Against Bilingual Education.* Culver City, CA: Language Education Associates.

———. 2003. *Explorations in Language Acquisition and Use.* Portsmouth, NH: Heinemann.

———. 2004. "The Acquisition of Academic English by Children in Two-Way Programs: What Does the Research Say?" [retrieved 24 March 2004]. Available from *www.sdkrashen.com/articles/the_2-way_issue/01.html.*

———. In press. "The Phonics Debate." *Language Magazine.*

Kucer, Stephen B., Cecilia Silva, and Esther L. Delgado-Larocco. 1995. *Curricular Conversations: Themes in Multilingual and Monolingual Classrooms.* York, ME: Stenhouse.

Kucer, Stephen, and Jenny Tuten. 2003. "Revisiting and Rethinking the Reading Process." *Language Arts* 80 (4): 284–90.

Lambert, Wallace E., and Richard Tucker. 1972. *Bilingual Education of Children: The St. Lambert Experiment.* Rowley, MA: Newbury House.

Lessow-Hurley, Judith. 1996. *The Foundations of Dual Language Instruction.* White Plains, NY: Longman.

Lindholm, Kathryn. J. 1992. "Two-Way Bilingual/Immersion Education: Theory, Conceptual Issues, and Pedagogical Implications." In *Critical Perspectives on Bilingual Education Research*, ed. R. Padilla and A. Benavides. Tucson: Bilingual Review/Press.

Lindholm-Leary, Kathryn J. 2001. *Dual Language Education.* Clevedon, England: Multilingual Matters.

Long, Michael, and Patricia Porter. 1985. "Group Work, Interlanguage Talk, and Second Language Acquisition." *TESOL Quarterly* 19 (1): 207–28.

López, Mary Jean Habermann. 2003. *History and Importance of Bilingualism and Bilingual Education in New Mexico.* Albuquerque: New Mexico State Department of Education and the University of New Mexico.

McCollum, Pam. 1999. "Learning to Value English: Cultural Capital in Two-Way Bilingual Programs." *Bilingual Research Journal* 23 (2 and 3): 113–14.

McGroarty, Mary. 1993. "Cooperative Learning and Second Language Acquisition." In *Cooperative Learning: A Response to Cultural and Linguistic Diversity*, ed. D. Holt. Washington, DC: Center for Applied Linguistics.

McQuillan, Jeff. 1998. *The Literacy Crisis: False Claims, Real Solutions.* Portsmouth, NH: Heinemann.

McTighe, Jay, and Grant Wiggins. 1999. *The Understanding by Design Handbook.* Alexandria, VA: Association for Supervision and Curriculum Development.

Montone, Christopher L., and Michael I. Loeb. 2000. *Implementing Two-Way Immersion Programs in Secondary Schools.* Education Practice Report No. 5. Santa Cruz, CA: CREDE.

Nagy, William, Richard Anderson, and Patricia Herman. 1987. "Learning Word Meanings for Context During Normal Reading." *American Educational Research Journal* 24 (2): 237–70.

OELA. 2002. *The Growing Number of Limited English Proficient Students 1991–2002.* U.S. Department of Education 2002 [retrieved 17 October 2002].

O'Malley, J. Michael, and Lorraine Valdez-Pierce. 1996. *Authentic Assessment for English Language Learners.* New York: Addison-Wesley-Longman.

Ovando, Carlos, and Virginia Collier. 1998. *Bilingual and ESL Classrooms: Teaching in Multicultural Contexts.* 2d ed. New York: McGraw-Hill.

Pally, Marcia, ed. 2000. *Sustained Content Teaching in Academic ESL/EFL: A Practical Approach.* Boston: Houghton Mifflin.

Paulson, Eric, and Ann Freeman. 2003. *Insight from the Eyes: The Science of Effective Reading Instruction.* Portsmouth, NH: Heinemann.

Pérez, Bertha. 2004. *Becoming Biliterate: A Study of Two-Way Bilingual Immersion Education.* Mahwah, NJ: Lawrence Erlbaum.

Pogrow, Stanley. 2000. "The Unsubstantiated 'Success' of Success for All: Implications for Policy, Practice, and the Soul of Our Profession." *Phi Delta Kappan* 81 (8): 596–600.

Providence Schools, Rhode Island. 2004. *Essential Components of a Balanced Literacy Program.* Providence Schools 2004 [retrieved 19 January 2004]. Available from *www.providenceschools.org.*

Ramírez, J. David. 1991. *Final Report: Longitudinal Study of Structured English Immersion Strategy, Early-Exit and Late-Exit Bilingual Education Programs.* Washington DC: U.S. Department of Education.

Richard-Amato, Patricia. 1996. *Making It Happen: Interactions in the Second Language Classroom: From Theory to Practice.* White Plains, NY: Longman.

Riley, Richard W. 2000. *Excelencia para todos—Excellence for All: The Progress of Hispanic Education and the Challenges of a New Century* [retrieved 24 April 2000]. Available from *www.ed.gov/Speeches/03-2000315.html.*

Rips, Geoff. 1999. "The Oasis in the Cane Fields." *Texas Co-op Power*: 8–11.

Rosenblatt, Louise. 1978. *The Reader, the Text, the Poem: The Transactional Theory of the Literary Work.* Carbondale, IL: Southern Illinois University Press.

Rossell, Christine. 1990. "The Effectiveness of Educational Alternatives for Limited-English-Proficient Children." In *Learning in Two Languages*, ed. G. Imhoff. New Brunswick, NJ: Transaction.

———. 1998. "Mystery on the Bilingual Express: A Critique of the Thomas and Collier Study 'School Effectiveness for Language Minority Students.'" *READ Perspectives* 5 (2): 5–32.

Rossell, Christine, and Keith Baker. 1996. "The Educational Effectiveness of Bilingual Education." *Research in the Teaching of English* 30: 7–74.

Ruíz, Richard. 1984. "Orientations in Language Planning." *Journal of the National Association for Bilingual Education* 8: 15–34.

Slavin, Robert, and Alan Cheung. 2004. "Effective Reading Programs for English Language Learners: A Best-Evidence Synthesis" [retrieved 25 March 2004]. Available from *www.csos.jhu.edu/crespar/techReports/Report66.pdf.*

Smith, Frank. 1985. *Reading Without Nonsense.* 2d ed. New York: Teachers College Press.

Smith, Patrick, and Elizabeth Arnot-Hopffer. 1998. "Exito Bilingüe: Promoting Spanish Literacy in a Dual Language Immersion Program." *Bilingual Research Journal* 22 (2, 3, 4): 261–77.

Snow, Marguerite, and Donna Brinton, eds. 1997. *The Content-Based Classroom: Perspectives on Integrating Language and Content.* White Plains, NY: Longman.

Soltero, Sonia White. 2004. *Dual Language: Teaching and Learning in Two Languages.* Boston: Pearson.

Soltero, Sonia White, and Martha Moya-Leang. 2002. *Dual Language Development Card.* Chicago: Chicago Public Schools.

Stanovich, Keith. 1998. "Twenty-Five Years of Research on the Reading Process: The Grand Synthesis and What It Means for Our Field." In *Forty-Seventh Yearbook of the National Reading Conference*, ed. T. Shanahan and F. Rodriguez-Brown. Chicago: National Reading Conference.

Strickland, Dorothy. 2004. *Balanced Literacy: Teaching the Skills and Thrills of Reading.* Scholastic 2004 [retrieved 19 January 2004]. Available from *http://teacher.scholastic .com /professional/teacherstrat/balanced.htm.*

Sutti, Domenica. 2003. "A Case Study of an English Language Learner: One Child's Journey." Unpublished manuscript. School of Education, University of Houston.

Swain, Merril. 1985. "Communicative Competence: Some Roles of Comprehensible Output in Its Development." In *Input in Second Language Acquisition*, ed. S. Gass and C. Madden. Rowley, MA: Newbury House.

Teachers of English to Speakers of Other Languages (TESOL). 1997. *ESL Standards for PreK–12 Students.* Alexandria, VA: TESOL.

Texas House of Representatives. 1999. *Resolution.* 75th, H.R. No. 1248.

Thomas, Wayne, and Virginia Collier. 1997. *School Effectiveness for Language Minority Students.* Washington, DC: National Clearinghouse of Bilingual Education.

———. 2002. *A National Study of School Effectiveness for Language Minority Students' Long-Term Academic Achievement* [electronic]. CREDE 2001 [retrieved 4 September 2002]. Available from *www.crede.ucsc.edu/research/llaa/1.1_es.html.*

Torres-Guzmán, María E. 2002. *Dual Language Programs: Key Features and Results.* No. 14. Washington, DC: National Clearinghouse for English Language Acquisition and Language Instruction Educational Programs.

Tregar, B., and B. Wong. 1984. "The Relationship Between Native and Second Language Reading Comprehension and Second Language Oral Ability." In *Communicative Competence Approaches to Language Proficiency: Education and Policy Issues*, ed. C. Rivera. Clevedon, England: Multilingual Matters.

Valdés, Guadalupe. 1997. "Dual-Language Immersion Programs: A Cautionary Note Concerning the Education of Language-Minority Students." *Harvard Educational Review* 67 (3): 391–429.

Verhoeven, Ludo. 1991. "Acquisition of Biliteracy." *AILA Review* 8: 61–74.

Villaseñor, Victor. 1991. *Rain of Gold*. New York: Dell.

Vygotsky, Lev. 1962. *Thought and Language*. Trans. E. H. G. Vakar. Cambridge, MA: MIT Press.

Waber, Bernard. 1972. *Ira Sleeps Over*. Boston: Houghton Mifflin.

Weaver, Constance. 2002. *Reading Process and Practice*. 3d ed. Portsmouth, NH: Heinemann.

Wells, Gordon, and Gen Chang-Wells. 1992. *Constructing Knowledge Together*. Portsmouth, NH: Heinemann.

Wiggins, Grant, and Jay McTighe. 2000. *Understanding by Design*. New York: Prentice-Hall.

Williams, J. 2001. "Classroom Conversations: Opportunities to Learn for ESL Students in Mainstream Classrooms." *The Reading Teacher* 54 (8): 750–57.

Index